Fodor's Inside

Berlin

CONTENTS

ABOUT THIS GUIDE

Inside Berlin shows you the city like you've never seen it. Written entirely by locals, it includes features on the city's street art and galleries and plenty of insider tips. The result is a curated compilation infused with authentic Berlin flavor, accompanied by easy-to-use maps and transit information.

Whether you're visiting Berlin for the first time or a seasoned traveler looking to explore a new neighborhood, this is the guide for you. We've handpicked the top things to do and rated the sights, shopping, dining, and nightlife in the city's most dynamic neighborhoods. Truly exceptional experiences in all categories are marked with a ★.

Restaurants, bars, and coffee shops are a huge part of Berlin's appeal, of course, and you'll find plenty to savor in its diverse neighborhoods. We cover cuisines at all price points, with everything from enduring institutions and groundbreaking chefs to the perfect late-night street snack. We cover hotels in the Experience section at the front of this guide. Use the $ to $$$$

price charts below to estimate meal and room costs. We list adult prices for sights; ask about discounts when purchasing tickets.

Berlin is constantly changing. All prices, opening times, and other details in this guide were accurate at press time. Always confirm information when it matters, especially when making a detour to a specific place. Visit Fodors.com for expanded restaurant and hotel reviews, additional recommendations, news, and features.

WHAT IT COSTS: Restaurants			
$	$$	$$$	$$$$
Under €15	€15–€20	€21–€25	Over €25

Prices are the average cost of a main course at dinner or, if dinner is not served, at lunch.

WHAT IT COSTS: Hotels			
$	$$	$$$	$$$$
Under €100	€100–€175	€176–€225	over €225

Prices are the lowest cost of a standard double room in high season.

1

Experience Berlin

WHAT'S WHERE IN BERLIN

The numbers refer to chapter numbers.

....

2. MITTE SOUTH OF THE SPREE (WITH MUSEUM ISLAND)

Mitte is, figuratively and literally, Berlin's "center." This huge neighborhood has been divided into two sections along the Spree River.

3. MITTE NORTH OF THE SPREE

One of Berlin's cultural hubs, Mitte is filled with shops, bars, restaurants—most of them on the north side of the Spree River.

4. PRENZLAUER BERG

Once a working-class neighborhood, Prenzlauer Berg is now one of the city's most gentrified—and international—areas.

5. KREUZBERG

Tenement blocks and anarchist squats have given way to sidewalk cafés and handsome canal-side apartments, but the remaining artists, punks, and Turkish immigrants continue to make this one of the most dynamic areas in Berlin.

6. NEUKÖLLN & ALT-TREPTOW

From bleak to chic, Neukölln's abandoned storefronts have turned into art galleries, fashion shops, bakeries, and wine bars. Next door, up-and-coming Alt-Treptow is fast becoming the next trendy Berlin neighborhood.

7. FRIEDRICHSCHAIN

Neo-baroque landmarks and socialist architecture compete for attention in this neighborhood in the former East, where cheap rent, offbeat bars, edgy clubs, and beautiful parks attract students and creative types from around the world.

8. SCHÖNEBERG

Historically Berlin's gay neighborhood, Schöneberg mixes the alternative vibe of Kreuzberg with the genteel residential feel of West Berlin.

9. TIERGARTEN AND POTSDAMER STRASSE

The glittery skyscrapers of Potsdammer Platz symbolize Germany's post-Cold War renaissance. Nearby Tiergarten, once a royal hunting estate, is Berlin's largest park.

10. CHARLOTTENBURG

This elegant West Berlin neighborhood is home to the bustling high-street commerce of Kurfürstendamm and elegant coffeehouses of Savignyplatz.

11. POTSDAM

A short trip from Berlin, the former center of the Enlightenment continues to draw learned visitors to its splendid Sanssouci Palace.

BEST FESTIVALS

You can always find something special to do in Berlin, but these are the standouts that Berliners plan their calendars around. They're organized by month, with ongoing events at the end.

FEBRUARY

Berlinale: International Film Festival
February is synonymous with international cinema in Berlin. Unlike the other red-carpet festivals around the world, all the showings in this 10-day celebration are open to the public, making the Berlinale the largest public movie festival in the world. Queue up for premieres of international films, or just party with an estimated 20,000 film professionals who brave the cold Berlin winter yearly. ⊕ *www.berlinale.de.*

MAY

Karneval der Kulturen
A celebration of Berlin's diversity, this multicultural street festival takes over bohemian Kreuzberg every Pentecost weekend (usually in May or June). From traditional ethnic arts to cutting-edge contemporary dance, the festival is a microcosm of present-day Berlin culture. The weekend peaks with a parade of musicians, dancers, and other performers showing off their skills to an enthusiastic crowd. ⊕ *www.karneval-berlin.de.*

JUNE

48 Stunden Neukölln
For two days in June, the working-class neighborhood of Neukölln, now home to boutiques and hip hangouts, celebrates the district's diversity and artsy-ness. An old brewery may host a concert, or an avant-garde opera performance may take over an art nouveau swimming pool; some venues are as intimate as someone's living room. From a modest block party in 1999, this homespun festival has evolved into a major cultural happening that the city's creative class looks forward to every year. ⊠ *Neukölln* ⊕ *www.48-stunden-neukoelln.de.*

JULY

Gay Pride Berlin
Originally a political rally commemorating the 1969 Stonewall riots, this flamboyant parade has become

one of the city's most popular street parties. The annual July celebration draws crowds from around the world, and culminates in a large open-air dance party at the Victory Column. ⊕ *www.csd-berlin.de*.

AUGUST
International Berlin Beer Festival
One August weekend each year, the socialist-style "workers' paradise" apartments of Karl-Marx-Allee provide the backdrop for Berlin's largest suds-themed party. Visitors sample 2,000 types of beer from around the world, including ales handcrafted by independent German brewers. ⊕ *www.bierfestival-berlin.de*.

DECEMBER
Christmas Markets
Berlin is home to more than 60 Christmas markets, from the traditional kitsch fest to hipster flea markets full of handmade goodies. Most are open from late November to the end of December. The Gendarmenmarkt Christmas Market is a classic cuckoo-clocks-and-wursts affair, with the opulent architecture of the square providing a Teutonic ambience. The Alt-Rixdorfer Christmas Market takes place every year on the historic Richardplatz in Neukölln during the second Advent weekend; it's a charming alternative to the more central and well-known markets.

ONGOING EVENTS
Lange Nacht der Museen
Taking place once in the spring and once in the fall, the Long Night of Museums is exactly what the name suggests: almost 100 museums open their doors to the public from 6 pm to 2 am with exhibitions, guided tours, and special programs. Browsing classical art late at night while a DJ spins ambient music is a quintessential Berlin experience. ⊕ *www.lange-nacht-der-museen.de*.

BEST TOURS

There's so much to see and do in Berlin; sometimes it makes sense to take a tour and leave the itinerary to someone else. Boat tours of central Berlin's Spree and the canals are especially popular and give up-close views of sights such as Museum Island, Charlottenburg Palace, the Reichstag, and the Berliner Dom.

BIKING TOURS

Fat Tire Bike Tours
The Fat Tire company runs bike tours in many major European cities. Their Berlin Wall bike tour is especially popular. There is also a general city tour. Bikes are included in the cost of the tour. ✉ *Berlin* ☎ *030/2404-7991* ⊕ *berlin.fattirebiketours.com* 🎫 *From €26.*

BOAT TOURS

Reederei Riedel
This family-run boat tour operator runs excursions of various durations on the Spree and on the Landwehr Canal. Their calendar is continually being updated with timely tours linked to the seasons and special events in the city. ✉ *Berlin* ☎ *030/6796-1470* ⊕ *www.reederei-riedel.de* 🎫 *From €12.*

Stern und Kreisschiffahrt
A variety of tours are offered by Stern und Kreisschiffahrt, in and around Berlin. Evening "Moonlight" cruises, with music, are especially popular. Some of their boat tours are run in conjunction with bus tours for excursions farther afield.

✉ *Berlin* ☎ *030/536-3600* ⊕ *www.sternundkreis.de* 🎫 *From €15.*

SPECIALIZED TOURS

Alternative Berlin
In addition to a free, tip-based walking tour that's given twice a day, Alternative Berlin has an excellent street art tour and a "Green Tour," which shows visitors how Berlin got its reputation as one of the most eco-friendly cities in Europe. In summer months, there is a "twilight" tour, which takes you through Berlin after hours. They also have a "Taste Berlin" tour. ✉ *Berlin* ☎ *0162/819-8264* ⊕ *www.alternativeberlin.com* 🎫 *From €15.*

Berliner Unterwelten
For a truly memorable experience, check out the "Berlin Underworlds" tour. The company

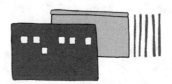

offers access to several of Berlin's best-preserved underground WWII bunkers that are normally closed to the public. ⊠ *Berlin* ☎ *030/499– 1517* ⊕ *www.berliner-unterwelten. de* ⊠ *From €11.*

Context Travel

Guides with expert credentials are the specialty of Context Travel, so expect an in-depth and intellectual look at Berlin history, art, and architecture. The best guides offer insight into niche aspects of Berlin, like Mitte's medieval roots, or the Tiergarten neighborhood known as the Hansaviertel, where top international architects competed to design housing in the 1957 International Building Exhibition. ⊠ *Berlin* ☎ *800/691–6036 international hotline* ⊕ *www.contexttravel. com* ⊠ *From €80.*

Gastro Rallye

Appetizers at one restaurant, main courses at another, and dessert at another—Gastro Rallye leads guests on restaurant crawls where you also get to see the neighborhood as you walk from spot to spot. Different neighborhoods offer different types of foodie experiences. The "Snacky" tour focuses on Berlin's international food scene. ⊠ *Berlin* ☎ *030/9168–5590* ⊕ *www. gastro-rallye.com* ⊠ *From €120.*

WALKING TOURS

Berlin Walks

The walking tours offered by this reputable company include a Sunday "Jewish Life" tour, a Potsdam tour on Thursday and Sunday, and visits to the Sachsenhausen concentration camp. ⊠ *Berlin* ☎ *030/301–9194* ⊕ *www.berlinwalks. com* ⊠ *From €12.*

Brewer's Berlin Tours

Firsthand accounts of the divided and reunified Berlin are a highlight of the all-day "Brewer's Best of Berlin" tour. ⊠ *Berlin* ☎ *0177/388– 1537* ⊠ *From €15.*

Insider Tours

Themed tours offered by Insider Tours include a "Cold War" Berlin tour about the Soviet era and a day trip to Dresden. ⊠ *Berlin* ☎ *030/692–3149* ⊕ *www.insidertour. com* ⊠ *From €12.*

BERLIN ITINERARIES

ONE DAY IN BERLIN

If you only have one day in Berlin, start the morning at two of the city's most iconic symbols, the **Reichstag** and the nearby **Brandenburg Gate** (note that if you want to visit the Reichstag dome you need to register in advance).

Head south to experience the moving silence in the maze of the Holocaust memorial, the **Denkmal für die Ermordeten Juden Europas.**Stop by **Potsdamer Platz,** which embodies the city's renaissance: once a no-go zone between East and West Berlin, the square now teems with glittering towers of optimism. A bit farther south is the **Topographie des Terrors,** an exhibition telling the story of the Nazi takeover in harrowing detail, built where the Gestapo headquarters used to be. Head back to Potsdamer Platz, where you can hop on the double-decker public bus 200, which travels down the grand, tree-lined boulevard Unter der Linden to the colossal **Berliner Dom** cathedral. You can then devote the entire afternoon to the stupendous collections of the **Museumsinsel.** The beautifully restored Neues Museum and the majestic Pergamon are standouts—the Pergamon Altar is closed for restoration until late 2019 but the rest of the museum, including the stunning Ishtar Gate,

remains open—as is the excellently curated Deutsches Historisches Museum (German History Museum). The delightful Café im Zeughaus, in the latter, is a perfect place for a mid-afternoon pick-me-up.

Later, you can wander the **Scheunenviertel,** the former working-class area and Jewish Quarter near Hackescher Markt for window-shopping and dinner at one of the neighborhood's German restaurants like Altes Europa, Hackescher Hof, or Weinbar Rutz. Finish the evening at the unpretentious **Clärchens Ballhaus,** a century-old dance hall that attracts everyone from cool twentysomethings to dressed-up senior citizens.

THREE DAYS IN BERLIN

Follow the one-day itinerary *above*, then spend the second day exploring the young side of Berlin, in Kreuzberg. This is a good time to rent a bicycle. Browse secondhand clothing stores and indie boutiques and have lunch at **Markthalle IX,** home to a bevy of excellent local food stalls, then head south to

Tempelhofer Park, the historic airfield turned popular park. These days you can share the runways, which the American bombers used during the Berlin Airlift, with kite-surfers and skateboarders.

Exit the park to Neukölln, a working-class neighborhood that has emerged as an epicenter of hipsterism. For lunch, there are many Middle Eastern eateries as well as the popular Italian restaurant **Lavanderia Vecchia**.

Continue east and cross the Spree over the redbrick **Oberbaum Bridge,** which served as a border crossing between East and West Berlin. On the other side of the river is Friedrichshain and the famous **East Side Gallery,** where international artists covered remnants of the Berlin Wall with colorful murals. Also in Friedrichshain, you can see the magnitude of socialist urban planning along **Karl-Marx-Allee,** a wide boulevard lined with the so-called workers' paradise apartments. Afterward, sample the food and nightlife offerings of youthful Simon Dach and Boxhagener Streets.

Go west on Day 3 and spend the day in Charlottenburg. Spend the morning at **Schloss Charlottenburg,** the largest palace in Berlin, with rococo flourishes and an impeccably manicured garden. Take Bus 109 to the **Käthe Kollwitz Museum** on Fasanenstrasse, featuring works by Berlin's best-known sculptor. Next door, the café in the **Literaturhaus,** set in a 19th-century villa, is a perfect place for a leisurely lunch.

Visit the **Kaiser Wilhelm Memorial Church,** a reminder of the devastations of WWII. Scour antiques on Bleibtreustrasse, or pop into big-name shops on Kurfürstendamm, one of the most famous avenues in Berlin. The top floor of the **Kaufhaus des Westens** (KaDeWe to the locals) department store is popular for its selection of gourmet food.

Take Bus M29 and get off on Potsdamer Bridge to take a walk down newly hip Potsdamer Strasse. Berlin's galleries are notorious for playing musical chairs, and this unassuming street has emerged in the past five years as the epicenter of Berlin's contemporary art scene. If you're short on time, however, beeline to the established **Gemäldegalerie** museum, West Berlin's collection of classical European paintings including Caravaggio and Rembrandt. Round off the evening with a classical concert at the world-famous Philharmonie nearby.

FIVE DAYS IN BERLIN

With five days in Berlin you'll have time to get out of the city and head to **Potsdam** on the fourth day. The former residence of the Prussian kings, Potsdam is a quick regional train or S-bahn ride away. Start the day at **Sanssouci Palace,** the Teutonic answer to Versailles. The summer home of Frederick the Great, this UNESCO World Heritage site is crisscrossed with gorgeously landscaped trails. You can try to plan your rambles with the free map from the tourist office, but you'll inevitably get lost—and that's the beauty of it. Put on your most comfortable shoes and lose yourself in the Prussian splendor.

On your final day, check out the up-and-coming district of Wedding, a multicultural working-class neighborhood once squeezed on two sides by the Berlin Wall. Walk around and then join a guided tour of the **Berlin Unterwelten,** which includes an underground WWII bunker filled with artifacts from the war.

Afterward, hop on the S-bahn and head to Schönhauser Allee to experience Prenzlauer Berg, arguably the most sought-after neighborhood in Berlin. Have lunch in the neighborhood or saunter to Kastanienallee, dubbed "Casting Alley" for its fashion-conscious denizens who strut up and down the street: perfect for people-watching. On weekends, a flea market pops up along the remnants of the Berlin Wall at Mauerpark. Later, head to Prater, Berlin's oldest beer garden, for a pint or two.

BERLIN WITH KIDS

For all its trendy reputation, Berlin is also quite a kid-friendly city. With abundant open space, family-friendly cafés, and fun educational attractions, the German capital is an ideal place for a family holiday.

BURNING OFF ENERGY

Berlin has plenty of room to run around. There are several excellent urban oases of greenery, aside from the vast, central **Tiergarten.** Those in the know, though, head to the relatively new **Tempelhofer Park,** which was converted from the old Tempelhof Airport into a fabulous outdoor area where families bike, picnic, and fly kites.

ANIMALS EVERYWHERE!

Berlin is home to the oldest zoo in Germany: the 1844-built Berlin Zoological Garden in the Tiergarten. It receives 3 million visitors a year, making it the most visited zoo in Europe. More than 1,570 species including pandas, orangutans, and other cuddly creatures call this central piece of greenery home. Next door is an adorably old-fashioned aquarium.

If the kids are into underwater creatures, you'll want to head to **Sea Life Berlin,** the urban aquarium near Alexanderplatz, where moray eels and sharks are on view. The highlight, however, is in the **Aquadom,** next door in the Radisson Blu Hotel, where the elevator travels through a 52-foot tropical fish tank (included in admission to Sea Life).

FUN LEARNING

At the **DDR Museum,** history comes alive with hands-on exhibits, like exploring a typical East German apartment or climbing into a Trabi automobile for a simulated ride. Kids and adults both get a kick out of the experience, and the museum is conveniently located in Mitte, right across from the Berliner Dom.

Another great museum that keeps the kids entertained is the **Deutsches Technikmuseum.** What used to be a train depot in Kreuzberg has become an expansive museum that displays the impressive evolution of modern transportation, from steamer trains to aircraft. Right next door, the newly developed Park am Gleisdreieck is also a wonderful place to romp: it's shaped out of an industrial landscape of train tracks, signals, and switches, some of which have been kept intact in a nod to its former life.

SIDE TRIPS
FROM BERLIN

Once you come to Berlin you may never want to leave—the city just has so much to offer in terms of art and architecture, history and culture, food and drink. But once you've had your fill, know that there are plenty of other exciting places to visit not far from the German capital. Whether your preference is for busy cities or tranquil countryside, vibrant art museums or lively shopping quarters, East or West German history, you'll find it just a few hours' drive or train ride from Berlin.

....

DRESDEN, GERMANY

The first stop for most Berlin visitors looking for a worthwhile overnight trip, this small city has gained a reputation as the "phoenix" of Germany. Almost entirely destroyed in a firebombing during WWII (you'll recognize it as the star of Kurt Vonnegut's iconic novel *Slaughterhouse-Five*) Dresden has truly been reborn. There's its gleaming old town, full of churches, museums, and palaces, and its thriving arts scene, complete with street murals, contemporary galleries, opera, and ballet. Any trip to Dresden should include a visit to the Frauenkirche, a reconstructed church, the Zwinger, a palatial art museum, and the Military History Museum, with a new wing designed by Daniel Liebeskind, the star architect also responsible for Berlin's Jewish Museum.

LEIPZIG, GERMANY

The perennial underdog, Leipzig is a city that few people think they'll find appealing, and most fall in love with once they get there. Banish those images of endless gray Communist blocks in favor of a gorgeous, bustling, beautifully rebuilt old town, full of covered shopping galleries, ornate, century-old cafés and some pretty great museums, and genteel residential neighborhoods with turn-of-the-century villas laced with leafy canals. Leipzig also has some pretty fascinating East German dissident history, and it's home to the world's most famous boys' choir, as well as the burial place of Bach. Add in trendy vegetarian restaurants, underground jazz clubs, and the hulking, bombastic Battle of the Nations Memorial and you've got yourself the makings of a world-class city just waiting for its moment.

GÖRLITZ, GERMANY

This town in Saxony gained recent fame as the setting for Quentin Tarantino's *Inglourious Basterds* and Wes Anderson's *Grand Budapest*

Hotel (although the candy-colored hotel is nowhere to be found here; its interior shots were filmed in a shuttered art nouveau department store). Thanks to rising real estate prices in cities like Berlin, though, and visitors looking to experience a bit of film lore, Görlitz has seen an uptick in international interest. Come here for centuries of architecture, including elegant apartment buildings and medieval churches, for glimpses into the lost art and culture of Silesia (a part of eastern Germany that reverted to Poland after the war), and a taste of meaty, rustic German cuisine and Polish favorites like pierogi, only a bridge away (it's right on the Polish border, with a river separating it from neighboring Zgorzelec).

SPREEWALD, GERMANY

This leafy, dreamy cluster of waterways is about as close as you'll get to that traditional image of Germany. Cheery villagers sell barrel pickles or sauerkraut, sausages, and traditional Sorbian painted eggs by the side of the road as you get off the train at the two main villages of Lübben and Lübbenau. Boats weave their way under bridges, past flowering meadows and charming country homes, and families sit down to coffee-and-cake hour at cafés in restored Prussian-era buildings. Just south of the German capital and less than an hour away by train, it's highly accessible as well, which probably makes it such a popular day trip for German if not international tourists (comparatively few locals speak English). Book kayaks, canoes, or bikes early during the high season, and be prepared for crowds on any nice sunny day in summer.

WEIMAR, GERMANY

Whether you're into art, architecture, music, or history, there's a lot to love about Weimar. It was once home to two giants of German culture—Goethe and Schiller—whose friendly rivalry produced novels, poetry, and plays that would become part of the country's literary canon. Then there was Franz Liszt, who ended his years of world traveling by moving here to teach and compose, forming a partnership with Richard Wagner. Finally, there's the Bauhaus movement, founded in Weimar in 1919 and about to celebrate its 100th anniversary, which upended countless aspects art and design, and truly ushered in the 20th century in the process. On top of all that, Weimar is truly a beautiful city, with parks and gardens, picturesque buildings and squares, and the Herzogin Anna Amalia Bibliothek, a magnificent rococo library so popular its timed tickets are sold out months in advance.

ERFURT, GERMANY

The capital of the region of Thuringia, Erfurt has a lot going for it. There's its grand Gothic cathedral, several centuries old and complete with original medieval interior, the enormous city fortress Zitadelle Petersburg, the Augustiner Kloster, a picturesque monastery where Martin Luther was a monk in the early 16th century, and the ruins of a thousand-year-old synagogue, possibly the oldest in Europe. Its most Insta-grammable sight, however, may be the Krämerbrücke or "merchant bridge," crowded with half-timber houses that once made it a major stop along a European trade route. Today, those picturesque buildings are home to shops, ateliers, and even private apartments. After you're done exploring, settle into an outdoor café in one the city's many bustling squares, joining locals to catch the late-afternoon sun over a cup of coffee or a glass of wine.

WITTENBERG, GERMANY

Nicknamed "Lutherstadt," this town in Thuringia will be forever be associated with Martin Luther and the Protestant Reformation, which he kicked off by nailing his "95 Theses" to the door of the local church. Countless city sights give insight into the Reformation, most of them refurbished or enhanced for its 500-year anniversary just one year ago: you can visit the Lutherhaus, where Luther once lived, to learn about his influence on history and his family life (he was a monk who married a nun—scandalous!), or the Melanchthon House, home to another famed German reformer. There's the Luther Garden with its 500 newly planted trees, and count-less memorials to Martin Luther as well. If you're experiencing religion overload, check out the Hunder-twasserschule, a school built according to the plans of the architect who also designed Vienna's famed

Hundertwasserhaus, or the Pies-teritz Workmen's Colony, an early-20th-century housing project.

DESSAU, GERMANY

Dessau may not have been the city where Bauhaus was founded (that would be Weimar), but it may be the one most closely associated with the movement, thanks to the iconic Bauhaus building, with its blocky design and striking font on its vertical sign. You can take a tour of the so-called Meisterhäuser or Masters' Houses, where Bauhaus professors lived with their families, or stay a night in the Prellerhaus, where a handful of the original studios have been made into guest rooms. The sprawling green Bau-haus campus is just a 15-minute walk from downtown, and students of architecture still come here from all over the world to study and marvel at a movement that existed for only a few short years, but had a worldwide impact.

HAMBURG, GERMANY

With its elegant town hall, green city parks and lakes, exciting art museums, famed nightlife centered around the notorious Reeperbahn, and large port that has made it a thriving center of trade for centu-ries, Hamburg is like an alternate-reality version of Berlin. It's enjoyed a healthy rivalry with the German capital for years, but Hamburg has its own personality, so you'd be forgiven for loving both. Just like the German capital, it's also in a constant state of flux, with new buildings being added, and old ones being repurposed. Check out the sparkly Elbphilharmonie, a striking new waterside concert venue, or the Speicherstadt, an entire neighborhood of century-old brick warehouses, now home to all sorts of businesses, cafés, and restaurants, and even a museum detailing the city's role in the spice trade.

POZNAN, POLAND

A favorite of Berliners looking for a weekend getaway, Poznan is a gorgeously restored Polish city that can feel a bit like a mini-Prague: the main town square is flanked by colorful and ornate buildings, there's a Renaissance-era town hall with a clock tower where mechanical animals prance every day at noon, and the old town is full of restaurants serving hearty regional fare, including ubiquitous pierogi, Polish beer brands like Żywiec, and bison-grass vodka. Churches and museums abound, including a striking cathedral on its own island and an imperial castle, but the city also has a thriving contemporary art scene, with plenty of indie galleries. The artificial Lake Malta is lined with early-20th-century villas, and is also the setting for the annual Malta Poznan Festival, a celebration of art, dance, theater, and music every June.

BERLIN OUTDOORS

Many first-time visitors to Berlin are surprised by how green it is: the city abounds with parks and gardens, leafy squares and picturesque canals. What's more, with a top-notch transit system, and regional trains that will have you halfway across the country in a matter of hours, there's no end to the national parks, lake districts, and mountain regions you can reach from the German capital.

....

TIERGARTEN

Once a royal hunting ground (its name translates as "animal garden") Berlin's central park is a respite from city life, full of ponds and streams, gardens and lawns, and cultural attractions like the English Garden, which hosts a jazz festival every summer, and Berlin's beloved zoo and aquarium. The easiest way to explore is by bike, though a long, meandering walk with a stop for coffee at the Café am Neuen See (a beloved café and restaurant beside a lake) isn't a bad way to spend an afternoon.

TEMPELHOFER PARK

Among Berlin's newest green spaces, this park is famous for its previous life: up until 2008 it was an airport, and the site of the famed Berlin Airlift, which saved the city from Soviet siege in 1948-49. Its runways are now full of bikers and rollerbladers, the green spaces in between taken over by community gardens and families grilling and picnicking. Meanwhile, its hulking

arrival halls host frequent events, and are open to several regular history and architecture tours.

GLEISDREIECKPARK

Another recent addition to Berlin's growing list of parks, Gleisdreieck used to be a rail depot. Industrial remnants still peek through the grass, including iron tracks and some watchtowers, but this is now a place where children run free on lawns and clamber across playgrounds, skateboarders strut their stuff at a skate park, and street artists decorate officially designated walls. Head to the park's southern end for wilder meadows, or its northern end for a glimpse of the striking German Technology Museum, with an airplane on its roof.

GRUNEWALD

More of a forest than a park, this sprawling bit of countryside at Berlin's western edge is dense and lush enough to entertain thoughts of witches, fairies, and the Brothers Grimm. It has a castlelike hunting lodge (Jagdschloss) that hosts a charming Christmas market, but also a Soviet-era listening station (Teufelsberg) on top of a hill made of WWII-era rubble. There are plenty of lakes for swimming in summer, but also an outdoor contemporary art collection (Haus am Waldsee) for those more culturally minded. This one is best explored by bike, but if you fancy a long hike in spring or summer, bring a spare basket to carry all the fruits, berries, and flowers you'll find here.

MAUERPARK

A bit dusty and scrappy but beloved by locals, Mauerpark has a name that hints at its history. This strip of green used to be part of the no-man's-land between East and West Berlin ("Mauer" means "wall" in German), notorious for its trip wires, watchtowers, and attack dogs. Today, it hosts a wildly popular Sunday flea market, complete with a beer garden and rollicking karaoke in an amphitheater. On a normal day, you'll see neighbors sprawling out on the grass or throwing a Frisbee, and kids rambling through the petting zoo at its northern end.

LANDWEHR CANAL

This waterway flows through several of Berlin's hippest neighborhoods, but the part that cuts through Kreuzberg is particularly picturesque, with sprawling grassy areas perfect for picnics, and bridges that act as impromptu gathering places for the city's buskers, beer drinkers, and layabouts. Although

it gets a bit industrial at its western end, the Landwehr Canal is mostly one long trail of trees and flowers perfect for cycling. Just make sure you budget time for all the photo stops you'll make along the way.

SPREEWALD

Just south of Berlin, this is a landscape of bright meadows, lush forests, and tranquil streams weaving their way past centuries-old half-timber houses and small farms. A biosphere reserve and UNESCO heritage site, Spreewald harks back to the early days of Berlin, when it was simply a series of settlements on a swamp. Organize a group of friends to take the train to one of two main villages, Lübben and Lübbenau, where you can rent canoes and kayaks, or simply get on one of the small barges that serve beer to boisterous locals as they wind along the canals.

TEGELER SEE

The city's second largest, this lake's proximity to the center makes it a favorite of Berliners looking to cool off in summer. Here's where you'll find a sprawling public beach perfect for setting up a picnic and taking a dip, but also plenty of sailing clubs and marinas, some of which offer yacht charters, or sailboat and houseboat rentals. Ringed by forest and freckled with seven tiny islands, Tegeler See is the perfect place for a mini adventure, especially if you have kids in tow.

SCHLACHTENSEE AND WANNSEE

Perhaps the most popular of Berlin's summer retreats, these two lakes in the southwest are absolutely teeming with swimmers the minute the weather gets warm. Schlachtensee is surrounded by a 7-km boardwalk that also makes it a popular spot for walking and running, while Wannsee, despite its gruesome history (the House of the Wannsee Conference sits on its banks) is one of Berlin's most picturesque spots, lined with villas and country clubs, dotted with countless sailboats, its public beach full of the traditional "Strandkörbe" or basketweave chairs.

MÄRKISCHE SCHWEIZ

Just beyond Berlin's eastern border, this reserve is a haven for hikers and cyclers, a European bird sanctuary, and a spa destination. Märkische Schweiz is Brandenburg's oldest nature park, and Berliners have been going here for years to traipse around woodlands, spot migrating geese in fall, and take a dip in the curative waters of the resort town of Buckow. Pack a bag full of snacks and head out into this vast forested area, weaving around its lakes, streams, and swamps, and enjoying the hilly terrain in an otherwise mostly flat region.

MADE IN BERLIN

Maybe it's the cheap rent and big spaces to work in, the layers of history to provide inspiration, or the vibrant art scenes to pick and choose from, but it seems Berliners have always been preternaturally creative. In the last decade or so, as the city's economy has picked up steam, attracting ambitious artists from around the globe, the worlds of fashion and design have produced some true luminaries. By no means an exhaustive list, here is a brief selection of Berlin's best designers, and where to find them.

LALA BERLIN

Founded by Tehran-born Leyla Piedayesh in 2004, this cult Berlin brand was one of the first to open in the area north of Hackescher Markt that has since become the center of the city's fashion scene. At first concentrating on playful, chunky knits—and signature patterned scarves—Lala Berlin has since moved on to offer a range of dresses and separates with a punk-rock vibe and an urban edge, perfect for hopping around to the many galleries that surround her store, or sipping drinks in a nearby hidden cocktail bar. ⌧ Alte Schönhauser Str. 3 ⊕ www.lalaberlin.com

KAVIAR GAUCHE

Founded in 2004 by Berlin fashion students Alexandra Fischer-Roehler and Johanna Kühl, this brand has made a name for itself with exceedingly elegant yet playful gowns that hug the body, or swirl around it in a fanciful, fairy-tale-like cloud. Just a glimpse through the window of their Linienstrasse shop could make even the most grounded woman want to grab someone off the street to marry, just so she could wear one of their gorgeous pieces. No worries if you can't: the label has a line of bags and shoes that could easily work for the everyday. ⌧ Linienstr. 44 ⊕ www.kaviargauche.com

DUMITRASCU

This Romanian-born designer made quite a splash with her recent guerilla fashion show in a Paris metro station, and indeed, her clothes feel a bit rebellious, with bright colors, oversized pieces, slouchy cuts, and fetish-inspired details that hark back to 1990s Berlin, when the city's techno clubbing scene was just beginning. Indeed, these are clothes to go out in, but they're also clothes that would work just as well in the newer, more grown-up Berlin of today, perfect for making a splash at an upscale Mitte restaurant or sleek cocktail bar. ✉ *Mulackstr. 34* ⊕ *www.dumitrascu.de*

THONE NEGRÓN

This German-born designer offers a bit of feminine whimsy, with silk print tops, smartly tailored dresses incorporating delicate lace and Japanese fabrics, and short jackets with a bit of Spanish flair. Her pieces have color and grace, and an elegance and playfulness that means they work just as well on the streets of London or Paris as they do in the German capital. They also work just as well paired with jeans for a casual day about town as they would on a party or a date, and their versatility is no doubt what has made them a favorite among Berlin fashionistas. ✉ *Novalisstr. 14* ⊕ *www.thonenegron.com*

RENÉ TALMON L'ARMÉE

There are plenty of Berlin souvenirs that everyone has, so why not return with a one-of-a-kind piece of jewelry, direct from this Linienstrasse store and workshop? Born in Berlin, the designer lived in London and Paris, and his pieces have a distinctly grown-up aesthetic, with molded metal rings, printed leather cuffs, and chunky earrings with dramatic stones. He also makes one-off pieces in discussion with clients, so perhaps this is the perfect time to get that black diamond ring you always dreamed about. ✉ *Linienstr. 109* ⊕ *www.renetalmonlarmee.com*

FRAU TONIS

What does Berlin summer smell like? What about a whiff of Hamburg or Munich? The scents at this Mitte shop go far beyond the traditional flowery or fruity notes to capture a whiff of a certain place or time: literally your favorite city in a bottle. Founded in 2009 and named after the owner's grandmother, Frau Tonis is adept at crafting nostalgia, but keeping things sleek, modern, and surprising. Drop in on any weekday to make your own customized scent at a workshop. That way, you'll be coming home with something entirely unique. ✉ *Zimmerstr. 13* ⊕ *www.frau-tonis-parfum.com/en/*

SCHOEMIG PORZELLAN

Claudia Schoemig's Prenzlauer Berg shop is full of sleek, simple ceramic pieces, some unpainted, with delicate lines traced to form an irregular grid over a white background, others showing off subdued pastel glazes. Schoemig brings expert craftsmanship and a sunny disposition to each bit of porcelain. One of her light, round cups feels beautifully natural in the hand, and is sure to brighten up your morning coffee routine. ✉ *Raumerstr. 35* ⊕ *schoemig-por-zellan.de*

WHAT TO EAT AND DRINK IN BERLIN

Like many world capitals, Berlin is a melting pot (or perhaps we should say a goulash stew) of cultures, nationalities, and religions that left their mark on the city. Its food scene is also a collage, with dishes from all over Germany. What's more, a growing international population has created a market for cuisines from outside Germany as well. That means it can be easier to rustle up a bowl of Vietnamese pho, a plate of Chinese dumplings, or a dish of Peruvian ceviche, than to find some of the authentic Berlin dishes on this list. Get 'em while they're hot...and while they're still around.

CURRYWURST

This perennial local favorite is nothing more than a sliced sausage doused in ketchup and sprinkled with curry powder. Sometimes, if you're lucky, the sausage will come premade with curry flavoring in it as well. A holdover from the post-WWII years that somehow became a symbol of the resurgent city, the invention of currywurst has been claimed by quite a few Berliners. The consensus falls on Herta Heuwer, who now has a plaque on the Charlottenburg spot where she first invented and sold it. It's best paired with French fries or "pommes" and eaten standing up at an outdoor high table.

DÖNER KEBAB

Like currywurst, this beloved Berlin snack is also famous enough to have disputed origins. Its invention is often attributed to Kadir Nurman, though several Turkish immigrants, no doubt part of the group brought over as "guest workers" to rebuild postwar Germany, have laid claim to it. It's easy to see why so many want to: it's the perfect handheld meal on-the-go. Made with sliced lamb or beef, chicken, or even tofu, and topped with salads and sauces (garlic or chili are the favorites), this simple flatbread sandwich (the name "döner" comes from the act of turning the meat on a spit) is endlessly customizable, and deliciously addictive.

BULETTE

Also referred to as *frikadelle*, this street snack is basically a hamburger without a bun. It's quite possible the citizens of Hamburg were the first ones to make it, but this snack has migrated all over Germany and is now still served at street stalls next to all manner of sausages. Expect it to be dryer than the average burger (no chance of ordering yours "medium rare" here), but that only means it should be washed down with a tall glass of pilsner.

BERLINER

When JFK made his famous proclamation "Ich bin ein Berliner," he never could have guessed he would become the butt of so many jokes for so many decades. The problem is, these jokes really only exist in English, since his expression of solidarity with Berlin residents makes perfect sense in German. That's because the jelly-filled doughnut everyone else in Germany calls a "Berliner" here is called a "Pfannkuchen," which means "pancake" everywhere else in Germany. Perplexed yet? You'll quickly drown your confusion in a dusting of powdered sugar, the crunch and chew of dough, and the ooze of jam. Just be careful if you're offered any at a New Year's party: one out of every batch is traditionally filled with mustard, giving its eater good luck for a year.

BIENENSTICHKUCHEN

Never fear, this sweet treat's name—"bee-sting cake"—is only a reference to its honey and sugar content. It combines a bottom layer of crumbly dough and a top layer of crisp, caramelized almond slices, its deeply burnished gold color and perfect combination of textures quite tempting on a brisk fall day. Some Germans like to make two layers of the cake, sandwiched around a buttercream or vanilla custard middle, but you'll find it without in most Berlin bakeries, and you may agree it's unnecessary.

KÖNIGSBERGER KLOPSE

Named after a city in East Prussia that's now part of Russia's Kalin ingrad, this was a classic Prussian dish that remained a staple in East Germany. Even today you can see why: the pillowy meatballs served in a creamy caper gravy with potatoes on the side is the perfect well-rounded meal (at least, if you lived in the GDR and had little access to fresh vegetables). Just like the people of the former East, this dish feels humble and unadorned; there's something warming, comforting, and nostalgic about it that explains why it's still on the menu at traditional German restaurants.

BRATWURST

The one that everyone knows, the standard by which all others are measured, this street snack is the closest you'll come to a Berlin version of a hot dog. Except instead of being served in a fluffy, elongated bun exactly its shape, the bratwurst will be handed to you in a tiny, crusty roll sliced nearly in half, which acts as an edible holder more than an important component of the meal. Get it with mustard or ketchup and then hightail it out of there: this lovingly browned, juicy grilled sausage is meant to be eaten on the go.

SCHNITZEL

Sure, it's most famous in Vienna (as the beloved Wiener schnitzel), but Germans love their meat pounded, breaded, and fried just as much as Austrians do. You're liable to find this veal cutlet (sometimes replaced with pork) at sit-down restaurants, served with potatoes and a lemon wedge, or tucked under a thick blanket of arugula. Sometimes, it'll be as big as your plate, sometimes even bigger: at Neukölln classic restaurant Louis, it's almost twice the size of whatever dish it's served on. What's more, if you happen to tell the waiter you want the rest to go, expect the entire restaurant to judge you for your small stomach. In Germany, finishing a schnitzel is a blood sport.

BERLINER WEISSE

As American craft beer lovers have adopted a taste for sour and fermented ales, the Berliner Weisse has achieved a kind of cult status. In Berlin, however, it's long been a classic warm-weather drink, prized for its refreshing taste and low alcohol content. In the United States, you may find it with all manner of fruit flavorings—Mango! Watermelon! Yuzu!—and cutesy names, but in the German capital there are only two: the one with the red syrup (raspberry) and the one with the green syrup (woodruff). No matter which one you choose, rest assured you'll be taking part in a Berlin summer tradition.

FEDERWEISSER

Not quite a Berlin drink but as much a part of Berlin summers as grill parties, long bike rides, and all-night raves, this fall beverage can only be found one month out of the year: it's a young wine (literally translated as "feather white") made from the pressed juice of just-picked grapes, bottled while still fermenting. That's why Federweisser, while delicious, is famously dangerous: caps are not screwed tightly to allow the gases to escape, so be careful to keep it upright. What's more, the longer you keep it around the drunker you'll be: the fermentation process continues over days, until the sweet grape juice you bought a week ago is all alcohol and ready for a party.

BERLIN'S
TOP EXPERIENCES

Hip, energetic Berlin has grabbed the world's attention with its exuberant urban life and vibrant arts scene. Gone are the days of drab Cold War Germany and a city divided by the wall. In this cosmopolitan and affordable capital, neighborhoods like Mitte, Friedrichshain, Prenzlauer Berg, and Kreuzberg bustle with restaurants, cafés, and nightlife. Museums and sights such as the Pergamon on Museum Island, the Brandenburg Gate, and the Jewish Museum provide a window into Berlin's rich history. Today the stitched-together heart of Germany beats fast.

THE REICHSTAG
Take a tour of the seat of Germany's Parliament to see where 20th-century world history was shaped and, especially, to check out the striking Norman Foster–designed glass cupola. The Reichstag (parliament building) was rebuilt with a special glass dome that offers sweeping views of the city and looks directly into the parliament chambers below in a nod to government transparency. The views of Berlin from here are spectacular.

THE SPREE RIVER
The Spree is one of the city's finest natural features. Clubs and cafés line its banks, and you can relax in a beach chair by the water in the summer months.

THE BERLIN WALL
When the wall fell in 1989, Berliners couldn't wait to get rid of it. The longest stretch left standing is the East Side Gallery. In 1990, the city invited artists to paint one side of the nearly mile-long wall in a tribute to peace, resulting in famous works such as the socialistic fraternal kiss. The Berlin Wall Memorial, located along another remaining segment, has a museum and open-air exhibition dedicated to the years of division. At the best-known border crossing, the Checkpoint Charlie Museum highlights ways people tried to escape the GDR.

STREET ART
Berlin is famous for edgy street art, with thousands of pieces in areas including Mitte, Friedrichshain, and Prenzlauer Berg. The East Side Gallery has some great examples.

BEER GARDENS
As soon as the sun comes out and temperatures allow, Germans set up tables and chairs under the open skies and offer a "Prost!" to their friends or colleagues. Bavaria is the home of the *Biergarten*, but you

can sample local variations of beer and bratwurst at outdoor tables almost anywhere in the country. If it's a beautiful day and you don't see a beer garden nearby, take your own drink to the park: Germany has no open-container laws.

HOLOCAUST MEMORIAL

The Memorial to the Murdered Jews of Europe is made up of 2,711 concrete slabs of different heights. Some visitors point out the memorial's resemblance to a cemetery.

BRANDENBURGER TOR

Berlin was the capital of Prussia, the German Empire, the Weimar Republic, and the Third Reich before being divided after World War II. The famed Brandenburger Tor (Brandenburg Gate), built in the late 1700s, became a symbol of both the country's division and reunification. Restored to Prussian glory after being partially destroyed, the Brandenburg Gate is one of Berlin's major landmarks. You can't miss it at the head of Unter den Linden.

SEASONAL DELICACIES

If you visit between April and June, you're in for a treat: it's white asparagus season. Germans go crazy for the stuff, which is thicker and larger than green asparagus. Enjoy it with a slice of ham and potatoes with butter or hollandaise sauce.

MUSEUMSINSEL

Five state museums on "Museum Island" showcase architectural monuments and art treasures. The Pergamonmuseum, with its artifacts from the ancient world, is a standout.

CHRISTMAS MARKETS

In Berlin, there are as many as 60 small Christmas markets each year, opening the last week of November and running through Christmas. Bundle up and shop for handmade gifts as you sip traditional, hot-spiced *Glühwein* to stay warm.

DDR MUSEUM

Experience a taste of life in Soviet East Germany at this interactive museum. Exhibits include a Trabi car you can "drive" and an apartment with a wiretapped phone.

THE DÖNER KEBAB

It would be hard to visit Berlin without trying this Turkish sandwich, whether for lunch, dinner, or a snack after a night out on the town. Made from some combination of lamb, chicken, pork, or beef roasted on a spit then sliced into pita pockets with lettuce, chopped tomato, yogurt, and spicy sauce, the *döner kebab* is the indisputable king of snack food. An inexpensive alternative to German fare, they're available on almost any city corner.

NEARBY LAKES

Berlin is surrounded by tranquil lakes, and when the weather is warm, locals strip down and jump right in. Don't worry if you don't have your suit. it's perfectly acceptable to swim in the nude. If swimming's not your thing, rent a paddleboat and cruise past the sunbathers.

BIKE TOURS

Seeing Berlin from the seat of a bike is one of the best ways to experience the city. Take a guided tour or rent a bike and set off on your own. As you wind your way along the river and through neighborhoods, you'll find that you see much more than you would from a tour bus.

CURRYWURST

Sausage with curried ketchup—it's a Berlin street food must. Stands around the city, like the renowned Curry 36, entice customers from morning till well past midnight.

POTSDAM'S PALACE

If you can tear yourself away from Berlin, take a day trip out to **Potsdam** and tour the opulent palaces and manicured gardens of **Sanssouci Park. Schloss Sanssouci,** a palace constructed to resemble Versailles, was used as a summer getaway for Frederick the Great and is a must-see (buy tickets in advance if you can). Return to Berlin in the evening to explore more of its distinct neighborhoods, like Turkish Kreuzberg or lively Prenzlauer Berg. The next day, fly home from Berlin.

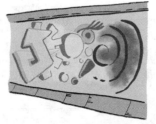

COOL PLACES TO STAY IN BERLIN

CASA CAMPER

Adopting a DIY approach, the slickly designed boutique hotel features a 24-hour snack bar—included in the room rate—in the top-floor lounge. The light-filled space, with its comfy leather seating, is a chill spot to hang out and soak in views of Berlin's rooftops. **Pros:** wood-lined rooms afford plenty of natural light. **Cons:** street noise in some rooms. *Rooms from: €165 ⊠ Weinmeisterstr. 1, Mitte, 10119. ☎ 49/30200–03410. ⊕ casacamper. com. 51 rooms, 24-hour buffet Ⓜ U-Bahn: Weinmeister Str.*

DAS STUE BERLIN

One of the city's most elegant hideaways, this hotel is situated in the former Danish Embassy, and its muted colors, mid-century modern furniture, and mix of wood and stone are a nod to restrained Scandinavian elegance. What's more, it's tucked into a corner of the Tiergarten, so guests will have the park as their own backyard. The elegant Cinco by Paco Pérez is billed as the city's first true molecular gastronomy restaurant. **Pros:** central location. **Cons:** small spa can book up quickly. *Rooms from: €153 ⊠ Drakestr. 1, Tiergarten, 10787. ☎ 49/3031–17220. ⊕ das-stue-com. 80 rooms, breakfast, lunch, and dinner available Ⓜ S-Bahn: Tiergarten.*

HOTEL ADLON KEMPINSKI BERLIN

Destroyed in World War II, this luxury hotel was rebuilt in 1997 with its golden past in mind. Rooms feature traditional mahogany furnishings, brocade silk bedspreads, and turn-of-the-century photos of the original hotel, while the lobby boasts a resplendent elephant fountain—presented to the Adlon in 1930 by India's Maharajah of Patiala—antique furnishings, and magnificent Murano glass chandeliers. **Pros:** excellent restaurants. **Cons:** crowded lobby, some noisy rooms. *Rooms from: €260 ⊠ Unter den Linden 77, Mitte, 10117. ☎ 49/302–2610. ⊕ Kempinski.com/ adlon. 382 rooms, breakfast, lunch, and dinner available Ⓜ S-Bahn/U-Bahn: Brandenburger Tor.*

HOTEL AM STEINPLATZ

In a century-old art nouveau building with Gaudí-esque touches designed by August Endell (also responsible for the Hackesche Höfe complex), this relatively new hotel has bright, airy rooms with high ceilings, understated patterns, and a minibar stocked with locally made snacks and drinks. **Pros:** the top-floor spa has views over Berlin's rooftops. **Cons:** sophisticated ambience might feel a bit stiff to some. *Rooms from: €150 ⊠ Steinpl. 4, Charlottenburg, 10623. ☎ 49/3055–44440. ⊕ hotelsteinplatz.com. 87 rooms,*

breakfast, lunch, and dinner available
Ⓜ *S-Bahn: Zoologischer Garten.*

HOTEL AMANO

This sleek, elegant, yet trendy hotel has made a name for itself as one of the city's premier hangout spots, filling up with hip Mitte locals at night who come for drinks on the roof and frequent parties in the ground-level bar. **Pros:** part of a growing mini-chain within the city, it puts Berlin at your fingertips with curated mini-maps and iPods preloaded with Berlin tips plus a cool Berlin soundtrack. **Cons:** can be noisy. *Rooms from: €85* ✉ *Auguststr. 43, Mitte, 10119.* ☎ *49/3080–94150.* ⊕ *amanogroup.de. 163 rooms, breakfast available* Ⓜ *U-Bahn: Rosenthaler-Platz.*

HOTEL DE ROME

Just off Unter den Linden in a former bank headquarters, this sumptuous hotel has retained many original historic touches, including a grand ballroom that was once a cashier's hall, and a mosaic-lined, columned swimming pool in the onetime vault. Rooms feel enormous even by Berlin standards, several with ornate wood paneling and marble bathrooms, and a classic afternoon tea is an elegant, unexpected touch. **Pros:** great location and large rooms. **Cons:** design might be over the top for some. *Rooms from: €260* ✉ *Behrenstr. 37, Mitte, 10117.* ☎ *49/3046–06090.* ⊕ *rocco-fortehotels.com/hotels-and-resorts/hotel-de-rome/. 145 rooms, breakfast, lunch, and dinner available* Ⓜ *U-Bahn: Franzözische Str.*

HOTEL ZOO BERLIN

Elegantly weaving together old and new, this boutique charmer features plenty of original prewar details in its preserved Altbau building on one of Kurfürstendamm's busiest stretches. Contemporary bespoke furnishings and whimsical design touches—including a 22-foot-long leopard carpet in the entryway—give the property a playful vibe that's much needed in the upscale west. **Pros:** its restaurant and rooftop bar have become an of-the-moment haunt for Charlottenburg artists and hipsters. **Cons:** street noise can be heard in some rooms. *Rooms from: €150* ✉ *Kurfürstendamm 25, Charlottenburg, 10719.* ☎ *49/3088–4370.* ⊕ *hotelzoo.de. 141 rooms, breakfast, lunch, and dinner available* Ⓜ *U-Bahn: Kurfürstendamm.*

LUX ELEVEN

Built into an "Altbau" (prewar apartment building) on one of Mitte's hippest streets, this hotel combines historic and contemporary details to give guests that coveted old Berlin feel with modern comfort. Neon-pink, acid-green, and bright-blue accents grant the sleek designer apartments a fresh, modern vibe. **Pros:** lavish penthouse suite has a view of the TV Tower. **Cons:** some rooms are a bit small. *Rooms from: €100* ✉ *Rosa-Luxemburg-Str. 9-13, Mitte, 10178.* ☎ *49/3093–62800.* ⊕ *lux-eleven.com. 73 rooms* Ⓜ *U-Bahn: Rosa-Luxemburg-Str.*

MICHELBERGER HOTEL

A youthful, artsy vibe pervades this budget design hotel, attracting nightlife-loving hipsters who come for cocktails at the buzzy bar-lounge area and, in summer, for the courtyard beer garden, which hosts live music. **Pros:** emphasis on using independent, organic producers in cuisine and cocktails; hip vibe. **Cons:** can be noisy; no phones in rooms. *Rooms from: €60 ⊠ W-arschauer Str. 39-40, Friedrichshain, 10243. ☎ 49/30297-78590. ⊕ michelbergerhotel.com. 113 rooms, breakfast, lunch, and dinner available* Ⓜ *S-Bahn/U-Bahn: Warschauer Str.*

NHOW BERLIN

Celebrated designer Karim Rashid created the playful, space-age interiors for this music-themed hotel, whose elevators entertain you with different musical genres. In keeping with its rock star-on-vacation vibe, you can also order electric guitars, keyboards, and speakers to your room, in case inspiration strikes and you feel you must compose a love song to the city. **Pros:** beautiful location on the Spree River. **Cons:** slightly isolated from neighborhood bars and restaurants. *Rooms from: €120 ⊠ Stralauer Allee 3, Friedrichshain 10245. ☎ 49/3029-02990. ⊕ nhow-berlin.com. 304 rooms, breakfast and dinner available* Ⓜ *S-Bahn/U-Bahn: Warschauer Str.*

PATRICK HELLMANN SCHLOSSHOTEL

High ceilings, multiple chandeliers, and an intricate wood-carved staircase give the lobby of this century-old baroque mansion turned luxury hotel a timeless feel. That holds true throughout many of its rooms—especially the fanciful, art deco–style Grunewald Suite. **Pros:** beautiful restaurant with garden terrace. **Cons:** might feel a bit stuffy. *Rooms from: €239 ⊠ Brahmsstr. 10, Grunewald, 14193. ☎ 49/3089-58430. ⊕ schlosshotel-berlin.com. 53 rooms, breakfast, lunch, and dinner available* Ⓜ *S-Bahn: Grunewald.*

PROVOCATEUR

A glamorous art deco hotel that pays homage to Paris of the 1920s, its award-winning interiors mix rich red velvet, ornate chandeliers, and contemporary artwork to great effect, creating a decadent, burlesque-style ambience. **Pros:** the Golden Phoenix restaurant, with cuisine by Berlin stalwart The Duc Ngo, is packed every night with Berliners drawn to its French-Asian fusion cuisine and slightly naughty mood. **Cons:** design and style not for everyone. *Rooms from: €85 ⊠ Brandenburgische Str. 21, Wilmersdorf, 10707. ☎ 49/30220-56060. ⊕ provocateur-hotel.com. 58 rooms, breakfast and dinner available* Ⓜ *U-Bahn: Adenauerplatz.*

THE RITZ-CARLTON BERLIN

The modern gray high-rise belies what's inside—a plush, old-school-style hotel dripping in gold leaf, marble, and European-style furnishings. A grand, white-marble lobby with a sweeping staircase and enormous chandelier is an appropriately sumptuous entry point to this luxury hotel. **Pros:** Curtain Club bar has a cool, old-school cigar-bar feel. **Cons:** popular with business travelers. *Rooms from: €215 ⊠ Potsdamer Pl. 3, Mitte, 10785 Berlin. ☎ 49/3033–7777. ⊕ www.ritzcarlton.com/en/hotels/germany/berlin. 303 rooms, breakfast available Ⓜ S-Bahn: Potsdamer Platz.*

SIR SAVIGNY

A hotel seemingly made for the Instagram generation in what has become the city's newly hip west side, Sir Savigny offers a retro lobby lounge lined with quirky contemporary artwork by German artists and tomes from indie bookseller Bücherbogen. **Pros:** the on-site burger bar The Butcher grills up some of the city's best meaty dishes. **Cons:** on-site dining can be pricey. *Rooms from: €113 ⊠ Kant-str. 144, Charlottenburg, 10623. ☎ 49/30217–82638. ⊕ sirhotels.com/savigny. 44 rooms, breakfast, lunch, and dinner available Ⓜ S-Bahn: Savignyplatz.*

SOHO HOUSE BERLIN

The Berlin outpost of this trendy hotel–private club is built into a 1920s department store that became a Communist Party headquarters after the war. Eclectic interiors, a hip rooftop bar scene, a swanky spa, and an industrial-chic lobby woo the millennial set. **Pros:** cleverly designed concept shop with its own café on-site. **Cons:** may feel too clubby for some. *Rooms from: €180 ⊠ Torstr. 1, Mitte, 10119. ☎ 49/3040–50440. ⊕ sohohouseberlin.com. 65 rooms, breakfast, lunch, and dinner available Ⓜ U-Bahn: Rosa-Luxemburg-Platz.*

WHAT TO WATCH AND READ

To learn more about Berlin, before or after you visit, consider these movies, TV shows, and books.

....

MOVIES

THE LIVES OF OTHERS

This Oscar-winning film is a moving and sympathetic portrayal of a group of people living behind the Iron Curtain in 1980s East Berlin. Stasi officer Gerd Wiesler is assigned to spy on a playwright and actress couple who are living out successful lives and careers as favorites of the East German government. A fascinating case study on how the act of watching a subject alters it, this film depicts what happens when one of them tries to subvert the system, and Wiesler is forced to make a decision to either report them or help them, thus putting himself in danger. Watch for the glimpses of a long-gone Berlin, but most of all, watch for a fascinating psychological portrait of people coping under a brutal totalitarian regime.

GOOD BYE LENIN

This fan favorite film brought fame to German actor Daniel Brühl with its unique storyline and dark humor. There's a revolution going on just outside young Alex's door, but the East German teenager can barely afford to take part in it, since his mother has just suffered a heart attack. The doctor says any great shock will likely kill her, so his entire family constructs an elaborate ruse to keep her calm: the Berlin Wall has not fallen, East Germany's chancellor has not just resigned, the end of the USSR is not on the horizon, and all is right in the (socialist) world. Watch for glimpses of the grand boulevard Karl-Marx-Allee and Alexanderplatz, and to find humor in the oddities of East German life and the lengths we'll go to deceive others and, when necessary, sometimes ourselves.

RUN, LOLA, RUN

Mention the name of this film and nearly any fan—plus a few people who've never seen it before—will immediately think of a young woman with a shock of magenta-red hair, dashing through the streets of the German capital. There's a lot more to this film than that, but also nothing more at all, because that's the entire premise: a young woman running through the streets of late-90s Berlin. She's punk and tough and cool as hell, but also terrified as she tries to save her boyfriend, who has lost a bag of money on a train platform, from being killed by the band of criminals who are expecting it. Then, the whole story starts over again and again, with slightly different results each time. Made less than a decade after the Berlin Wall fell, *Lola* explores how chance encounters can change people's lives and how minor decisions can have major consequences. It is an ode to a world capital finally coming into its own.

WINGS OF DESIRE

The ultimate love letter to a divided Berlin, this 1987 Wim Wenders classic film has inspired adulation ever since it was made, with late-night screenings, exhibitions, and one unfortunate U.S. remake: 1998's *City of Angels*. Its main character, the angel Damiel, played by the exquisite Swiss actor Bruno Ganz, falls in love with a circus performer and decides to give up his wings. There are special appearances by Peter Falk of *Columbo* fame and the musician Nick Cave (both playing themselves), but the real star of the film is Berlin itself—its shabby, old-fashioned corners, its new wave and punk spirit, and its historic center still ripped in two. The film's original name—*Der Himmel über Berlin* or "the heaven over Berlin"—was a far more fitting one: you see much of the city from Damiel's perspective, and even in its tragicomic moments, it offers a vision of Berlin that truly soars.

TV SHOWS

BABYLON, BERLIN

Colorful characters intertwine in this Weimar epic TV series that's a delicate dance of money, corrupt politics, scandalous cabaret, and decadent settings, the drama heightened since you know the war is about to end it all. Gereon Rath is a police inspector who's trying to uncover an organized crime ring while also battling a morphine addiction, and Charlotte Ritter is a typist by day and sometimes prostitute by night, who dreams of becoming the nation's first female police inspector. Anyone familiar with Germany's prewar history will spot countless signposts pointing the way towards the 20th century's greatest catastrophe. That's the tragedy in it, but also the beauty: pre-WWII Berlin was a lost world before it was even over, but visitors still come to the city for a whiff of it, nearly a century later.

BOOKS

THE BERLIN STORIES BY CHRISTOPHER ISHERWOOD

Blame this book for Berlin's loafers, layabouts, and "life artists" (that would be *Lebenskünstler* in German). Nearly a century on, Isherwood's version of Weimar-era Berlin—surreal and grotesque, romantic and poignant—is still the dominant one. That's thanks in no small part to the masterful story-telling in these twin novellas—*The Last of Mr. Norris* and *Goodbye to Berlin*—which introduced us to the "divinely decadent" Sally Bowles, who would go on to become an everlasting symbol of Berlin thanks to many stage and film versions. Semiautobiographical, sardonic, and slightly manic, the novellas feel like a breathless chance encounter, a story told by a stranger on a fast-moving train. In other words, they capture what it's like to discover Berlin for the first time, to never want to leave, and to be aware that one day, you must.

STASILAND BY ANNA FUNDER

This astonishing work of nonfiction is a juggling act of multiple stories, starting with its clever framing conceit: it was written from the point of view of the Australian author, who lived and worked in Berlin just after the wall fell. Now back in Germany and curious about what happened in its first decade as a reunited country, she tells the story of her attempt to locate and interview East German heroes and victims. These are the people who tried to escape, both under and over the Berlin Wall, and were caught, who fought the regime and ended up beaten, in prison, or unexpectedly banished, or who simply tried to live their lives as far as possible from the ever-present Stasi (state secret police). In the process, the author comes to grips with her role in documenting these stories, preserving history in a rapidly changing city, and how to identify heroes and victims in a regime where nearly everyone was complicit.

BERLIN: IMAGINE A CITY BY RORY MACLEAN

This epic tale tells the story of Berlin through its people, from the world-famous (David Bowie) to the well-known (Karl Friedrich Schinkel, the architect who shaped the city) to the obscure (Dieter Werner, who helped build the Berlin Wall). Interspersed with MacLean's own observations as a long-time British Berliner, it is both fiction and nonfiction, true stories embellished with details no living writer could have known. The book is perhaps a better reflection of the city than many others, thanks to its broadness: most of us know what happened in Berlin in the 20th century, but MacLean delves into 19th-century Prussia, and goes even further back, to a time when the capital was just a cluster of Slavic villages on a swamp. Those who wax poetic about Berlin often evoke its "layers of history" all visible at once; this book documents that history through the eyes of 21 people who lived it.

THE WALL JUMPER BY PETER SCHNEIDER

Technically a novel with journalistic elements, this book delves into the psychological, spiritual, and historical impact of the Berlin Wall: what it did to the city divided by it, the regime that maintained it, and the people who would long live with its consequences. Of course, there are wall jumpers to be found here, both literal and figurative: those who crossed the border from East to West Berlin at the beginning, before there really was a wall, or those who took their chances later on by burrowing under it or braving the legendary armed guards, tripwires, and attack dogs of "no-man's-land." This is a book to carry around Berlin like a guide: every time you come across a line of bricks demarcating the wall's original path, you will appreciate just what it means to cross over it in a single, simple step.

RUSSIAN DISCO BY WLADIMIR KAMINER

A novel for the new Berlin, this book's author isn't just an outsider—a Russian Jew who first arrived in the 1990s—but he's an outsider who created his own world, founding the legendary "Russian Disco" DJ night at Berlin club Kaffee Burger, becoming a central player in the city's literary and nightlife scenes. In a welcome deviation from most Berlin literature, the book is a series of comical vignettes about Kaminer's own life there in the '90s, many of which will be familiar to anyone who has recently moved to the German capital. Twenty years ago, he met with the same Kafkaesque bureaucracy, hedonistic nightlife, bad weather, and maddeningly difficult language, and somehow found it all noteworthy and hilarious enough to write about. Some have called this book a contemporary *Goodbye to Berlin*. There's no Sally Bowles in it, but its clever storytelling may just satisfy fans of Isherwood.

BERLIN CITY TIMELINE

PREHISTORY

ca. 5000 BC Indo-Germanic tribes settle in the Rhine and Danube valleys.

ca. 2000–800 BC Distinctive German Bronze Age culture emerges, with settlements ranging from coastal farms to lakeside villages.

ca. 450–50 BC Salzkammergut people, whose prosperity is based on abundant salt deposits (in the area of upper Austria), trade with Greeks and Etruscans; Salzkammerguts spread as far as Belgium and have first contact with the Romans.

9 BC–AD 9 Roman attempts to conquer the "Germans"—the tribes of the Cimbri, the Franks, the Goths, and the Vandals—are only partly successful; the Rhine becomes the northeastern border of the Roman Empire (and remains so for 300 years).

212 Roman citizenship is granted to all free inhabitants of the empire.

ca. 400 Pressed forward by Huns from Asia, such German tribes as the Franks, the Vandals, and the Lombards migrate to Gaul (France), Spain, Italy, and North Africa, scattering the empire's populace and eventually leading to the disintegration of central Roman authority.

486 The Frankish kingdom is founded by Clovis; his court is in Paris.

497 The Franks convert to Christianity.

EARLY MIDDLE AGES

776 Charlemagne becomes king of the Franks.

800 Charlemagne is declared Holy Roman Emperor; he makes Aachen capital of his realm, which stretches from the Bay of Biscay to the Adriatic and from the Mediterranean to the Baltic. Under his enlightened patronage there is an upsurge in art and architecture—the Carolingian renaissance.

843 The Treaty of Verdun divides Charlemagne's empire among his three sons: West Francia becomes France; Lotharingia becomes Lorraine (territory to be disputed by France and Germany into the 20th century); and East Francia takes on, roughly, the shape of modern Germany.

911 Five powerful German dukes (of Bavaria, Lorraine, Franconia, Saxony, and Swabia) establish the first German monarchy by electing King Conrad I; Henry I (the Fowler) succeeds Conrad in 919.

962 Otto I is crowned Holy Roman Emperor by the pope; he establishes Austria—the East Mark. The

Ottonian renaissance is marked especially by the development of Romanesque architecture.

MIDDLE AGES

1024–1125 The Salian dynasty is characterized by a struggle between emperors and the Church that leaves the empire weak and disorganized; the great Romanesque cathedrals of Speyer, Trier, and Mainz are built.

1138–1254 Frederick Barbarossa leads the Hohenstaufen dynasty; there is temporary recentralization of power, underpinned by strong trade and Church relations.

1158 Munich, capital of Bavaria, is founded by Duke Henry the Lion; Henry is deposed by Emperor Barbarossa, and Munich is presented to the House of Wittelsbach, which rules it until 1918.

1241 The Hanseatic League is founded to protect trade; Bremen, Hamburg, Köln, and Lübeck are early members. Agencies are soon established in London, Antwerp, Venice, and along the Baltic and North Seas; a complex banking and finance system results.

mid-1200s The Gothic style, exemplified by the grand Köln Cathedral, flourishes.

1349 The Black Death plague kills one-quarter of the German population.

RENAISSANCE AND REFORMATION

1456 Johannes Gutenberg (1400–68) prints the first book in Europe.

1471–1553 Renaissance flowers under the influence of painter and engraver Albrecht Dürer (1471–1528); Dutch-born philosopher and scholar Erasmus (1466–1536); Lucas Cranach the Elder (1472–1553), who originates Protestant religious painting; portrait and historical painter Hans Holbein the Younger (1497–1543); and landscape-painting pioneer Albrecht Altdorfer (1480–1538). Increasing wealth among the merchant classes leads to strong patronage of the revived arts.

1517 The Protestant Reformation begins in Germany when Martin Luther (1483–1546) nails his 95 Theses to a church door in Wittenberg, contending that the Roman Church has forfeited divine authority through its corrupt sale of indulgences. Luther is outlawed, and his revolutionary doctrine splits the Church; much of north Germany embraces Protestantism.

1524–30 The (Catholic) Habsburgs rise to power; their empire spreads throughout Europe (and as far as North Africa, the Americas, and the Philippines). Erasmus breaks with Luther and supports reform within the Roman Catholic Church. In 1530 Charles V (a Habsburg) is crowned Holy Roman Emperor; he brutally crushes the Peasants' War, one in a series of populist uprisings in Europe.

1545 The Council of Trent marks the beginning of the Counter-Reformation. Through diplomacy and coercion, most Austrians, Bavarians, and Bohemians are won back to Catholicism, but the majority of Germans remain Lutheran; persecution of religious minorities grows.

THIRTY YEARS' WAR

1618–48 Germany is the main theater for the Thirty Years' War. The powerful Catholic Habsburgs are defeated by Protestant forces, swelled by disgruntled Habsburg subjects and the armies of King Gustav Adolphus of Sweden. The bloody conflict ends with the Peace of Westphalia (1648); Habsburg and papal authority are severely diminished.

ABSOLUTISM AND ENLIGHTENMENT

1689 Louis XIV of France invades the Rhineland Palatinate and sacks Heidelberg. At the end of the 17th century, Germany consolidates its role as a center of scientific thought.

1708 Johann Sebastian Bach (1685–1750) becomes court organist at Weimar and launches his career; he and Georg Friederic Handel (1685–1759) fortify the great tradition of German music. Baroque and, later, rococo art and architecture flourish.

1740–86 Reign of Frederick the Great of Prussia; his rule sees both the expansion of Prussia (it becomes the dominant military

force in Germany) and the spread of Enlightenment thought.

ca. 1790 The great age of European orchestral music is raised to new heights with the works of Joseph Haydn (1732–1809), Wolfgang Amadeus Mozart (1756–91), and Ludwig van Beethoven (1770–1827).

early 1800s Johann Wolfgang von Goethe (1749–1832) is part of the Sturm und Drang movement, which leads to Romanticism. Painter Caspar David Friedrich (1774–1840) leads early German Romanticism. Other luminary cultural figures include writers Friedrich Schiller (1759–1805) and Heinrich von Kleist (1777–1811); and composers Robert Schumann (1810–56), Hungarian-born Franz Liszt (1811–86), Richard Wagner (1813–83), and Johannes Brahms (1833–97). In architecture, the severe lines of neoclassicism become popular.

ROAD TO NATIONHOOD

1806 Napoléon's armies invade Prussia; it briefly becomes part of the French Empire.

1807 The Prussian prime minister Baron vom und zum Stein frees the serfs, creating a new spirit of patriotism; the Prussian army is rebuilt.

1813 The Prussians defeat Napoléon at Leipzig.

1815 Britain and Prussia defeat Napoléon at Waterloo. At the Congress of Vienna the German Confederation is created as a loose union of 39 independent states, reduced from more than 300 principalities. The Bundestag (national assembly) is established at Frankfurt. Already powerful Prussia increases its territory, gaining the Rhineland, Westphalia, and most of Saxony.

1848 The "Year of the Revolutions" is marked by uprisings across the fragmented German Confederation; Prussia expands. A national parliament is elected, taking the power of the Bundestag to prepare a constitution for a united Germany.

1862 Otto von Bismarck (1815–98) becomes prime minister of Prussia; he is determined to wrest German-populated provinces from Austro-Hungarian (Habsburg) control.

1866 Austria-Hungary is defeated by the Prussians at Sadowa; Bismarck sets up the Northern German Confederation in 1867. A key figure in Bismarck's plans is Ludwig II of Bavaria. Ludwig—a political simpleton—lacks successors, making it easy for Prussia to seize his lands.

1867 Karl Marx (1818–83) publishes *Das Kapital.*

1870–71 The Franco-Prussian War: Prussia lays siege to Paris. Victorious Prussia seizes Alsace-Lorraine but eventually withdraws from all other occupied French territories.

1871 The four South German states agree to join the Northern Confederation; Wilhelm I is proclaimed first kaiser of the united empire.

MODERNISM

1882 The Triple Alliance is forged between Germany, Austria-Hungary, and Italy. Germany's industrial revolution blossoms, enabling it to catch up with the other great powers of Europe. Germany establishes colonies in Africa and the Pacific.

ca. 1885 Daimler and Benz pioneer the automobile.

1890 Kaiser Wilhelm II (rules 1888–1918) dismisses Bismarck and begins a new, more aggressive course of foreign policy; he oversees the expansion of the navy.

1890s A new school of writers, including Rainer Maria Rilke (1875–1926), emerges. Rilke's *Sonnets to Orpheus* gives German poetry new lyricism.

1905 Albert Einstein (1879–1955) announces his theory of relativity.

1906 Painter Ernst Ludwig Kirchner (1880–1938) helps organize *Die Brücke,* a group of artists who, along with *Der Blaue Reiter,* create the avant-garde art movement expressionism.

1907 Great Britain, Russia, and France form the Triple Entente, which, set against the Triple Alliance, divides Europe into two armed camps.

1914–18 Austrian archduke Franz-Ferdinand is assassinated in Sarajevo. The attempted German invasion of France sparks World War I; Italy and Russia join the Allies, and four years of pitched battle ensue.

By 1918 the Central Powers are encircled and must capitulate.

WEIMAR REPUBLIC

1918 Germany is compelled by the Versailles Treaty to give up its overseas colonies and much European territory (including Alsace-Lorraine to France) and to pay huge reparations to the Allies; Kaiser Wilhelm II repudiates the throne and goes into exile in Holland. The tough terms leave the new democracy (the Weimar Republic) shaky.

1919 The Bauhaus school of art and design, the brainchild of Walter Gropius (1883–1969), is born. Thomas Mann (1875–1955) and Hermann Hesse (1877–1962) forge a new style of visionary intellectual writing.

1923 Germany suffers runaway inflation. Adolf Hitler's Beer Hall Putsch, a rightist revolt, fails; leftist revolts are frequent.

1925 Hitler publishes *Mein Kampf* (*My Struggle*).

1932 The Nazi party gains the majority in the Reichstag (parliament).

1933 Hitler becomes chancellor; the Nazi "revolution" begins. In Berlin, Nazi students stage the burning of more than 25,000 books by Jewish and other politically undesirable authors.

NAZI GERMANY

1934 President Paul von Hindenburg dies; Hitler declares himself Führer (leader) of the Third Reich. Nazification of all German social institutions begins, spreading a policy that is virulently racist and anti-Communist. Germany recovers industrial might and rearms.

1936 Germany signs anti-Communist agreements with Italy and Japan, forming the Axis; Hitler reoccupies the Rhineland.

1938 The *Anschluss* (annexation): Hitler occupies Austria. Germany occupies the Sudetenland in Czechoslovakia. *Kristallnacht* (Night of Broken Glass), in November, marks the Nazis' first open and direct terrorism against German Jews. Synagogues and Jewish-owned businesses are burned, looted, and destroyed in a night of violence.

1939–40 In August Hitler signs a pact with the Soviet Union; in September he invades Poland; war is declared by the Allies. Over the next three years there are Nazi invasions of Denmark, Norway, the Low Countries, France, Yugoslavia, and Greece. Alliances form between Germany and the Baltic states.

1941–45 Hitler launches his anti-Communist crusade against the Soviet Union, reaching Leningrad in the north and Stalingrad and the Caucasus in the south. In 1944 the Allies land in France; their combined might brings the Axis to its knees. In addition to the millions killed in the fighting, more than 6 million Jews and other victims die in Hitler's concentration camps. Germany is again in ruins. Hitler kills himself in April 1945. East Berlin and what becomes East Germany are occupied by the Soviet Union.

THE COLD WAR

1945 At the Yalta Conference, France, the United States, Britain, and the Soviet Union divide Germany into four zones; each country occupies a sector of Berlin. The Potsdam Agreement expresses the determination to rebuild Germany as a democracy.

1946 East Germany's Social Democratic Party merges with the Communist Party, forming the SED, which would rule East Germany for the next 40 years.

1948 The Soviet Union tears up the Potsdam Agreement and attempts, by blockade, to exclude the three other Allies from their agreed zones in Berlin. Stalin is frustrated by a massive airlift of supplies to West Berlin.

1949 The three western zones are combined to form the Federal Republic of Germany; the new West German parliament elects Konrad Adenauer as chancellor (a post he held until his retirement in 1963). Soviet-held East Germany becomes the Communist German Democratic Republic (GDR).

1950s West Germany, aided by the financial impetus provided by the Marshall Plan, rebuilds its devastated cities and economy— the *Wirtschaftswunder* (economic miracle) gathers speed. The writers

Heinrich Böll, Wolfgang Koeppen, and Günter Grass emerge.

1957 The Treaty of Rome heralds the formation of the European Economic Community (EEC); West Germany is a founding member.

1961 Communists build the Berlin Wall to stem the outward tide of refugees.

1969–74 The vigorous chancellorship of Willy Brandt pursues *Ostpolitik,* improving relations with Eastern Europe and the Soviet Union and acknowledging East Germany's sovereignty.

mid-1980s The powerful German Green Party emerges as the leading environmentalist voice in Europe.

REUNIFICATION

1989 Discontent in East Germany leads to a flood of refugees westward and to mass demonstrations; Communist power collapses across Eastern Europe; the Berlin Wall falls.

1990 In March the first free elections in East Germany bring a center-right government to power. The Communists, faced with corruption scandals, suffer a big defeat but are represented (as Democratic Socialists) in the new, democratic parliament. The World War II victors hold talks with the two German governments, and the Soviet Union gives its support for reunification. Economic union takes place on July 1, with full political unity on October 3. In December, in the first democratic national German elections in 58 years, Chancellor Helmut Kohl's three-party coalition is reelected.

1991 Nine months of emotional debate end on June 20, when parliamentary representatives vote to move the capital from Bonn—seat of the West German government since 1949—to Berlin, the capital of Germany until the end of World War II.

1998 Helmut Kohl's record 16-year-long chancellorship of Germany ends with the election of Gerhard Schröder. Schröder's Social Democratic Party (SPD) pursues a coalition with the Greens in order to replace the three-party coalition of the Christian Democratic Union, Christian Social Union, and Free Democratic Party.

1999 The Bundestag, the German parliament, returns to the restored Reichstag in Berlin on April 19. The German federal government also leaves Bonn for Berlin, making Berlin capital of Germany again.

1999–2003 For the first time since 1945, the German army (the Bundeswehr) is deployed in combat missions in the former Yugoslavia and Afghanistan.

2005 Chancellor Schröder asks for a vote of confidence in parliament and fails. After a new election in September, Angela Merkel (CDU) becomes the new chancellor with a "grand coalition" of CDU/CSU and SPD.

2007 Angela Merkel as German chancellor and also in her role as the then President of the Council of the European Union hosts the G-8 summit in Heiligendamm, Germany.

2009 In Bundestag elections the alliance of the CDU/CSU and FDP receives an outright majority of seats, ensuring that Angela Merkel continues as chancellor.

2019 The 30th anniversary of the fall of the Berlin Wall marks a high point for the restored German capital. Decreasing unemployment and an increasingly gentrified cityscape have made Berlin more livable than ever, and expats are still flocking to the city. Berlin also continues to top lists as one of the fastest-growing tourism destinations in Europe.

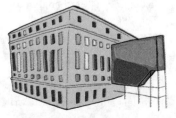

BEST BETS
FOR BERLIN

With so many places to go and things to do in Berlin, how will you decide? Fodor's writers and editors have chosen our favorites to help you plan. Search the neighborhood chapters for more recommendations.

ACTIVITIES AND SIGHTS

ARCHITECTURE
Altes Museum, Mitte

Berliner Dom, Mitte

Brandenburger Tor, Mitte

Reichstag, Tiergarten

MUSEUMS AND GALLERIES
Berlinische Galerie, Kreuzberg

East Side Gallery, Friedrichshain

Hamburger Bahnhof - Museum für Gegenwart (Museum of Contemporary Art), Mitte

Kulturforum, Tiergarten

Museum Insel, Mitte

PARKS AND GREEN SPACES
Tempelhofer Feld, Neukölln

Volkspark Friedrichshain, Friedrichshain

VIEWS
Berliner Fernsehturm, Mitte

SHOPPING

BOOK STORES
Do You Read Me?, Mitte

CLOTHING
Andreas Murkudis, Tiergarten

Baerck, Mitte

MARKETS
Gendarmenmarkt Christmas Market, Mitte

Markt am Kollwitzplatz, Prenzlauer Berg

Markt am Winterfeldtplatz, Schöneberg

Mauerpark Flohmarkt, Prenzlauer Berg

Trödelmarkt Arkonaplatz, Prenzlauer Berg

VINTAGE
The Corner Berlin, Mitte

Das Neue Schwarz, Mitte

Garments Vintage, Prenzlauer Berg

FOOD

COFFEE SHOPS
The Barn Café, Mitte

Distrikt Coffee, Mitte

CAFES AND BISTROS

Café Einstein Stammhaus, Schöneberg

Paris-Moskau, Tiergarten

ASIAN

Cocolo Ramen, Mitte

Curry 36, Kreuzberg

893 Ryotei, Charlottenburg

Kushinoya, Charlottenburg

Monsieur Vuong, Mitte

GERMAN

Die Henne, Kreuzberg

Einsunternull, Mitte

Konnopke's Imbiss, Prenzlauer Berg

Nobelhart und Schmutzig, Mitte

Pauly Saal, Mitte

HEALTHY

Cookies Cream, Mitte

MEDITERRANEAN

Bandol sur Mer, Mitte

Mädchenitaliener, Mitte

Lavanderia Vecchia, Neukölln

ROMANTIC

Facil, Tiergarten

Tulus Lotrek, Kreuzberg

Mrs. Robinson's, Prenzlauer Berg

Katz Orange, Mitte

DRINKS

COCKTAILS

Buck and Breck, Mitte

REDWOOD Bar Berlin, Mitte

Stagger Lee, Schöneberg

BEER

Prater Garten, Prenzlauer Berg

BRLO Brwhouse, Kreuzberg

NIGHTLIFE AND PERFORMING ARTS

CINEMA

Kino Tilsiter Lichtspiele, Friedrichshain

Moviemento Kino, Neukölln

CLUBBING

House of Weekend, Mitte

Berghain, Friedrichshain

LIVE MUSIC

b-flat, Mitte

THEATER AND PERFORMANCES

Staatsoper Unter den Linden, Mitte

Volksbühne, Mitte

Berliner Philharmonie, Tiergarten

2

Mitte South of the Spree River (with Museum Island)

WEDDING

GESUNDBRUNNEN

PRENZLAUER BERG

MOABIT

HANSA-VIERTEL

SPREE

MITTE

CHARLOTTENBURG

TIERGARTEN

FRIEDRICHSHAIN

SPREE

HALENSEE

KREUZBERG

WILMERSDORF

ALT-TREPTOW

SCHÖNEBERG

PLÄNTERWALD

FRIEDENAU

NEUKÖLLN

TEMPELHOF

BAUMSCHULENWEG

MARIENDORF

BRITZ

Sightseeing ★★★★★ | Shopping ★☆☆☆☆ | Dining ★★★☆☆ | Nightlife ★★☆☆☆

B ordering Tiergarten and the government district are the meticulously restored Brandenburger Tor (Brandenburg Gate), the unofficial symbol of the city, and the Memorial to the Murdered Jews of Europe, whose design and scope engendered many debates. The historic boulevard Unter den Linden proudly rolls out Prussian architecture and world-class museums—now the site of increased construction related to the extension of U-bahn U5 line, slated to open in 2020. Its major cross street is Friedrichstrasse, revitalized in the mid-1990s with upscale malls and an enormous showroom for Volkswagen. Two of Berlin's most important opera houses, the Staatsoper Unter den Linden (State Opera) and the Komische Oper, offer world-class entertainment. Further south, the Gendarmenmarkt, one of East Berlin's loveliest squares, includes the Konzerthaus, the Deutscher Dom and Französischer Dom (German and French cathedrals), and Berlin's most popular Christmas market.—*by Liz Humphreys*

◎ Sights

★ Alte Nationalgalerie *(Old National Gallery)*

The permanent exhibit here is home to an outstanding collection of 18th-, 19th-, and early-20th-century paintings and sculpture, by the likes of Cézanne, Rodin, Degas, and one of Germany's most famous portrait artists, Max Liebermann. Its collection has masterpieces from such 19th-century German painters

as Karl Friedrich Schinkel and Caspar David Friedrich, the leading members of the German Romantic school. ✉ *Museumsinsel, Bodestr. 1–3, Mitte* ☎ *30/2664–24242* ⊕ *www. smb.museum* 💰 *€10 (combined ticket for all Museum Island museums €18)* ⊙ *Closed Mon.* Ⓜ *Hackescher Markt (S-bahn).*

Altes Museum *(Old Museum)*

This red-marble neoclassical building abutting the green Lustgarten was Prussia's first structure purpose-built to serve as a museum. Designed by Karl Friedrich Schinkel, it was completed in 1830. The permanent collection consists of everyday utensils from ancient Greece as well as vases and sculptures from the 6th to 4th century BC. Etruscan art is the highlight here, and there are also a few examples of Roman art. Antique sculptures, clay figurines, and bronze art of the Antikensammlung (Antiquities Collection) are also here (the other part of the collection is in the **Pergamonmuseum**). ⊠ *Museumsinsel, Am Lustgarten, Mitte* ☎ *30/2664-24242* ⊕ *www.smb. museum* ☎ *From €10* ⊙ *Closed Mon.* Ⓜ *Hackescher Markt (S-bahn).*

Bebelplatz

After he became ruler in 1740, Frederick the Great personally planned the buildings surrounding this square (which has a huge parking garage cleverly hidden beneath the pavement). The area received the nickname "Forum Fridericianum," or Frederick's Forum. On May 10, 1933, Joseph Goebbels, the Nazi minister for propaganda and "public enlightenment," organized one of the nationwide book burnings here. The books, thrown on a pyre by Nazi officials and students, included works by Jews, pacifists, and Communists. In the center of Bebelplatz, a modern and subtle memorial (built underground but viewable through a window in the cobblestone pavement) marks where 20,000 books went up in flames. The **Staatsoper Unter den Linden** (State Opera) is on the east side of the square. **St. Hedwigskathedrale** is on the south side of the square. The **Humboldt-Universität** is to the west. ⊠ *Mitte* Ⓜ *Französische Strasse (U-bahn), Bhf Hausvogteiplatz (U-bahn).*

GETTING HERE

As the most central area of Berlin, Southern Mitte is extremely accessible by all forms of public transportation. The U-bahn (which goes underground), the S-bahn (which runs aboveground), trams, and buses will get you everywhere you need to go. Museum Island is accessed by the S-bahn or by bus. Nearby Hauptbahnhof (Central Station) will take you to destinations throughout the city and elsewhere in Germany and Europe.

Berliner Dom *(Berlin Cathedral)*
A church has stood here since 1536, but this enormous version dates from 1905, making it the largest 20th-century Protestant church in Germany. The royal Hohenzollerns worshipped here until 1918, when Kaiser Wilhelm II abdicated and left Berlin for Holland. The massive dome wasn't restored from World War II damage until 1982; the interior was completed in 1993. The climb to the dome's outer balcony is made easier by a wide stairwell, plenty of landings with historic photos and models, and even a couple of chairs. The 94 sarcophagi of Prussian royals in the crypt are significant, but to less-trained eyes can seem uniformly dull. Sunday services include communion. ⊠ *Am Lustgarten 1, Mitte* ☎ *030/2026-9136* ⊕ *www.berlinerdom.de* ☎ *€7; audio guide €4* Ⓜ *Hackescher Markt (S-bahn).*

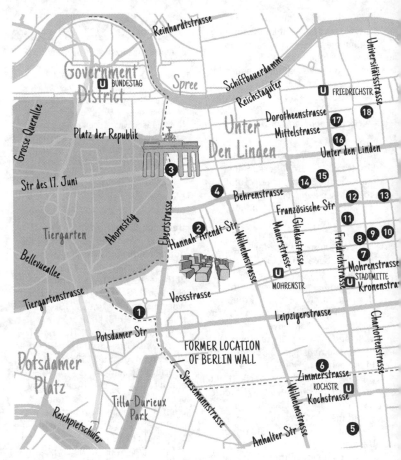

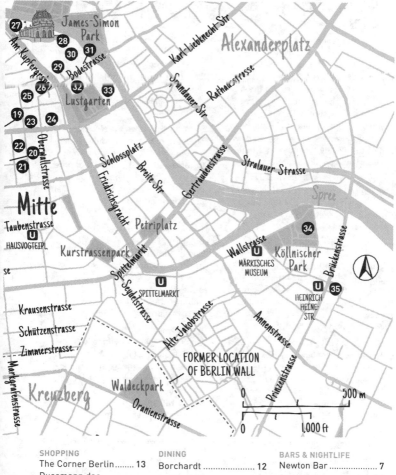

HOW TO NAVIGATE MUSEUM ISLAND

The five excellent museums found in Mitte's Museum Island (Museuminsel)—the Pergamonmuseum, the Bode-Museum, the Neues Museum, the Alte Nationalgalerie, and the Altes Museum—should be on the must-see list of every visitor to Berlin. But if you only have limited time—and who doesn't?—we've got the best strategies to navigate the museums' highlights while preserving your sanity.

Buy Your Tickets Online in Advance
Advance tickets are crucial to avoid having to stand in line, especially during high season. You can buy a one-day pass or a three-day pass (recommended if you have a bit more time so you won't go into art overload).

Consider Visiting on a Monday
Only the Pergamon and the Neues are open on Monday—which means fewer crowds, so you can see the highlights in peace, and save the other museums for another day.

Plan Your Visit Around the Pergamonmuseum
The Pergamon is (arguably) the one museum you absolutely have to see, particularly the Pergamon Altar, the Ishtar Gate, and the Roman Market Gate of Miletus. (The rest of the museum showcases classical antiquities, ancient Near Eastern art, and Islamic art.) Your Museum Island ticket will include timed entry for the Pergamonmuseum, which is always the busiest of the five museums, so you can schedule the rest of your day around that.

Set Your Sights on the Neues
The other can't-miss exhibit is the bust of Nefertiti in the Neues Museum. Other than that, the amount of time you spend here will depend upon how interested you are in Egyptian art and prehistoric art.

If You Prefer Paintings...
Then head over to the Alte Nationalgalerie next, for its wonderful collection of 18th- to early-20th-century paintings and sculpture. Otherwise, pick and choose from the Bode-Museum's stunning European sculpture and the Alte Museum's Greek and Etruscan art.

Fit in a Break
Don't try to see everything all at once. Instead, stop for snacks and coffee at one of the eateries alongside the Spree River—or better yet, fit in a boat ride if you're able. Once you're refreshed, return to catch any museums you've missed.

Bode-Museum

At the northern tip of Museum Island is this somber-looking gray edifice graced with elegant columns. The museum is home to the state museum's stunning collection of German and Italian sculptures since the Middle Ages, as well as the Museum of Byzantine Art, and a huge coin collection. ⊠ *Museumsinsel, Am Kupfergraben, Mitte* ☎ *030/2664–24242* ⊕ *www.smb. museum* ⊡ *From €12* ⊙ *Closed Mon.* Ⓜ *Hackescher Markt (S-bahn).*

★ Brandenburger Tor
(Brandenburg Gate)
Once the pride of Prussian Berlin and the city's premier landmark, the Brandenburger Tor was left in a desolate no-man's-land when the wall was built. Since the wall's dismantling, the sandstone gateway has become the scene of the city's Unification Day and New Year's Eve parties. This is the sole remaining gate of 14 built by Carl Langhans in 1788–91, designed as a triumphal arch for King Frederick Wilhelm II. Troops paraded through the gate after successful campaigns—the last time in 1945, when victorious Red Army troops took Berlin. The upper part of the gate, together with its chariot and Goddess of Victory, was destroyed in the war. In 1957 the original molds were discovered in West Berlin, and a new quadriga was cast in copper and presented as a gift to the people of East Berlin. A tourist information center is in the south part of the gate. ⊠ *Pariser Pl., Mitte* 🚆 *Free* Ⓜ *Unter den Linden (S-bahn).*

Contemporary Fine Arts
From its perch on Am Kupfergraben, Contemporary Fine Arts (CFA) Berlin has a perfect view of Museum Island and its hordes of daily visitors. Those looking for a different kind of Berlin art scene will find it in this elegant gallery. Housed in a David Chipperfield–constructed, ultramodern building, it stands out from its Prussian surroundings. CFA has been a fixture in Berlin since the early 1990s, showing Berlin-based artists like Jonathan Meese and Anselm Reyle, and big-timers like Juergen Teller and Julian Schnabel. ⊠ *Am Kupfergraben 10, Mitte* ☎ *030/288-7870* ⊕ *www.cfa-berlin.com* Ⓜ *Hackescher Markt (S-bahn).*

Deutsches Historisches Museum
(German History Museum)
The museum is composed of two buildings. The magnificent pink, baroque Prussian arsenal (Zeughaus) was constructed between 1695 and 1730, and is the oldest building on Unter den Linden. It also houses a theater, the Zeughaus Kino, which regularly presents a variety of films, both German and international, historic and modern. The new permanent exhibits offer a modern and fascinating view of German history since the early Middle Ages. Behind the arsenal, the granite-and-glass Pei-Bau building by I. M. Pei holds often stunning and politically controversial changing exhibits. The museum's café is a great place to stop and restore your energy. ⊠ *Unter den Linden 2, Mitte* ☎ *030/203–040* ⊕ *www.dhm.de* 🚆 *€8* Ⓜ *Französische Strasse (U-bahn), Friedrichstrasse (S-bahn and U-bahn), Hackesher Markt (S-bahn).*

Friedrichstrasse
The once-bustling street of cafés and theaters of prewar Berlin has risen from the rubble of war and Communist neglect to reclaim the crowds with shopping emporiums.

North of the train station you will see the rejuvenated heart of the entertainment center of Berlin's Roaring Twenties, including the **Admiralspalast** and the somewhat kitschy **Friedrichstadt Palast**. ⊠ *Mite* Ⓜ *Französische Strasse (U-bahn), Friedrichstrasse (S-bahn and U-bahn).*

Gendarmenmarkt
This is without a doubt the most elegant square in former East Berlin. Anchored by the beautifully reconstructed 1818 **Konzerthaus** and the **Deutscher Dom** and **Französischer Dom** (German and French cathedrals), it also hosts one of Berlin's classiest annual Christmas markets. ⊠ *Mite* Ⓜ *Stadtmitte (U-bahn), Hausvogteiplatz (U-bahn).*

Hotel Adlon Kempinski Berlin
The Adlon's prime setting adjacent to the Brandenburg Gate, wonderful spa, and highly regarded restaurants (including Michelin-starred Lorenz Adlon) make this one of the top addresses to stay in Berlin. The elegant lobby and world-class restaurants make this worth a visit, even if you're not staying here. ⊠ *Unter den Linden 77, Mitte* ☎ *030/22610* ⊕ *www. kempinski.com/adlon* Ⓜ *Brandenburger Tor (U-bahn and S-bahn).*

Humboldt-Universität
Running the length of the west side of Bebelplatz, the former royal library is now part of Humboldt-Universität, whose main campus is across the street on Unter den Linden. The university building was built between 1748 and 1766 as a palace for Prince Heinrich, the brother of Frederick the Great. With its founding in 1810, the university moved in. The fairy-tale-collecting Grimm brothers taught here, and political philosophers Karl Marx and Friedrich Engels studied within its hallowed halls. Albert Einstein taught physics from 1914 to 1929, when he left Berlin for the United States. ⊠ *Unter den Linden 6, Mitte* Ⓜ *Friedrichstrasse (S-bahn and U-bahn), Französische Str. (U-bahn).*

Märkisches Museum
(Brandenburg Museum)
This redbrick museum includes exhibits on the city's theatrical past, its guilds, and its newspapers. A permanent exhibit, *Here is Berlin!,* tells the story of Berlin's history through its different neighborhoods. Paintings capture the look of the city before it crumbled during World War II. ⊠ *Am Köllnischen Park 5, Mitte* ☎ *030/2400–2162* ⊕ *www. en.stadtmuseum.de* 💶 *€5* 🕐 *Closed Mon.* Ⓜ *Märkisches Museum (U-bahn).*

★ Memorial to the Murdered Jews of Europe *(Denkmal für die Ermordeten Juden Europas)*
An expansive and unusual memorial dedicated to the 6 million Jews who were killed in the Holocaust,

the Memorial to the Murdered Jews of Europe was designed by American architect Peter Eisenman. The stunning place of remembrance consists of a grid of more than 2,700 concrete stelae, planted into undulating ground. The abstract memorial can be entered from all sides and offers no prescribed path. An information center that goes into specifics about the Holocaust lies underground at the southeast corner. Just across Eberstrasse, inside the Tiergarten, is the **Memorial to the Homosexuals Persecuted under the National Socialist Regime**: a large concrete block with a window through which visitors can see a short film depicting a kiss. ✉ *Cora-Berliner-Str. 1, Mitte* ☎ *030/263–9430* ⊕ *www.stiftung-denkmal.de* 🎫 *Free* Ⓜ *Unter den Linden (S-bahn).*

★ **Museumsinsel** *(Museum Island)* On the site of one of Berlin's two original settlements, this unique complex of five state museums is a UNESCO World Heritage site and a must-visit in Berlin. The museums are the **Alte Nationalgalerie**, the **Altes Museum** (Old Museum), the **Bode-Museum**, the **Pergamonmuseum**, and the **Neues Museum** (New Museum). If you get tired of antiques and paintings, drop by any of the museums' cafés. A state-of-the-art visitor center is expected to open here in 2019. To avoid standing in long lines (especially during the summer), buy a combined day ticket that covers all Museum Island museums in advance online at ⊕ *www.smb. museum/en* or ⊕ *www.visitberlin. dc/cn*, or at any of the individual museum ticket offices (the Altes Museum tends to be less busy). ✉ *Museumsinsel, Mitte* ☎ *030/2664-24242* ⊕ *www.visitberlin.de/en/ museum-island-in-berlin* 🎫 *€18 combined ticket to all Museum Island museums* Ⓜ *Hackescher Markt (S-bahn).*

Neue Wache *(New Guardhouse)* One of many Berlin projects by the early-19th-century architect Karl Friedrich Schinkel, this building served as both the Royal Prussian War Memorial (honoring the dead of the Napoleonic Wars) and the royal guardhouse until the kaiser abdicated in 1918. In 1931 it became a memorial to those who fell in World War I. Badly damaged in World War II, it was restored in 1960 by the East German state and rededicated as a memorial for the victims of militarism and fascism. After unification it regained its Weimar Republic appearance and was inaugurated as Germany's central war memorial. Inside is a copy of Berlin sculptor Käthe Kollwitz's *Pietà*, showing a mother mourning over her dead son. The inscription in front of it reads, "to the victims of war and tyranny." ✉ *Unter den Linden, Mitte* Ⓜ *Friedrichstrasse (S-bahn and U-bahn), Französische Str. (U-bahn).*

★ **Neues Museum** *(New Museum)* Originally designed by Friedrich August Stüler in 1843–55, the building housing the Neues

Museum was badly damaged in World War II and has only in the 21st century been elaborately redeveloped by British star architect David Chipperfield. Instead of completely restoring the Neues Museum, the architect decided to integrate modern elements into the historic landmark, while leaving many of its heavily bombed and dilapidated areas untouched. The result is a stunning experience, considered by many to be one of the world's greatest museums. Home to the Egyptian Museum, including the famous bust of Nefertiti (who, after some 70 years, has returned to her first museum location in Berlin), it also features the Papyrus Collection and the Museum of Prehistory and Early History. ⊠ *Museumsinsel, Bodestr. 1–3, Mitte* ☏ *030/2664–24242* ⊕ *www. smb.museum* 🚇 *From €12* Ⓜ *Hackescher Markt (S-bahn).*

★ Pergamonmuseum

The Pergamonmuseum is one of the world's greatest museums and its name is derived from its principal display, the Pergamon Altar, a monumental Greek temple discovered in what is now Turkey and dating from 180 BC. The altar was shipped to Berlin in the late 19th century. Equally impressive are the gateway to the Roman town of Miletus, the Ishtar Gate, and the Babylonian processional way. At the end of 2014, the hall with the Pergamon Altar closed for refurbishment and is expected to reopen in 2019; other construction

works will be ongoing until at least 2025. That said, the majority of the Pergamonmuseum will continue to be open to the public, and it is still very much worth a visit. ⊠ *Museumsinsel, Bodestr. 1–3, Mitte* ☏ *030/2664–24242* ⊕ *www.smb. museum* 🚇 *From €12* Ⓜ *Hackescher Markt (S-bahn).*

The Ritz-Carlton Berlin

Judging from the outside of this gray, high-rise hotel that soars above Potsdamer Platz, you would never guess that inside it's all luxurious, 19th-century grandeur, with exquisite furniture, marble bathrooms, and great views of bustling Potsdamer Platz and the Tiergarten. ⊠ *Potsdamer Pl. 3, Mitte* ☏ *030/337–777* ⊕ *www.ritzcarlton. com* Ⓜ *Potsdamer Platz (U-bahn and S-bahn).*

St. Hedwigs-Kathedrale *(St. Hedwig's Cathedral)*

The green-patina dome is a striking feature of St. Hedwigs-Kathedrale. Begun in 1747, it was modeled after the Pantheon in Rome, and was the first Catholic church built in resolutely Protestant Berlin since the 16th-century Reformation. This was Frederick the Great's effort to appease Prussia's Catholic population after his invasion of Catholic Silesia (then Poland). A treasury lies inside. ⊠ *Bebelpl., Mitte* ☏ *030/203–4810* ⊕ *www.hedwigs-kathedrale.de* ☞ *Tours (€3) available in English, call ahead* Ⓜ *Französische Strasse (U-bahn).*

Unter den Linden

The name of this historic Berlin thoroughfare, between the Brandenburg Gate and Schlossplatz, means "under the linden trees," and it was indeed lined with fragrant and beloved lindens until the 1930s. Imagine Berliners' shock when Hitler decided to fell the trees in order to make the street more parade-friendly. The grand boulevard began as a riding path that the royals used to get from their palace to their hunting grounds (now the central Berlin park called Tiergarten). It is once again lined with linden trees planted after World War II. ⊠ *Mitte*.

🛍 Shopping

★ The Corner Berlin

In the heart of the stunning Gendarmenmarkt, this luxury concept store sells a contemporary collection of new and vintage clothing from high-end designers like Yves Saint Laurent and Chloé, as well as cosmetics, home furnishings, and art books. There's also a men's shop next door and a second store near Kurfürstendamm. ⊠ *Französischestr. 40, Mitte* ☎ *030/2067–0940* ⊕ *www. thecornerberlin.de* Ⓜ *Französische Strasse (U-bahn)*.

Dussmann das KulturKaufhaus

Berlin's largest general bookstore, this five-story emporium has two levels of English-language titles, including unusual books, new releases, and classics. The store is open until midnight on weekdays,

and until 11:30 pm on Saturday. ⊠ *Friedrichstr. 90, Mitte* ☎ *030/2025–1111* ⊕ *www.kulturkaufhaus.de* ⊗ *Closed Sun.* Ⓜ *Friedrichstrasse (S bahn and U-bahn)*.

★ Frau Tonis Parfum

This elegant perfumery will help you create a completely personal scent; choose from vials filled with perfumes like acacia, linden tree blossoms, cedarwood, or pink peppercorns. All the perfumes are produced locally in Berlin, creating a really one-of-a-kind gift. ⊠ *Zimmerstr. 13, Potsdamer Platz* ☎ *030/2021–5310* ⊕ *www.frau-tonis-parfum.com* Ⓜ *Kochstrasse, Checkpoint Charlie (U-bahn)*.

☕ Coffee and Quick Bites

★ Cookies Cream

$$$ | Vegetarian. The name might have you thinking something different, but this is actually a vegetarian fine-dining restaurant that serves fantastic food (it's above what used to be a club called Cookies, owned by a nightlife mogul by the same moniker); the chef steers away from "easy" vegetarian dishes like pasta and stir-fries and instead focuses on innovative preparations. The entrance, too, is misleading: the only access is via a dingy alley between the Westin Grand Hotel and the Komische Oper next door, but once you're inside the vibe is industrial-chic, and the service is friendly, casual, and fun. **Known for:** Michelin-starred creative vegetarian cuisine; three- and four-course tasting menus, plus à la carte dishes; interesting organic wine pairings. *Average main: €25* ⊠ *Behrenstr. 55, Mitte* ☎ *030/2749–2940* ⊕ *cookiescream.com* ⊘ *Closed Sun. and Mon. No lunch* Ⓜ *Friedrichstrasse (S-bahn and U-bahn), Französische Strasse (U-bahn), Brandenburger Tor (S-bahn).*

🍴 Dining

Borchardt
$$ | **German.** The menu changes daily at this celebrity meeting place—the location near Gendarmenmarkt makes it a popular power lunch spot for politicians and influential people, though the food and service are not what you'd expect from the high prices. The setting is wonderful, though, with high ceilings, plush maroon benches, marble columns, and an Art Nouveau mosaic that was discovered during renovations. **Known for:** elegant decor; distinguished clientele; classic cuisine. *Average main: €19* ⊠ *Französischestr. 47, Mitte* ☎ *030/8188–6262* ⊕ *www.borchardt-restaurant.de* Ⓜ *Französische Strasse (U-bahn).*

Lutter & Wegner
$$$ | **Austrian.** The dark-wood-paneled walls, parquet floor, and multiple rooms of this bustling restaurant across from Gendarmenmarkt have an air of 19th-century Vienna, and the food,
too, is mostly German and Austrian, with game served in winter and classic dishes offered year-round. In the Weinhandlung, a cozy room lined with wine shelves, meat and cheese plates are served until 1 am. **Known for:** Sauerbraten (marinated pot roast) with red cabbage; Weiner schnitzel with potato and cucumber salad; traditional Austrian apple strudel. *Average main: €25* ⊠ *Charlottenstr. 56, Mitte* ☎ *030/2029–5415* ⊕ *www.l-w-berlin.de* Ⓜ *Französische Strasse (U-bahn), Stadtmitte (U-bahn).*

★ Nobelhart und Schmutzig
$$$$ | **German.** The locavore obsession is taken seriously at this trendy spot that uses only the most local ingredients in the simple but sublime preparations that come from the open kitchen and are served at a long, shared counter. One 10-course menu is served each evening (dietary restrictions can usually be accommodated) and everything—from the bread and butter through several vegetable, meat, and fish courses—is gorgeously presented and delicious. **Known for:** one nightly 10-course tasting menu; all-natural wines, best experienced when paired with each dish; friendly servers who share the stories behind every plate. *Average main: €95* ⊠ *Friedrichstr. 218, Mitte* ☎ *030/2594–0610* ⊕ *www.nobelhartundschmutzig.com* ⊘ *Closed Sun. and Mon.* Ⓜ *Kochstrasse (U-bahn).*

Sra Bua

$$$ | Thai. Spicy, flavorful curries are front and center on the menu at this upscale Thai restaurant, excellently complemented by salads and raw fish starters that play with some of the freshest ingredients around. Save room for the "deconstructed" yuzu cheesecake dessert, and make sure to sample the cocktails, which also pay homage to Southeast Asia with ingredients like chili, ginger, mango, and sesame oil. **Known for:** attentive service; dim sum; locations in Bangkok and St. Moritz. *Average main: €24* ⊠ *Adlon Kempinski Hotel, Behrenstr. 72, Mitte* ☎ *030/2261–1590* ⊕ *www.srabua-adlon.de* Ⓜ *Brandenburger Tor (S-bahn and U-bahn).*

🍸 Bars and Nightlife

Newton Bar

This posh bar in Mitte has been around for ages. Helmut Newton's larger-than-life photos of nude women decorate the walls. ⊠ *Charlottenstr. 57, Mitte* ☎ *030/2029–5421* ⊕ *www.newton-bar.de* Ⓜ *Stadtmitte (U-bahn).*

Sage Club

Affiliated with nearby Sage Restaurant, this eclectic club is open only on Thursday. Different floors play different music, from rock to electro, so expect to see diverse crowds depending on the vibe (check the program on the website). ⊠ *Köpenicker Str. 76, Mitte* ☎ *030/278–9830* ⊕ *www.sage-club.de* Ⓜ *Heinrich-Heine-Strasse (U-bahn).*

🎭 Performing Arts

Komische Oper

The operas performed here are sung in their original language (often with English subtitles), but the lavish and at times over-the-top and kitschy staging and costumes make for a fun night even if you don't speak the language. ⊠ *Behrenstr. 55–57, Mitte* ☎ *030/4799–7400* ⊕ *www.komische-oper-berlin.de.*

Konzerthaus Berlin

The beautifully restored hall at Konzerthaus Berlin is a prime venue for classical music concerts. The box office is open from noon to curtain time. ⊠ *Gendarmenmarkt, Mitte* ☎ *030/2030–92101* ⊕ *www.konzerthaus.de.*

Maxim Gorki Theater

With the radical slogan *More Love!*, the Maxim Gorki Theater produces eclectic plays about our society in transition, touching on economic crises, identity conflict, and the human condition in contemporary times. Under the guidance of artistic director Shermin Langhoff, the theater mixes live music, dance, and theater—almost every show with English subtitles. ⊠ *Am Festungsgraben 2, Mitte* ☎ *030/2022–1115* ⊕ *gorki.de.*

★ Staatsoper Unter den Linden
(State Opera)

Frederick the Great was a music lover and he made the Staatsoper Unter den Linden, on the east side of Bebelplatz, his first priority. The lavish opera house was completed in 1743 by the same architect who built Sanssouci in Potsdam, Georg Wenzeslaus von Knobelsdorff. The house reopened in late 2017 after a major seven-year renovation. There are guided tours of the opera house's interior on weekends at 2 and 4 pm (book online), but they are offered in German only. ⊠ *Unter den Linden 7, Mitte* ☎ *030/2035–4555* ⊕ *www.staatsoper-berlin.de* 🎫 *Tours €15.*

Mitte North of the Spree River

WEDDING

GESUNDBRUNNEN

PRENZLAUER BERG

MOABIT

HANSA-VIERTEL

SPREE

MITTE

CHARLOTTENBURG

TIERGARTEN

FRIEDRICHSHAIN

SPREE

HALENSEE

KREUZBERG

WILMERSDORF

ALT-TREPTOW

SCHÖNEBERG

PLÄNTERWALD

FRIEDENAU

NEUKÖLLN

TEMPELHOF

BAUMSCHULENWEG

MARIENDORF

BRITZ

Sightseeing ★★★★★ | Shopping ★★★★★ | Dining ★★★★★ | Nightlife ★★★★☆

After the fall of the wall, Mitte, which had been in East Germany, once again became the geographic center of Berlin. The area comprises several mini-districts, each with its own distinctive history and flair. Alexanderplatz, home of the iconic TV Tower, was the center of East Berlin. With its Communist architecture, you can still get a feel for the GDR aesthetic here. The nearby Nikolaiviertel is part of the medieval heart of Berlin. The Scheunenviertel, part of the Spandauer Vorstadt, was home to many of the city's Jewish citizens. Today, the narrow streets that saw so much tragedy house art galleries, excellent restaurants, and upscale shops. Treasures once split between East and West Berlin museums are reunited on Museuminsel, the stunning Museum Island, a UNESCO World Heritage site.—*by Liz Humphreys*

⊙ Sights

Alexanderplatz

This bleak square, bordered by the train station, the Galeria Kaufhof department store, and the 37-story Park Inn Berlin-Alexanderplatz hotel, once formed the hub of East Berlin and was originally named in 1805 for Czar Alexander I. German writer Alfred Döblin dubbed it the "heart of a world metropolis" (a quote from his 1929 novel *Berlin Alexanderplatz* is written on a building at the northeastern end of the square).

Today it's a basic center of commerce and the occasional festival. The unattractive modern buildings are a reminder not just of the results

of Allied bombing but also of the ruthlessness practiced by East Germans when they demolished what remained. A famous meeting point in the south corner is the World Time Clock (1969), which even keeps tabs on Tijuana. ⊠ *Mitte.*

Berliner Fernsehturm *(TV Tower)*

Finding Alexanderplatz is no problem: just head toward the 1,207-foot-high tower piercing the sky. Built in 1969 as a signal to the West (clearly visible over the wall, no less) that the East German economy was thriving, it is deliberately higher than both western Berlin's broadcasting tower and the Eiffel Tower in Paris. You can get the best view of Berlin from within the tower's disco ball–like observation level (also home to Berlin's highest bar); on a clear day you can see for 40 km (25 miles). One floor above, the city's highest restaurant rotates for your panoramic pleasure. During the summer season, order fast track tickets online to avoid a long wait. ✉ *Panoramastr. 1a, Mitte* ☎ *030/247–5750 for restaurant* ⊕ *www.tv-turm.de* 💶 *From €16* Ⓜ *Alexanderplatz (U-bahn and S-bahn).*

Brecht-Weigel-Gedenkstätte

You can visit the former working and living quarters of playwright Bertolt Brecht and his wife, actress Helene Weigel, and scholars can browse through the Brecht library (by appointment only). The downstairs restaurant serves Viennese cuisine using Weigel's recipes. Brecht, Weigel, and more than 100 other celebrated Germans are interred in the **Dorotheenstädtischer Friedhof** (Dorotheenstadt Cemetery) next door. The house can only be visited on tours, which take place every half hour, in German. Call ahead to schedule an English tour. ✉ *Chausseestr. 125, Mitte* ☎ *030/2005–71844* 💶 *Apartment €3, library free* Ⓜ *Naturkundemuseum (U-bahn).*

★ DDR Museum

Half museum, half theme park, the DDR Museum is an interactive and highly entertaining exhibit about life during Communism. It's difficult to say just how much the museum benefits from its prime location beside the Spree, right across from the Berliner Dom, but it's always packed, filled with tourists, families, and student groups trying to get a hands-on feel for what the East German experience was really like. Exhibitions include

GETTING HERE

Northern Mitte is accessible by all forms of public transportation. The U-bahn (which goes underground), the S bahn (which runs above ground), trams, and buses will get you everywhere you need to go, though the distances from one point to the next can be long. You'll probably pass through Alexanderplatz, the major transportation hub, at some point during your stay, and you can leave from the Hauptbahnhof (Central Station) for destinations throughout the city and elsewhere in Germany and Europe.

a re-creation of an East German kitchen, all mustard yellows and bilious greens; a simulated drive in a Trabi, the only car the average East German was allowed to own; and a walk inside a very narrow, very claustrophobic interrogation cell. ✉ *Karl-Liebknecht-Str. 1, at Spree opposite Berliner Dom, Mitte* ☎ *030/8471–23731* ⊕ *www. ddr-museum.de* 💶 *€10 (€9 online)* Ⓜ *Alexanderplatz (U-bahn and S-bahn), Hackescher Markt (S-bahn).*

Direktorenhaus

Just as much a draw for its architecture and history as for the quirky, off-kilter art shows and events that take place here, Direktorenhaus is a relative newcomer to the Berlin art scene and also the producer of the annual Illustrative Festival each September. This Spree-side building was once part of the State Mint. The large, Berlin-heavy

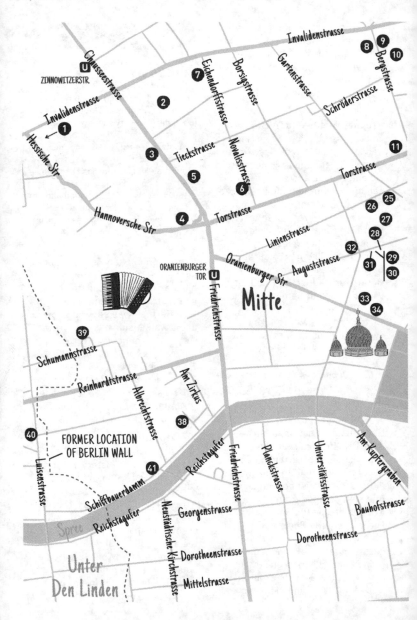

roster of artists includes Olaf Hajek, Daniel Becker, and Lauren Coleman. The gallery has no public hours, and viewings are by appointment. ⊠ *Am Krögel 2, Mitte* ☎ *030/4849-1929* ⊕ *www.direk-torenhaus.com* ☞ *Free* Ⓜ *Alexan-derplatz (S-bahn and U-bahn) and Klosterstrasse (U-bahn).*

★ Ehemalige Jüdische Mädchenschule

This boxy brick building in central Berlin, which formerly served as a Jewish girls' school and then a military hospital during WWII, sat neglected until recently. Now it is one of the city's newest star attractions: a renovated multiplex with art galleries, restaurants, and a bar. The former gymnasium is now the restaurant Pauly Saal; upstairs, art galleries share space with the newly relocated Kennedys museum. Berlin's now-thriving Jewish community still owns the building and leases it out to the current management. Both Jewish and non-Jewish visitors will rejoice at the inclusion of Mogg & Melzer, a deli dedicated to Jewish delica-cies like matzo ball soup, pastrami, and *shakshuka.* ⊠ *Auguststr. 11–13, Mitte* ⊕ *www.maedchenschule.org/* Ⓜ *Oranienburger Strasse (S-bahn).*

Hackesche Höfe *(Hacke Courtyards)*

Built in 1905–07, this series of eight connected courtyards is the finest example of art nouveau indus-trial architecture in Berlin. Most buildings are covered with glazed white tiles, and additional Moorish mosaic designs decorate the main

BACK IN THE DAY

In the nearby neighborhood of Wedding, don't miss the Gedenk-stätte Berliner Mauer. This open-air site, located on the former border strip between East and West Berlin, includes a portion of the Berlin Wall and a thorough exhibition on the city's division, which can be viewed 24/7. The creation of the wall was particularly heart-wrenching on Bernauer Strasse, where neighbors and families on opposite sides of the street were separated overnight. The site includes the Reconciliation Chapel, completed in 2000, which replaced the community church dynamited by the Communists in 1985; the church had been walled into the "death strip" and was seen as a hindrance to security patrols. Head into the visitor center for a wealth of images and information, including a film on the history of the wall and a specialized bookstore.

courtyard off Rosenthaler Strasse. Shops, restaurants, the variety theater Chamäleon Varieté, and a movie theater populate the spaces once occupied by ballrooms, a poets' society, and a Jewish girls' club. ⊠ *Rosenthaler Str. 40–41, and Sophienstr. 6, Mitte* ⊕ *www. hackesche-hoefe.com* Ⓜ *Hackescher Markt (S-bahn).*

★ Hamburger Bahnhof - Museum für Gegenwart *(Museum of Contemporary Art)*

This light-filled, remodeled train station is home to a rich survey of post-1960 Western art. The perma-nent collection includes installations by German artists Joseph Beuys and Anselm Kiefer, as well as paintings by Andy Warhol, Cy Twombly, Robert Rauschenberg, and Robert Morris. An annex presents the Friedrich Christian Flick Collection, a collection of the latest in the world's contemporary art. The more than 1,500 works rotate, but you're bound to see some by Bruce Naumann, Rodney Graham, and Pipilotti Rist. ⊠ *Invalidenstr. 50–51, Mitte* ☎ *030/2664–24242* ⊕ *www.smb.museum* 🎟 *€14 (free 1st Thurs. of month 4–8 pm)* Ⓜ *Naturkundemuseum (U-bahn), Hauptbahnhof (S-bahn).*

The Kennedys

In West Berlin in 1963, John F. Kennedy surveyed the recently erected Berlin Wall and said, "Ich bin ein Berliner" (I am one with the people of Berlin). And with that, he secured his fame throughout Germany. He's honored in this small but intriguing museum, which used to reside opposite the American embassy on Pariser Platz, but has since found a new home in the Ehemalige Jüdische Mädchenschule. With photographs, personal memorabilia, documents, and films, the collection traces the fascination JFK and the Kennedy clan evoked in Berlin and elsewhere. ⊠ *Auguststr. 11–13, in Ehemalige Jüdische Mädchenschule, Mitte* ☎ *030/2065–3570* ⊕ *www. thekennedys.de* 🎟 *€5* ⊘ *Closed Mon.* Ⓜ *Oranienburger Strasse (S-bahn).*

Built in 1969 as a signal to the West that the East German economy was thriving, the Berliner Fernsehturm (TV Tower) is deliberately higher than both western Berlin's broadcasting tower and the Eiffel Tower in Paris. You can get the best view of Berlin from within the tower's disco ball–like observation level (also home to Berlin's highest bar); on a clear day you can see for 40 km (25 miles). One floor above, the city's highest restaurant rotates for your panoramic pleasure.

Share your photo with us!
@FodorsTravel #FodorsOnTheGo

KW Institute for Contemporary Art

This gallery cum museum got its start in the 1990s, when a group of art fans and aficionados led by Klaus Biesenbach came upon a practically collapsing former margarine factory and decided it would be a great place for their project. Since then, KW (which stands for "Kunst Werke" or "art works") has been presenting exhibitions, site-specific works, and various events in the three-floor space (there's also an enclosed courtyard with a café). ✉ *Auguststr. 69, Mitte* ☎ *030/243–4590* ⊕ *www. kw-berlin.de* 🎟 *€8* 🕐 *Closed Tues.* Ⓜ *Oranienburger Strasse (S-bahn) and Oranienburger Tor (U-bahn).*

Neue Synagoge *(New Synagogue)*
This meticulously restored landmark, built between 1859 and 1866, is an exotic amalgam of styles, the whole faintly Middle Eastern. Its bulbous, gilded cupola stands out in the skyline. When its doors opened, it was the largest synagogue in Europe, with 3,200 seats. The synagogue was damaged on November 9, 1938 (*Kristallnacht*—Night of the Broken Glass), when Nazi looters rampaged across Germany, burning synagogues and smashing the few Jewish shops and homes left in the country. It was destroyed by Allied bombing in 1943, and it wasn't until the mid-1980s that the East German government restored it. The effective exhibit on the history of the building and its congregants includes fragments of the original architecture and furnishings. Sabbath services are held in a modern addition. ✉ *Oranienburger Str. 28–30, Mitte* ☎ *030/8802–8300*

ART IN THE WILD

As befitting a city known for its street art, be sure to look up wherever you walk in Mitte to not miss murals painted on the sides of buildings. But to catch some of the most interesting art, stop by the Haus Schwarzenberg Street Art Alley, to the right of Café Cinema near Hackescher Markt. The fascinating murals and collages here are constantly changing, with only a painting of Anne Frank remaining always the same.

⊕ *www.centrumjudaicum.de* 🎟 *€7; audio guides €3* 🕐 *Closed Sat.* Ⓜ *Oranienburger Tor (U-bahn), Oranienburger Strasse (S-bahn).*

Neugerriemschneider
One of Berlin's heavy hitters, this Mitte gallery with a seemingly unpronounceable name (it's actually the names of the two founders combined), has either represented or hosted shows by such art world luminaries as Olafur Eliasson, Ai Weiwei, Billy Childish, and Keith Edmier. ✉ *Linienstr. 155, Mitte* ☎ *030/2887–7277* Ⓜ *Oranienburger Strasse (S-bahn) and Oranienburger Tor (U-bahn).*

Nikolaiviertel *(Nicholas Quarter)*
Renovated in the 1980s and a tad concrete-heavy as a result, this tiny quarter grew up around Berlin's oldest parish church, the medieval, twin-spire **St. Nikolaikirche** (St. Nicholas's Church), dating from 1230 and now a museum. The adjacent Fischerinsel (Fisherman's Island) area was the heart of Berlin almost 800 years ago, and retains

a bit of its medieval character. At Breite Strasse you'll find two of Berlin's oldest buildings: No. 35 is the **Ribbeckhaus**, the city's only surviving Renaissance structure, dating from 1624, and No. 36 is the early-baroque **Marstall**, built by Michael Matthais between 1666 and 1669. The area feels rather artificial, but draws tourists to its gift stores, cafés, and restaurants. ⊠ *Church: Nikolaikirchpl., Mitte* ☎ *030/2400-2162* ⊕ *www.stadtmuseum.de* ◎ *Nikolaikirche museum €5* Ⓜ *Alexanderplatz (U-bahn and S-bahn).*

St. Marienkirche *(St. Mary's Church)*
This medieval church, one of the finest in Berlin, is best known for its late-Gothic, macabre fresco *Der Totentanz* (Dance of Death), which is in need of restoration. Tours on Tuesday at 2 pm highlight the fresco. ⊠ *Karl-Liebknecht-Str. 8, Mitte* ☎ *030/2475-9510* ⊕ *www.marienkirche-berlin.de* Ⓜ *Alexanderplatz (U-bahn and S-bahn), Hackescher Markt (S-bahn).*

🛍 Shopping

A.D. Deertz
This tiny shop on Torstrasse is the flagship menswear outlet for designer Wibke Deertz, who uses fabrics and inspirations from her travels around the world to create a collection of handmade, limited-edition pieces, including pants, shirts, jackets, and accessories. ⊠ *Torstr. 106, Mitte* ☎ *030/9120-6630* ⊕ *www.addeertz.com* Ⓜ *Rosenthaler Platz (U-bahn).*

Absinthe Depot Berlin
This old-fashioned-style liquor store harkens back to the age of the green fairy—complete with antique wooden cabinets and vintage absinthe fountains—although the primary ingredient, thujone, is now strictly regulated in countries around the world. A friendly proprietor is on hand to help you choose which of the more than 100 different varieties you'd like to carry home. ⊠ *Weinmeisterst. 4, Mitte* ☎ *030/281-6789* ⊕ *absinthdepot.de* Ⓜ *Weinmeisterstrasse (U-bahn).*

Ampelmann
This gallery shop opened in the mall-like Hackesche Höfe shopping area in 2001, promoting the red and green Ampelmännchen, the charming symbol used on the former East traffic lights. The brand now operates eight shops in Berlin, and you can find the logo on everything from T-shirts and umbrellas to ice cube trays and candy. ■TIP→ It's a perfect stop for souvenirs. ⊠ *Hackesche Höfe, Hof 5, Rosenthalerstr. 40–41, Mitte* ☎ *030/4472-6438* ⊕ *www.ampelmann.de* Ⓜ *Weinmeisterstrasse (U-bahn), Hackescher Markt (S-bahn).*

Apartment
Don't be deterred when you arrive at this seemingly empty storefront: the real treasure lies at the bottom of the black spiral staircase. On the basement level you'll find one of Berlin's favorite shops

for local designs and wardrobe staples for both men and women. Think distressed tops, shoes, leather jackets, and skinny jeans. ⊠ *Memhardstr. 8, Mitte* ☎ *030/2804–2251* ⊕ *www.apartmentberlin.de* Ⓜ *Weinmeisterstrasse (U-bahn), Alexanderplatz (U-bahn and S-bahn).*

ausberlin

This shop near Alexanderplatz provides a wide range of Berlin memories, all designed and manufactured in the city. There is everything from Berlin-themed emergency candy bars and tote bags with city landmark designs to Berlin-produced liquors. ⊠ *Karl-Liebknechtstr. 9, Mitte* ☎ *030/9700–5640* ⊕ *www.ausberlin. de* Ⓜ *Alexanderplatz (U-bahn and S-bahn).*

★ Baerck

Baerck artfully displays its mix of European and Berlin men's and women's wear on wheeled structures, allowing them to be rearranged in the store whenever necessary. Along with designers like Henrik Vibskov and Hope, you'll find the store's eponymous accessories line of handbags and scarves, as well as their clothing label NIA for blouses and trousers, and their product line llot llov—a play on the German word *toll* meaning great or cool. ⊠ *Mulackstr. 12, Mitte* ☎ *030/2404–8994* ⊕ *baerck. net* Ⓜ *Weinmeisterstrasse (U-bahn).*

Bonbonmacherei

Tucked into a small courtyard near the New Synagogue, this charming candy store has been making and selling handmade sweets for more than 100 years. The brightly colored sugar bonbons are pressed on vintage molds into leaf, raspberry, and diamond shapes, and more than 30 different varieties are available. ⊠ *Oranienburgerstr. 32, Mitte* ☎ *030/4405–5243* ⊕ *www.bonbon-macherei.de* Ⓜ *Oranienburger Strasse (U-bahn and S-bahn).*

Claudia Skoda

One of Berlin's top avant-garde designers, Claudia Skoda's creations are mostly for women, but there's also a selection of men's knitwear. ⊠ *Mulackstr. 8, Mitte* ☎ *030/4004–1884* ⊕ *www.clau-diaskoda.com* Ⓜ *Weinmeisterstrasse (U-bahn), Rosa-Luxemburg-Platz (U-bahn).*

★ Das Neue Schwarz

Whether you want a new little black dress or a cool vintage bag to carry around this season, a peek into Das Neue Schwarz (The New Black) is guaranteed to result in some special finds. In the midst of Mitte's fashionista neighborhood of avant-garde designers and exclusive boutiques, this shop holds its own with a collection of secondhand items—many never worn—from big-name designers including Vivienne Westwood, Helmut Lang, and Yves Saint Laurent. ⊠ *Mulackstr. 38, Mitte* ☎ *030/2787–4467* ⊕ *www.dasneue-schwarz.de* Ⓜ *Weinmeisterstrasse (U-bahn), Rosa-Luxemburg-Platz (U-bahn).*

★ Do You Read Me?

Whether you're looking for something to read on the plane or a special present, this charming bookstore is guaranteed to have something to pique your literary interests. The wide selection of magazines and literature—many of the titles are in English—comes from around the world and spans fashion, photography, architecture, interior design, and cultural topics. ⊠ *Auguststr. 28, Mitte* ☎ *030/6954–9695* ⊕ *www.doyoureadme.de* Ⓜ *Weinmeisterstrasse (U-bahn), Rosa-Luxemburg-Platz (U-bahn).*

Esther Perbandt

An avant-garde pioneer with a penchant for black, Esther Perbandt's buzzed-about runway shows during Berlin Fashion Week are as adventurous as the designs sold in her shop. Expect androgynous silhouettes for men and women including tailored trousers, blazers, wrap dresses with generous, draping fabric, and her signature, military-inspired hats. ⊠ *Almstadtstr. 3, Mitte* ☎ *030/8853–6791* ⊕ *estherperbandt. com* Ⓜ *Weinmeisterstrasse (U-bahn), Alexanderplatz (U-bahn and S-bahn).*

14 oz.

Inside a beautiful old building in the heart of Mitte's Hackescher Markt shopping district, 14 oz. sells high-end denim (Denham the Jeanmaker, Momotaro Jeans, Edwin), along with sneakers, accessories, knitwear, and outerwear. For true VIP treatment, a private shopping area is available on the second floor. ⊠ *Neue Schönhauserstr. 13, Mitte* ☎ *030/2804–0514* ⊕ *14oz.com* Ⓜ *Weinmeisterstrasse (U-bahn), Hackescher Markt (S-bahn).*

Hay

The Danish product line has been operating its popular Berlin outpost since 2011. Unexpected creative delights like polka-dotted tablecloths, designer coat hangers, tie-dyed stationery, and mirrored trays are all found here at reasonable prices. ⊠ *Auguststr. 77/78, Mitte* ☎ *030/2809–4878* ⊕ *www.hayberlin. de* ☉ *Closed Sun.* Ⓜ *Oranienburger Strasse (S-bahn), Oranienburger Tor (U-bahn).*

Jünemann's Pantoffeleck

The Jünemann family has owned this basement shop on Torstrasse for more than 100 years, producing their quality handmade felt *hausschuhe*, or slippers, for four generations. The shoes come in a variety of colors and two simple styles, a classic backless version or the full slipper. Either is the perfect way to bring a piece of German tradition back home. ⊠ *Torstr. 39, Mitte* ☎ *030/442–5337* ⊕ *www.pantoffeleck. de/* ☉ *Closed weekends* Ⓜ *Rosa-Luxemburg-Platz (U-bahn).*

★ Konk

Since 2003, this Mitte hot spot has nurtured Berlin independent designers who are as visionary in their aesthetics as they are in their production mode: most items are handmade and sustainably sourced. Look for local favorite NCA for hats, and elegant gold earrings and rings by Savoir Joaillerie. ⊠ *Kleine Hamburger Str. 15, Mitte* ☎ *030/2809–7839* ⊕ *www. konk-berlin.de* Ⓜ *Oranienburger Strasse (S-bahn), Rosenthaler Platz (U-bahn).*

Lala Berlin

Originally from Tehran, former MTV editor Leyla Piedayesh is one of Berlin's top design talents. Her popular boutique showcases her high-quality fabric scarves, sweaters, and accessories that use the reinterpreted Palestinian keffiyeh pattern she's become known for. ⊠ *Alte Schonhauser Str. 3, Mitte* ☎ *030/2576–2924* ⊕ *www. lalaberlin.com* Ⓜ *Weinmeisterstrasse (U-bahn), Rosa-Luxemburg-Platz (U-bahn).*

Puppenstube im Nikolaiviertel

This is the ultimate shop for any kind of (mostly handmade) dolls, including designer models as well as old-fashioned German dolls. It's for collectors, not kids. ⊠ *Propststr. 4, Mitte* ☎ *030/242–3967* ⊕ *www.puppen1.de* Ⓜ *Klosterstrasse (U-bahn).*

R.S.V.P.

Housed in two charming storefronts across the street from each other, this is the go-to place when looking for beautiful paper, notebooks, and other stationery needs. Along with designer parchment, high-end writing tools, and notebooks from Moleskine and others, the store carries international stationery brands, calendars, and other desk accessories. ⊠ *Mulackstr. 14 and 26, Mitte*

☎ *030/2809–4644* ⊕ *rsvp-berlin. de/en/online-shop* ☉ *Closed Sun.* Ⓜ *Weinmeisterstrasse (U-bahn), Rosa-Luxemburg-Platz (U-bahn).*

s.wert

Products here are inspired by Berlin's facades (pillows), graffiti (etched drinking glasses), and civic symbols (on polo shirts). ⊠ *Brunnenstr. 191, Mitte* ☎ *030/4005–6655* ⊕ *www.s-wert-design.de* ☉ *Closed Sun.* Ⓜ *Rosenthaler Platz (U-bahn).*

Sabrina Dehoff

The flagship store of German jewelry designer Sabrina Dehoff balances bling and minimalism—bright crystals are paired with chunky metals. ⊠ *Auguststr. 26A, Mitte* ☎ *030/9700–4160* ⊕ *www.sabrinadehoff.com* Ⓜ *Rosenthaler Strasse (U-bahn).*

soda. BERLIN

Opened in early 2015, this branch of the Munich bookstore started by Isabell Hummel and Sebastian Steinacker gives the many mainstream and DIY magazines and books carried here plenty of room to breathe. Hummel and Steinacker's goal for their spaces is to offer "curious publications for curious people." Here you'll find plenty of both. ⊠ *Weinbergsweg 1, Mitte* ☎ *030/4373–3700* ⊕ *www.soda-books.com* ☉ *Closed Sun.* Ⓜ *Rosenthaler Platz (U-bahn).*

SOTO

SOTO is the name of the hip, fashion-forward area of Mitte, south of Torstrasse, filled with charming side streets and

The Uferhallen complex, constructed in 1873 in the nearby neighborhood of Wedding, was originally part of the Grosse Berliner Pferdeeisenbahn (Great Berlin Horse Railway), before being used for electric trolleys at the beginning of the 20th century, and finally as a bus terminal and repair shop after World War II. In 2010, the Uferhallen were transformed into a series of artists' studios and workshops along the tiny Panke canal. Nowadays, Wedding residents and intrepid visitors can catch a contemporary dance performance at the Uferstudios, an intimate piano concert at the Piano Salon Christophori, or a meal at Café Pförtner. If you're feeling adventurous, just wander around and knock on a few doors.

numerous fashion boutiques. So, it's appropriate that it's also the name of this boutique where you'll find a mix of timeless and trendsetting menswear including brands like Norse Projects and Our Legacy, grooming products, and accessories ranging from cameras to lanyards. ⊠ *Torstr. 72, Mitte* ☎ *030/2576–2070* ⊕ *www.sotostore. com* Ⓜ *Rosa-Luxemburg-Platz (U-bahn).*

★ The Store Berlin

In a stunning interior of marble tables, Moroccan rugs, and oversize couches, you'll find discerning labels like The Row and Alexander Wang, as well as cosmetics and jewelry. The unpretentious, 30,000-square-foot space encourages you to stay awhile and take advantage of other amenities like British Salon Barber & Parlour, laptop-friendly workstations, and an organic café. ⊠ *Torstr. 1, Mitte* ☎ *030/405–0440* ⊕ *www.thestores. com/berlin* Ⓜ *Alexanderplatz (U-bahn and S-bahn).*

★ Wheadon's Beauty Shop

This cool beauty shop offers an assortment of goods. You'll find everything from lovely scented candles to lotions and body products to makeup and cosmetics, with popular, ethical brands like Dr. Bronner, Börlind, and Susanne Kaufmann. But the real gem is the basement-level men's spa and barbershop, which welcomes guest barbers from around the world, and the women's beauty salon, which offers makeovers and hair care. ⊠ *Steinstr. 17, Mitte* ☎ *017636144509* ⊕ *www.wheadon.de* ⊙ *Closed Sun.* Ⓜ *Weinmeisterstrasse (U-bahn).*

Wood Wood Annex

The avant-garde street-wear brand out of Copenhagen stocks its Berlin annex with its eponymous line of bags, shoes, and clothing for men and women. Also in-store are contemporary labels like Comme des Garçons, Opening Ceremony, and Kenzo. ⊠ *Rochstr. 3, Mitte* ☎ *030/2759–59770* ⊕ *www.wood-wood.dk* ⊙ *Closed Sun.* Ⓜ *Weinmeisterstrasse (U-bahn), Alexanderplatz (U-bahn and S-bahn).*

☕ Coffee and Quick Bites

★ The Barn Café
$ | Café. One of Berlin's original third-wave coffee joints, this tiny café in the heart of Mitte's gallery district serves up superlative hand-brewed coffees (always served black) and espresso drinks with trendy add-ons like oat milk, alongside a small but tasty selection of baked goods and sandwiches. There's limited indoor seating and laptops are banned, so this is a better place to sit outside when the weather's nice or to get your coffee to go. **Known for:** top-notch filtered coffee; sustainable, single-origin beans roasted in-house; delicious daily changing pastries. *Average main: €4 ⊠ Auguststr. 58, corner of Koppenpl., Mitte ☏ 1512/410–5136 ⊕ thebarn.de Ⓜ Rosenthaler Platz (U-bahn).*

★ Distrikt Coffee
$ | Café. Known for having one of the best breakfasts in Berlin (think avocado toast and toasted brioche with berry preserves), the filtered coffee at Distrikt is far from an afterthought, with beans chosen from some of Europe's top roasteries. Tea lovers aren't left out with a fine selection from Kreuzberg's Companion Coffee & Tea, served up with a scrumptious choice of cakes. **Known for:** breakfast served every day till 4 pm; Instagrammable brick-walled interiors; hipsters waiting outside. *Average main: €9 ⊠ Bergstr. 68, Mitte ☏ 030/5459–4033 ⊕ distriktcoffee.de Ⓜ Rosenthaler Platz (U-bahn).*

Hermann's Berlin
$ | Café. In a bright and contemporary white space, you have your choice of seating at communal or individual tables or on couches, depending on whether you want to work, socialize, or simply fill up on the frequently changing organic dishes offered for breakfast or lunch. Seasonal salads, sandwiches, and quiche are always available, or just drop by for a coffee, tea, or glass of wine while observing neighborhood hipsters in their element. **Known for:** organic, sustainable food; friendly service; large, open coworking space. *Average main: €10 ⊠ Torstr. 118, Mitte ☏ 030/3982–19880 ⊕ www.hermanns.com ⊘ Closed weekends Ⓜ Rosenthaler Platz (U-bahn).*

Oslo Kaffebar
$ | Café. With a mix of industrial concrete interiors and a cozy, woodsy Scandinavian vibe, this Norwegian-run café near Nordbahnhof makes the perfect place to catch up on some work or chill over a cup of coffee and homemade croissants. They also feature rotating art exhibitions each month and occasional live concerts. **Known for:** espresso and drip coffee from a variety of roasters; ultrafresh and often gluten-free pastries; local artwork. *Average main: €5 ⊠ Eichendorffstr. 13, Mitte ☏ 1578/520–6625 ⊕ www.oslokaffebar.com Ⓜ Nordbahnhof (U-bahn, S-bahn).*

Rosenthaler Grill und Schlemmerbuffet

$ | **Turkish.** *Döner kebab* aficionados love this bright, casual spot for the delicious food—the fact that it's in the middle of the city and open 24 hours a day is an added bonus. The friendly staff expertly carve paper-thin slices of perfectly cooked meat from the enormous, revolving spit; if you like things spicy, ask for the red sauce. **Known for:** döner kebab, either as a meal with salad and fries, or as a sandwich; other food choices including falafel, chicken, and even pizza; long hours, open around the clock. *Average main: €5* ⊠ *Torstr. 125, Mitte* ☎ *030/283–2153* ▄ *No credit cards* Ⓜ *Rosenthaler Platz (U-bahn).*

Shiso Burger

$ | **Burger.** Though casual burger joints abound in Berlin, only Shiso offers up patties with an Asian twist, from a Bulgogi Burger with marinated beef and a Korean chili base to a Shiso Burger with marinated tuna and teriyaki sauce to an Ebi Burger with black tiger shrimp, all served inside dim sum baskets in a stripped-down environment. Vegetarians are also well catered to with a choice of tofu or portobello mushroom options. **Known for:** Asian-fusion burgers; sweet potato, kimchi, and edamame sides; daily discounts between noon and 5 pm. *Average main: €7* ⊠ *Auguststr. 29C, Mitte* ☎ *030/8894–4687* ⊕ *www.shisoburger.com* Ⓜ *Weinmeisterstrasse (U-bahn).*

🍴 Dining

Altes Europa

$ | **German.** By day, this is a quiet café reminiscent of a classic Viennese coffeehouse (the name means "Old Europe"), with shabby but trendy decor, and fashionable Mitte-ites chatting and paging through newspapers and magazines. At night, it turns into a comfortable but bustling neighborhood pub serving classic Berlin dishes, just crowded enough to look like a scene but never too packed. **Known for:** traditional Berlin dishes like meatballs, schnitzel, and spätzle; daily changing seasonal dishes; being a locals' hangout. *Average main: €12* ⊠ *Gipsstr. 11, Mitte* ☎ *030/2809–3840* ⊕ *www.alteseuropa.com* Ⓜ *Hackescher Markt (S-bahn).*

Bandol sur Mer

$$$$ | **French.** This tiny and hip 20-seat eatery serves inspired French cuisine in rotating six- or seven-course menus celebrating a mix of seasonal regional and international ingredients. If you can't get a reservation here, try the sister restaurant next door: the larger and slightly more casual 3 Minutes Sur Mer. **Known for:** casual, industrial setting; creative interpretations of French cooking; well-selected wine pairings. *Average main: €95* ⊠ *Torstr. 167, Mitte* ☎ *030/6730–2051* ⊕ *www.bandolsurmer.de* ☉ *Closed Tues. and Wed. No lunch* Ⓜ *Rosenthaler Platz (U-bahn).*

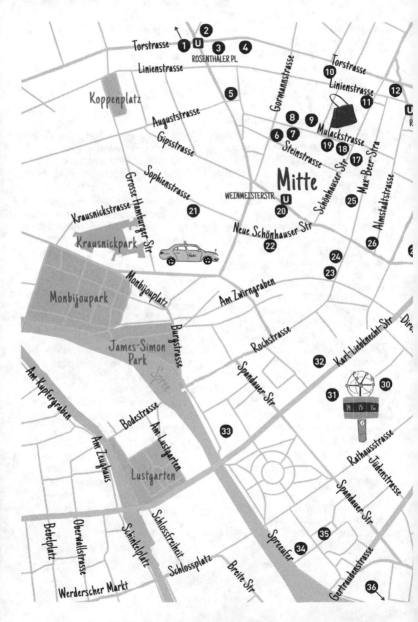

SIGHTS

Alexanderplatz 29
Berliner
Fernsehturm 30
DDR Museum 33
Direktorenhaus........36
Nikolaiviertel...........34
St. Marienkirche 31

SHOPPING

Absinthe Depot
Berlin 20
A.D.Deertz 4
Ampelmann 21
Apartment 27
ausberlin 32
Baerck 8
Claudia Skoda 9
Das Neue Schwarz...19
Esther Perbandt 26
14 oz........................22
Jünemann's
Pantoffeleck.............13
Lala Berlin...............11
Puppenstube im
Nikolaiviertel...........35
R.S.V.P. 7
soda. Berlin...............2
SOTO 10
The Store Berlin 14
Trodelmarkt
Arkonaplatz 1
Wheadon's
Beauty Shop 6
Wood Wood Annex ...24

COFFEE & QUICK BITES

Hermann's Berlin 3

DINING

Monsieur Vuong 17
Mädchenitaliener.....18
Shiori 25
The Store Kitchen....15
Zur Letzten
Instanz 37

BARS & NIGHTLIFE

b-flat 23
Hotel Amano 5
House of Weekend...28
Kaschk 12

PERFORMING ARTS

Volksbühne 16

Chén Chè

$ | Asian. Tucked into a court-yard behind the bflat jazz club, this elegant restaurant benefits from fresh ingredients, expert cooking, and an enticing exotic tea list. It has a lovely location; the outdoor space is adorned with paper lamps and canopies. *Average main: €8* ⊠ *Rosenthalerstr. 13, Mitte* ☎ *030/2888–4282* ⊕ *www.chenche-berlin.de* ▭ *No credit cards.*

Cocolo Ramen

$ | Japanese. The narrow, blink-and-you-miss-it ramen joint Cocolo, run by German chef Oliver Prestele, has obviously got it right; the noodle kitchen is packed almost every night of the week and has gained a devoted following—and it doesn't take reservations, so prepare to wait in line. Tasty pork-based broths come in flavors like creamy *tonkotsu* with pork belly, salty *shio* with smoked chicken, or rich *shoyu* with wakame and scallion. **Known for:** authentic-seeming ramen; busy, lively atmosphere; gentle prices. *Average main: €10* ⊠ *Gipsstr. 3, Mitte* ☎ *0172/304–7584* ⊕ *kuchi.de/restaurant/cocolo-ramen* ▭ *No credit cards* ⊗ *Closed Sun.* Ⓜ *Rosenthaler Platz, Weinmeisterstrasse (U-bahn), Hackescher Markt (S-bahn).*

★ Einsunternull

$$$$ | German. In a clean and modern Scandinavia-like space done up in woods and light colors, chef Andreas Rieger, formerly of two–Michelin star Reinstoff, aims to serve up German culture on a plate, using all regional ingredients in sometimes nostalgic dishes presented in innovative ways (think back bacon served with dried plums and rose petals). The four- to five-course lunch menu is served upstairs with open kitchen views, while the 10-course dinner is eaten downstairs; natural wines, many from Germany, perfectly balance each plate. **Known for:** German terroir–driven plates, with many foraged and preserved ingredi-ents; inspired wine or alcohol-free beverage pairings; "memories of our childhood" dessert with brown bread and honey. *Average main: €109* ⊠ *Hannoversche Str. 1, Mitte* ☎ *030/2757–7810* ⊕ *restaurant-einsunternull.de* ⊗ *Closed Sun. and Wed. No lunch Mon.* Ⓜ *Oranien-burger Tor (U-bahn).*

Habel am Reichstag

$$$ | German. Under the arches of the S-bahn tracks connecting Friedrichstrasse with Hauptbahnhof, Habel am Reichstag seems unassuming from outside, but inside you'll find old Berlin elegance melded with industrial chic: leather banquettes, crystal chandeliers dangling from the arched brick ceilings, and rumbling trains overhead. The no-nonsense waiters serve local classics, like lamb, Wiener schnitzel, *weisser Spargel* (asparagus), and *Knödel* (dumplings) with mushrooms and ham. **Known for:** huge wine selec-tion; cool underground location; seasonal menu. *Average main: €24* ⊠ *Luisenstr. 19, Mitte* ☎ *030/2809–8484* ⊕ *www.wein-habel.de* ⊗ *No* dinner Sun. Ⓜ *Brandenburger Tor (S-bahn and U-bahn).*

Hackescher Hof

$$$ | German. This beautiful, wood-paneled restaurant is spacious but almost always crowded, but it's right in the middle of the action at bustling Hackesche Höfe, and a solid place to eat German food while doing some excellent people-watching. The clientele is a fun mix of tourists and locals, which gives the place a vibrant, lively atmosphere; when the weather is good there are tables outside in the courtyard, too. **Known for:** good-quality German dishes; Brandenburg wild boar (when available); convenient, central location. *Average main: €23* ✉ *Rosenthalerstr. 40–41, inside Hackesche Höfe, Mitte* ☎ *030/283–5293* ⊕ *www.hackescher-hof.de* Ⓜ *Hackescher Markt (S-bahn).*

★ Katz Orange

$$ | Contemporary. This lovely restaurant, hidden in a courtyard off a quiet, residential street, is both elegant enough for a special occasion and homey enough to be a favorite local haunt. Local ingredients are used whenever possible on the inventive menu, and the restaurant is best known for its slow-cooked meats for two: choose pork or lamb, along with fresh vegetable-focused side dishes. **Known for:** beautiful setting with courtyard seating; 12-hour slow-roasted Duroc pork; interesting craft cocktails. *Average main: €20* ✉ *Bergstr. 22, Mitte* ☎ *030/9832–*

08430 ⊕ *www.katzorange.com* ⊗ *No lunch* Ⓜ *Nordbahnhof (S-bahn).*

Lokal

$$$ | German. This popular restaurant, located on the corner of one of Berlin's prettiest streets, serves locally sourced dishes like Brandenburg wild boar, lake trout, or venison on stylish long wooden tables to an equally stylish crowd. The unfussy German standards have become fast favorites with local gallerists and shop owners, and on warm weekend nights the place opens up to the street, beckoning passersby with the cozy sound of clinking glasses and the low hum of conversation. **Known for:** seasonal, local ingredients; daily changing menus; welcoming, casual vibe. *Average main: €23* ✉ *Linienstr. 160, Mitte* ☎ *030/2844–9500* ⊕ *lokal-berlin.blogspot.de* ⊗ *No lunch* Ⓜ *Oranienburger Tor (U-bahn), Oranienburger Strasse (S-bahn).*

★ Mädchenitaliener

$ | Italian. This cozy Mitte spot has two different spaces: the bustling and sometimes drafty front room with high tables where walk-ins are seated, and a darker, more romantic back room for those who remember to reserve ahead—as you should. The short but well-thought-out menu includes small and large antipasti plates of grilled vegetables, olives, cheeses, and meats, as well as unusual pastas like a tagliatelle with crawfish in a lemon-mint sauce, or one with pine nuts and balsamic-roasted figs. **Known for:** chestnut-filled ravioli with pears; affordable lunch specials; panna cotta. *Average main: €11* ✉ *Alte Schönhauserstr. 12, Mitte* ☎ *030/4004–1787* ▭ *No credit cards* Ⓜ *Rosa Luxemburg-Platz (U-bahn).*

Mogg

$ | Café. In the renovated Ehemalige Jüdische Mädchenschule (Old Jewish Girls' School), this deli-style café serves delicious versions of Jewish deli standards along with regularly changing vegetarian-based salads and mains. The space, with wood floors and tables, blue walls, and low, deep purple banquettes is trendier than any traditional deli. **Known for:** New York–style deli sandwiches, like Reubens and pastrami on rye; chicken liver brûlée with grilled challah; New York cheesecake. *Average main: €12* ✉ *Ehemalige Jüdische Mädchenschule, Auguststr. 11–13, Mitte* ☎ *030/3300–60770* ⊕ *www. moggmogg.com* Ⓜ *Tucholskystrasse (S-bahn).*

Monsieur Vuong

$ | Vietnamese. This hip Vietnamese eatery is a convenient place to meet before hitting Mitte's galleries or bars, or for a light lunch after browsing the area's popular boutiques. There are only a handful of items and daily specials to choose from, but the delicious curries, pho (noodle soup), and noodle salads keep the regulars coming back. **Known for:** lively atmosphere with a nice mix of Berlin locals and tourists; well-prepared and gently priced

Vietnamese dishes; tasty shakes, with flavors including mango and raspberry. *Average main: €8* ✉ *Alte Schönhauserstr. 46, Mitte* ☎ *030/9929–6924* ⊕ *www.monsieur-vuong.de* Ⓜ *Weinmeisterstrasse (U-bahn), Rosa-Luxemburg-Platz (U-bahn).*

★ Pauly Saal

$$$$ | German. With an airy, high-windowed space in what used to be the school gym of the converted Ehemalige Jüdische Mädchenschule (Old Jewish Girls' School), and outdoor tables taking over the building's expansive courtyard, the setting here alone is a draw, but the food is also some of the most exquisite in this part of Mitte. The menu focuses on artful presentation and local ingredients, like meat from Brandenburg, prawns from Pomerania, and cheese from Bad Tölz; the lunch prix fixe is a great way to sample the restaurant's best dishes. **Known for:** only serving three- to seven-course tasting menus; extensive wine list; quirky artwork and setting. *Average main: €100* ✉ *Ehemalige Jüdische Mädchenschule, Auguststr. 11–13, Mitte* ☎ *030/3300–6070* ⊕ *www. paulysaal.com* ⊘ *Closed Sun. and Mon.* Ⓜ *Tucholskystrasse (S-bahn).*

Rutz Restaurant and Weinbar

$$$$ | German. The narrow, unassuming facade of this Michelin-starred restaurant, tucked away on a sleepy stretch of Chausseestrasse, belies the elegant interior and stellar food you'll find inside. "Inspiration"

tasting menus of six or nine courses (limited à la carte choices are also available for parties of four or fewer) make the most of ingredients like duck and beef and combine unusual items like black radishes and mushrooms, or asparagus and wild violets; you can find more casual and heartier fare at the Weinbar downstairs. **Known for:** one of the most extensive wine lists in Berlin; mostly adventurous tasting menus using mainly local ingredients; prices on the high side. *Average main: €64* ⊠ *Chausseestr. 8, Mitte* ☎ *030/2462–8760* ⊕ *www.rutz-restaurant.de* ⊗ *Closed Sun. and Mon.* Ⓜ *Oranienburger Tor (S-bahn).*

Shiori
$$$$ | **Japanese.** Sparsely decorated, with a collection of hand-made bowls behind the counter, the focus at this Japanese *izakaya* is solely on the food; there are just 10 seats around a small counter where you can watch chef Shiori Arai at work. The 10 to 12 exquisitely presented seasonal courses fuse local German ingredients with Japanese technique and can be paired with a small but smart selection of sake for some of the most authentic Japanese cuisine in town. **Known for:** wide-ranging selection of Japanese dishes, from soup to sashimi to tofu; surprisingly affordable prix-fixe menu; cozy atmosphere where diners feel like part of the experience. *Average main: €70* ⊠ *Max-Beer-Str. 13, Mitte* ☎ *030/2433–7766* ⊕ *www.shiorib-erlin.com* ⊗ *Closed Sun. No lunch*

Ⓜ *Weinmeisterstrasse (U-bahn), Rosa-Luxemburg-Platz (U-bahn).*

The Store Kitchen
$ | **International.** Much more than just a place to eat, this bright, sprawling, and modern concept store on the ground floor of the SoHo House hotel is open to everyone, not just SoHo House guests. The Store Kitchen, in the front of the space, focuses on healthy cuisine and excels at salad and grain dishes, while soups, sandwiches, and desserts round out the menu—order one of the set plates and you'll get to try a variety of what's available that day. **Known for:** Middle Eastern flavors; juice bar; craft cocktails. *Average main: €12* ⊠ *Torstr. 1, Mitte* ⊕ *Ground fl. of the SoHo House* ⊗ *Closed Sun.* ▭ *No credit cards* Ⓜ *Rosa-Luxemburg-Platz (U-bahn).*

Zur Letzten Instanz
$$ | **German.** Berlin's oldest restaurant (established in 1621) is half hidden in a maze of medieval streets, though it's welcomed some illustrious diners over the centuries: Napoléon is said to have sat by the tile stove, and Mikhail Gorbachev sipped a beer here in 1989. The small, well-priced menu focuses on some of Berlin's most traditional specialties, including *Eisbein* (pork knuckle), and takes its whimsical dish titles from classic legal jargon—the national courthouse is around the corner, and the restaurant's name is a rough equivalent of the term "at the 11th hour." **Known for:** roasted pork knuckle

with red cabbage; meatballs with mashed potatoes; historic setting with charming ambience. *Average main: €18* ✉ *Waisenstr. 14–16, Mitte* ☎ *030/242–5528* ⊕ *www.zurletzteninstanz.de* ☽ *Closed Mon.* Ⓜ *Klosterstrasse (U-bahn).*

🍸 Bars and Nightlife

★ b-flat

Young German artists perform most nights at b-flat. The well-known and well-attended Wednesday jam sessions focus on free and experimental jazz, and once a month on Thursday the Berlin Big Band takes over the small stage. ✉ *Dircksenstr. 40, Mitte* ☎ *030/283–3123* ⊕ *b-flat-berlin.de* Ⓜ *Weinmeisterstrasse (U-bahn), Hackescher Markt (S-bahn).*

Bar Tausend

In the grand tradition of upscale clubs, Bar Tausend is well hidden behind a steel door under the Friedrichstrasse S-bahn tracks and guarded by a discerning doorman. The futuristic main bar area, basically a long tunnel with circular lights at either end and mirrors above, looks like something out of the classic German film *Metropolis*. It would feel a bit claustrophobic if not for the excellent cocktails and stylish clientele. Hidden behind the bar is an even harder-to-get-into restaurant, whispered about by Berlin foodies—the so-called Tausend Cantina. For an unforgettable meal, call in advance for reservations. ✉ *Schiffbauerdamm 11, under S-bahn tracks, Mitte*

☎ *030/2758–2070* ⊕ *www.tausend-berlin.com* Ⓜ *Friedrichstrasse (U-bahn, S-bahn).*

★ Buck and Breck

The entrance is so Berlin: an unmarked, nondescript door across from Weinsbergpark has a buzzer that reads "Bar." But once you're let inside this dark and moody speakeasy and perched at the long table in its main room, which only seats 12, you'll be treated to classic, well-executed cocktails and a hip and lively crowd. ✉ *Brunnenstr. 177, Mitte* ⊕ *www.buckandbreck.com* Ⓜ *Rosenthaler Platz (U-bahn).*

★ Clärchen's Ballhaus

A night out at Clärchen's Ballhaus (Little Clara's Ballroom) is like a trip back in time; opened in 1913, the club is an impressive sight. On summer nights, lines often stretch out the door, while the front courtyard comes alive with patrons dining alfresco on brick-oven pizzas. The main ballroom features a different style of music every night and there are often dance lessons before the party starts. One of the best things about this place, though, is the variety of people of different ages, nationalities, and social backgrounds. ✉ *Auguststr. 24, Mitte* ☎ *030/282–9295* ⊕ *www.ballhaus.de* Ⓜ *Oranienburger Strasse (S-bahn).*

Hotel Amano

This designy boutique hotel is in the center of the action in Mitte. The happening bar scene and popular rooftop garden attract a hip group of locals. ✉ *Auguststr. 43, Mitte* ☎ *030/809–4150* ⊕ *www. hotel-amano.com* Ⓜ *Rosenthaler Platz (U-bahn).*

House of Weekend

More like a lounge and party venue than a club, House of Weekend has great views of East Berlin's skyline and several different floors of music, including the occasional international DJ act. But beware: the crowd is young, and on weekends you may find yourself caught in a throng of tourists, or rowdy study-abroad students on their night out. In the summer, it's open nightly from 6 pm, with table reservations available. ✉ *Alexanderstr. 7, Mitte* ☎ *030/2463–1676.*

Kaschk

Like most Berlin bars, this new space doubles during the day as a breakfast café. What sets it apart is the basement, home to Germany's first shuffleboard court. The selection of international craft beers and the open atmosphere make it an enjoyable place to hang out in the city center—day or night. ✉ *Linienstr. 40, Mitte.*

Kunstfabrik Schlot

Schlot hosts Berlin jazz scenesters, aspiring musicians playing Monday-night free jazz sessions, and local heavy hitters. It's a bit hard to find—it's in the cellar of the Edison Höfe—but enter the courtyard via Schlegelstrasse and follow the music. ✉ *Invalidenstr. 117, entrance at Schlegelstr. 26, Mitte* ☎ *030/448–2160* ⊕ *kunstfabrik-*

schlot.de Ⓜ *Nordbahnhof (S-bahn), Naturkundemuseum (U-bahn).*

Mr. Susan

American transplant Susan Choi helms this airy and innovative cocktail haven. Though the drinks list is small, it focuses on seasonal ingredients (think peaches in summer and mushrooms in fall) and interesting flavor combinations you won't find elsewhere—plus it's nonsmoking, rare for a Berlin bar. ✉ *Krausnickstr. 1, Mitte* ☎ *160/536–7463* ⊕ *www.facebook. com/hellomrsusan* Ⓜ *Oranienburger Strasse (S-bahn).*

REDWOOD Bar Berlin

Run by a California native, this simple, solid cocktail bar serves near-perfect concoctions that belie the bare wood surroundings. If loud crowds and smoky rooms aren't your thing, this is the place for you—the cocktails are excellent and you'll be able to carry on a conversation in a normal voice. ✉ *Bergstr. 25, Mitte* ☎ *030/7024–8813* ⊕ *redwoodbar.de* Ⓜ *Nordbahnhof (S-bahn).*

🎭 Performing Arts

Berliner Ensemble

The excellent Berliner Ensemble is dedicated to Brecht and works of other international playwrights. ✉ *Bertolt Brecht-Pl. 1, off Friedrichstr., just north of train station, Mitte* ☎ *030/2840–8155* ⊕ *www.berliner-ensemble.de.*

Deutsches Theater

The theater most renowned for both its modern and classical productions is the Deutsches Theater. ✉ *Schumannstr. 13a, Mitte* ☎ *030/2844–1225* ⊕ *www.deutsches-theater.de*.

★ Volksbühne

The Volksbühne is unsurpassed for its aggressively experimental style, and the 824 seats are often sold out. The unusual building was reconstructed in the 1950s using the original 1914 plans. It also houses two smaller performance spaces—the Roter Salon and the Grüner Salon—which host everything from retro Motown nights and salsa classes for all levels to touring pop and rock acts. ✉ *Rosa-Luxemburg-Pl. 1, Mitte* ☎ *030/2406–5777* ⊕ *www.volksbuehne.berlin/en*.

Prenzlauer Berg

GO FOR

Fine dining

Charming atmosphere

Good bar scene

Sightseeing ★☆☆☆☆ | Shopping ★★★★☆ | Dining ★★★★★ | Nightlife ★★★★☆

Once a spot for edgy art spaces, squats, and all manner of alternative lifestyles, Prenzlauer Berg has morphed into a lively, upscale neighborhood filled with restaurants and bars, independent boutiques, and young German and expat couples with baby strollers. It's a lovely area to stroll, with gorgeous prewar buildings and cobblestone streets shaded by giant chestnut trees. The famous Mauerpark flea market and open-air karaoke attract throngs of hipsters and tourists every Sunday. —by Jennifer Ceaser

◉ Sights

Jüdischer Friedhof Weissensee
(Jewish Cemetery)
Some 115,000 graves make up Europe's largest Jewish cemetery, in Berlin's Weissensee district, near Prenzlauer Berg. Covering more than 100 acres, the grounds resemble a forest, with tall trees and large ferns; scattered throughout are tombstones and mausoleums in various states of repair. Wandering through them is like taking an extremely moving trip back in time through the history of Jewish Berlin. Men are required to cover their heads with a *kippah*, available at the entrance. ⊠ *Herbert-Baum-Str. 45* ☎ *030/925–3330* ⊕ *jewish-cemetery-weissensee.org* ⬚ *Free* ⊙ *Closed Sat.* Ⓜ *Albertinenstrasse (M4 or M13 tram).*

Kollwitzplatz
(Kollwitz Square)
Named for the painter, sculptor, and political activist Käthe Kollwitz (1867–1945),

who lived nearby, the square is the center of the old working-class district of Prenzlauer Berg. Kollwitz, who portrayed the hard times of area residents, is immortalized here in a sculpture based on a self-portrait. Ironically, this image of the artist now has a view of the upwardly mobile young families who have transformed the neighborhood since reunification. Bars and restaurants peel off from the square, and one of the best organic markets in town takes over on weekends. ⊠ *Kollwitzpl., Prenzlauer Berg* Ⓜ *Senefelderplatz (U-bahn).*

Kulturbrauerei *(Culture Brewery)*
The redbrick buildings of the old Schultheiss brewery are typical of late-19th-century industrial architecture. Parts of the brewery were built in 1842, and at the turn of the 20th century the complex expanded to include the main brewery of Berlin's famous Schultheiss beer, then the world's largest brewery. Today, the multiplex cinema, pubs, clubs, and a concert venue that occupy it make up an arts and entertainment nexus (sadly, without a brewery). Pick up information at

the Prenzlauer Berg tourist office here, and come Christmastime, visit the Scandinavian-themed market, which includes children's rides. ✉ *Schönhauser Allee 36, entry at Sredzkistr. 1 and Knaackstr. 97, Prenzlauer Berg* 🕾 *030/4435-2170* ⊕ *www.kulturbrauerei.de* Ⓜ *Eberswalder Strasse (U-bahn).*

Mauerpark

This former no-man's-land between East and West Berlin (the name translates to "Wall Park") was off-limits to the public from 1961 to 1989, when the Berlin Wall fell. After reconstruction, the area reopened as a park in 1994, and though it's still a bit rough around the edges, it's filled with hipsters, musicians, and tourists on sunny days and for the weekly Sunday flea market. It's also home to the hugely popular open-air Bearpit Karaoke Show, which runs Sunday afternoon from spring through late fall and attracts a boisterous mix of people of all ages. ✉ *Prenzlauer Berg* ✛ *Between Gleimstr. to north, Bernauer Str. and Topsstr. to south, Cantianstr. to east, and Graunstr. and Wolliner Str. to west* 🕾 *Free* Ⓜ *Eberswalder Strasse (U-bahn).*

Soho House Berlin

The Berlin branch of this luxury hotel–club, inside a grand, restored Bauhaus building, brings the chic atmosphere of London and New York's Soho to the German capital for a moderate price. Visit the shop, cafe, restaurant, or bar while you're exploring the neighborhood. ✉ *Torstr. 1, Prenzlauer Berg*

GETTING HERE

The beating heart of Prenzlauer Berg is in and around Eberswalder Strasse, Kastanienallee, and Kollwitzplatz, where you'll find most of the district's bars, restaurants, and shopping. Three tram lines—the M1, M10, and M12—will take you here, as will the U-bahn (U2). There's also a nearby S-bahn station at Schönhauser Allee. To reach the popular Sunday flea market at Mauerpark, take the M10 tram and get off at the Friedrich-Ludwig-Jahn-Sportpark stop.

🕾 *030/405-0440* Ⓜ *Rosa-Luxemburg-Platz (U-bahn).*

🛍 Shopping

Calypso Shoes

A must-visit for shoe lovers, this shop has an impressive collection of exotic and vintage footwear, including suede heels, leather-trimmed boots, embroidered flats, and men's work boots—all spanning the last six decades. Because of its diverse collection, the shop also regularly works with film and theater stylists. ✉ *Oderbergerstr. 14, Prenzlauer Berg* 🕾 *030/281-6165* ⊕ *www.facebook.com/calypsovintageshoes* ⊘ *Closed Sun.* Ⓜ *Eberswalder Strasse (U-bahn).*

Dear

This secondhand shop, on one of Prenzlauer Berg's most charming streets, offers a well-curated selection of designer clothing, shoes, and accessories for both men and women. You'll find stylish labels

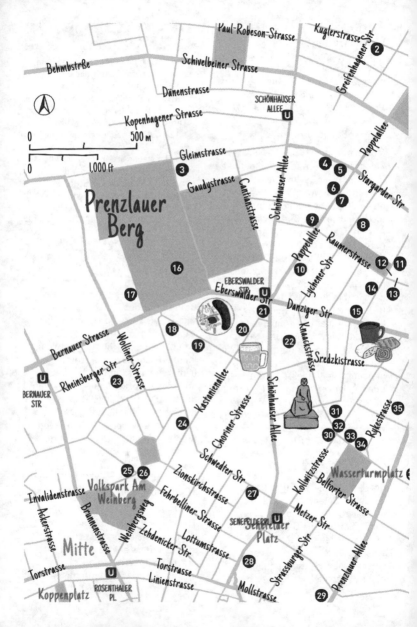

SUNDAYS IN MAUERPARK

The rather shabby Mauerpark holds little aesthetic appeal, but every Sunday, it transforms into one of the liveliest spots in the city. Locals and tourists alike descend by the thousands to the sprawling open-air Floh-markt am Mauerpark (Fleamarket at Mauerpark), jam-packed with second-hand goods and original handmade designs. Throngs weave their way through row upon row of local vendors peddling vintage clothing, antiques, retro furniture, GDR memorabilia, old vinyl, artwork, crafts, jewelry, and knickknacks galore. Though much of it is junk, you can find the occasional treasure. Fuel up after shopping at one of many street food stands, selling everything from currywurst to empanadas to vegan cookies, or make a pit stop at one of the park's two shady beer gardens, Mauersegler and Schönwetter. Afternoons, crowds start streaming over to the nearby hillside amphitheater for one of the day's biggest draws, Bearpit Karaoke. When the clock strikes three, the performances begin; amateur singers and dancers are cheered—or booed—depending on their talent. The rowdy event takes place spring through late fall, weather permitting.

like Acne, Nike, Marni, and Miu Miu. Be prepared for somewhat steep prices. ⊠ *Stargarder Str. 9, Prenzlauer Berg* ☎ *030/4908–1169* ⊗ *Closed Sun.* Ⓜ *Schönhauser Allee (U-bahn and S-bahn).*

★ **Dr. Kochan Schnapskultur**
This small shop embodies traditional German liquor culture; there are schnapps and fruit brandies from family farms and independent distilleries for sale, among other items to pique a tippler's interest. ⊠ *Immanuelkirchstr. 4, Prenzlauer Berg* ☎ *030/3462–4076* ⊕ *www.schnapskultur.de* ⊗ *Closed Sun.* Ⓜ *Senefelderplatz (U-bahn).*

Garments Vintage
This chic store offers Prenzlauer Berg's fashion lovers an excellent selection of vintage and second-hand designer clothing, costume jewelry, shoes, and accessories. There is also a branch in Mitte, at Linienstrasse 204. ⊠ *Stargarderstr. 12 A, Prenzlauer Berg* ☎ *030/7477–9919* ⊕ *www.garments-vintage.de* ⊗ *Closed Sun.* Ⓜ *Schönhauser Allee (U-bahn and S-bahn).*

Goldhahn und Sampson
A food-lover's paradise, this epicurean shop sells a wide range of products, from gourmet, artisanal pantry ingredients and kitchen tools to an extensive collection of cookbooks and food magazines. Handmade breads, pastries, and chocolates are available to satiate your appetite. There's also a nice

selection of cheeses, as well as fine wines and craft beer. A second outpost is in Charlottenburg, at Wilmersdorfer Strasse 102/103. ✉ *Dunckerstr. 9, Prenzlauer Berg* ☎ *No phone* ⊕ *www.goldhahnundsampson.de* ⊙ *Closed Sun.* Ⓜ *Eberswalder Strasse (U-bahn), Prenzlauer Allee (S-bahn).*

Kauf Dich Glücklich

With an odd assortment of retro furnishings, this ice-cream café and waffle shop takes over the entire corner of a Prenzlauer Berg sidewalk, especially on sunny days. Head to the second story and you'll find a shop that captures young Berliner style, with vintage pieces, bold prints, and skinny fits, as well as shoes and jewelry. There's a second outpost on Oderberger Strasse as well as one in Mitte, plus an outlet shop in Wedding. ✉ *Kastanienallee 54, Prenzlauer Berg* ☎ *030/4862–3348* ⊕ *www.kaufdichgluecklich-shop.de* Ⓜ *Rosenthaler Platz (U-bahn).*

Majaco

Just off the lovely Zionskirchplatz, this shop is home to Berlin designers Anna Franke and Janine Weber. Their collection has a whimsical, feminine style and incorporates flowing fabrics and clean cuts. The shop also carries beautiful bags and accessories from Scandinavian and German designers. ✉ *Fehrbelliner Str. 24, Prenzlauer Berg* ☎ *303/38304–00566* ⊕ *www.majaco-berlin.de* ⊙ *Closed Sun.* Ⓜ *Rosenthaler Platz (U-bahn).*

Markt am Kollwitzplatz

One of the city's best farmers' markets sits on the pretty Kollwitzplatz square in Prenzlauer Berg. During its smaller Thursday and bustling Saturday markets, you'll not only find a superb selection of organic produce, meats, cheeses, and pantry items, but also an array of prepared foods and sellers offering handmade home goods and gifts. ✉ *Kollwitzpl., Prenzlauer Berg* Ⓜ *Senefelderplatz (U-bahn).*

Mauerpark Flohmarkt

The enormous Sunday flea market at Mauerpark, a favorite among hipsters and tourists, is absolutely packed in nice weather, turning the intersection of Bernauer Strasse and Oderberger Strasse (where the unofficial market outside the market begins) into a veritable Times Square of fun- and sun-loving young people. Head out early to find the best pickings, as most of the selection here is junkyard mixed in with the occasional handmade or repurposed product. ✉ *Bernauer Str. 63–64, Prenzlauer Berg* ☎ *0176/292–5002* ⊕ *www.flohmarktimmauerpark. de* Ⓜ *Eberswalder Strasse (U-bahn), Bernauer Strasse (U-bahn).*

MDC

Melanie Dal Canton (MDC), stocks her elegant beauty shop with hard-to-find labels like Malin + Goetz, Santa Maria Novella from Florence, and Berlin's Frank Leder. She takes time with every client, offering recommendations, and when you need even more care, there's a treatment room in back for facials and manicure/pedicures. ✉ *Knaackstr. 26, Prenzlauer Berg* ☎ *030/4005–6339* ⊕ *mdc-cosmetic. com* ⊘ *Closed Sun.* Ⓜ *Senefelderplatz (U-bahn).*

NO WÓDKA
This minimal showroom is offset by a playfully curated selection of Polish art, fashion, and design items. The store's name hints at irony, and indeed no vodka can be found here—just rather covetable contemporary products that reinterpret the meaning of "made in Poland."✉ *Pappelallee 10, Prenzlauer Berg* ☎ *030/4862–3086* ⊕ *nowodka. com* ⊘ *Closed Sun.* Ⓜ *Eberswalder Strasse (U-bahn).*

Schoemig Porzellan
Germany has a long history of porcelain manufacturing and this small artisan studio and shop carries on the tradition. Watch as delicate, nearly translucent porcelain tableware is crafted by hand, and choose from an array of modern ceramic designs including vases, cups, bowls, plates, and platters. ✉ *Raumerstr. 35, Prenzlauer Berg* ☎ *030/6954-5513* ⊕ *schoemig-porzellan.de* ⊘ *Closed Sun. to Wed.* Ⓜ *Eberswalder Strasse (U-bahn or tram).*

Temporary Showroom
This sleek, multilevel concept store showcases a revolving collection of eclectic European and international designers, spanning high fashion, avant-garde labels, street wear, and accessories. Look for interesting limited-edition and capsule collections as well. ✉ *Kastanienallee 36a,*

> **BACK IN THE DAY**
>
> Stadtbad Oderberger opened as a public bathhouse in 1902. The palatial landmarked building on Oderberger Strasse closed in 1986 and sat vacant for three decades until it was entirely renovated and reopened as a boutique hotel in 2016. But the historic 65-foot-long heated indoor pool, set beneath a glorious vaulted stone ceiling, is still open to the public for swimming; the cost is 6 euro for two hours or 15 euro for the pool and sauna.

Prenzlauer Berg ☎ *030/6220–4563* ⊕ *www.temporaryshowroom.com* ⊘ *Closed Sun.* Ⓜ *Rosenthaler Platz (U-bahn), Eberswalder Strasse (U-bahn).*

★ Trödelmarkt Arkonaplatz
This is a smaller Sunday market tucked on a neighborhood square in Prenzlauer Berg, but one that many locals say is Berlin's best, especially for its wide selection of vintage and secondhand furniture, housewares, books, and records. ✉ *Arkonpl., Prenzlauer Berg* ☎ *030/786–9764* ⊕ *www.troedelmarkt-arkonaplatz.de/* Ⓜ *Bernauer Strasse (U-bahn).*

☕ Coffee and Quick Bites

The Barn Roastery
$ | Café. The Barn roasts their coffee beans on the premises and offers a limited menu of near-perfect brews—they take coffee seriously, and can get a bit dictatorial about how much milk or sugar you should add. There are baked

goods and sandwiches on the menu as well, but the focus here is definitely on the coffee. *Average main: €3 ⊠ Schönhauser Allee 8, Prenzlauer Berg ⊕ thebarn.de ⊟ No credit cards Ⓜ Rosa-Luxemburg-Platz (U-bahn and tram), Senefelder Platz (U-bahn).*

Bonanza Coffee Heroes

$ | Café. The name isn't an exaggeration: Bonanza really was one of the first "coffee heroes" to champion artisanal roasting and brewing methods in the German capital. From its tiny home next to Mauerpark in Prenzlauer Berg, Bonanza roasts its own beans, runs a catering business, offers their beans wholesale to customers all over the city, and serves some of the smoothest, tastiest coffee in town. *Average main: €3 ⊠ Oderbergerstr. 35, Prenzlauer Berg ☎ 0171/563-0795 ⊕ www.bonanzacoffee.de ⊟ No credit cards Ⓜ Eberswalder Strasse (U-bahn).*

Café Liebling

$ | Café. A local favorite, this cozy, casual café is open from early morning into the wee hours, making it the perfect spot for everything from breakfast to a light lunch to evening drinks. There's an affordable daily quiche and salad plate as well as a nice selection of cakes. *Average main: €7 ⊠ Raumerstr. 36A, Prenzlauer Berg ☎ 030/4119-8209 ⊟ No credit cards Ⓜ Eberswalder Strasse (U-bahn).*

Godshot

$ | Café. The eclectic mix of oddly matched couches, chairs, and tables in this tiny space create a cozy setting for enjoying excellent coffee and pastries. The latte art and the "godshot" logo on the coffee cups make for some Instagram-worthy photos, too. *Average main: €3 ⊠ Immanuelkirchstr. 32, Prenzlauer Berg ⊕ www.godshot.de ⊟ No credit cards Ⓜ Knaackstrasse (tram).*

🍴 Dining

Allan's Breakfast Club & Wine Bar

$ | Café. There are a whole host of reasons why this small, friendly, Aussie-owned spot is always packed at brunch. First and foremost, it's one of the few places in Berlin where you can find a Bloody Mary—and it's a good, spicy one, complete with all the requisite garnishes. **Known for:** busy weekend brunch; excellent Bloody Marys; friendly service. *Average main: €8 ⊠ Rykestr. 13, Prenzlauer Berg ☎ No phone ☺ Closed Tues. No dinner Sat. to Mon. ⊟ No credit cards Ⓜ Senefelderplatz (U-bahn), Marienburger Str. (tram).*

The Bird

$ | American. Yes it's run by Americans, and yes it serves burgers, but the Bird, overlooking a corner of Mauerpark in Prenzlauer Berg, is more than just an expat burger joint—it serves some of the best burgers in Berlin, and it's one of the few spots where "rare" actually means pink and juicy on the inside. Besides cheekily named burgers like the "Bronx Jon" (mushrooms and Swiss cheese), "Da Works" (everything, including guacamole if you ask for it), and the "Lousy Hunter," which is a vegetarian burger, the Bird also serves a mean steak frites suitable for two. **Known for:** classic American burgers; friendly service; creative topping combos. *Average main: €12* ✉ *Am Falkpl. 5, Prenzlauer Berg* ☎ *030/5105–3283* ⊕ *www.thebirdin-berlin.com* 🚻 *No credit cards* ☉ *No lunch weekdays* Ⓜ *Schönhauser Allee (S-bahn and U-bahn).*

Gugelhof

$$ | French. Although far from Alsatian France and the Mosel and Saar regions of Germany's southwest that inspire the hearty fare here, a visit to this busy but homey Kollwitzplatz restaurant will leave you pleasantly surprised at the authenticity of the food—and deliciously full. The raclette is the best you're likely to get this side of the Rhine, and classic choucroute comes with *Blutwurst* (blood sausage). **Known for:** excellent raclette; weekly changing dishes plus constant favorites; pleasant location in the heart of charming Prenzlauer Berg. *Average main: €18* ✉ *Knaackstr. 37, Prenzlauer Berg* ☎ *030/442–9229* ⊕ *www.gugelhof.de* ☉ *Closed Tues. No lunch weekdays* Ⓜ *Senefelder Platz (U-bahn).*

häppies

$ | Austrian. These are not your typical dumplings. Out of this tiny, cheery space come big, yeasty, steamed balls of dough known as *germknödel,* stuffed with all manner of savory or sweet fillings and topped with imaginative sauces. **Known for:** a rotating selection of savory and sweet dumplings; local favorite; homemade rhubarb-vanilla lemonade. *Average main: €5* ✉ *Dunckerstr. 85, Prenzlauer Berg* ☎ *1511/498–4140* ☉ *Closed Mon. and Tues. No dinner* 🚻 *No credit cards* Ⓜ *Eberswalder Strasse (U-bahn or tram).*

★ Konnopke's Imbiss

$ | German. Under the tracks of the elevated U2 subway line is Berlin's most beloved sausage stand. Konnopke's is a family business that's been around since 1930 and, though there are several options on the menu, this place is famous for its currywurst, which is served on a paper tray with a plastic prong that

can be used to spear the sauce-covered sausage slices; with French fries and a pilsner, this is one of the quintessential Berlin meals. **Known for:** much-loved currywurst with fries (there's also a vegan option); throngs of people all day long; quick, cheap eats. *Average main: €4 ⌧ Schönhauser Allee 44b, Prenzlauer Berg ☏ 030/442–7765 ⊕ www. konnopke-imbiss.de ▭ No credit cards ◔ Closed Sun. Ⓜ Eberswalderstrasse (U-bahn).*

Maria Bonita

$ | Mexican. This Mexican restaurant is an unassuming space on Prenzlauer Berg's Danziger Strasse. The young owners (hailing from Texas and Australia) had different ideas of what Mexican food could be, but shared one dream: to bring the authentic cuisine to Berlin. **Known for:** authentic Mexican tacos, burritos, and quesadillas; classic Mexican egg dishes including chilaquiles; fresh mezcal margaritas. *Average main: €7 ⌧ Danzigerstr. 33, Prenzlauer Berg ☏ ⊕ www. mariabonita.de ▭ No credit cards Ⓜ Eberswalder Strasse (U-bahn).*

★ Mrs. Robinson's

$$ | Eclectic. Intimate and effortlessly cool, this pint-size modern restaurant specializes in creative, affordable small plates with an Asian touch, such as their signature *bao* (filled buns) in varying flavors, served alongside expertly mixed cocktails or inspired wine choices. Snag one of the few tables if you've come with a group, but it's most fun to sit on a bar stool near the kitchen where you can chat with

the friendly staff and feel like a part of the action. **Known for:** small, Asian-inflected plates; unusual ingredient combinations; relaxed, fun atmosphere. *Average main: €17 ⌧ Pappelallee 29, Prenzlauer Berg ☏ 030/5462–2839 ⊕ www.mrsrobinsons.de ◔ Closed Tues. and Wed. No lunch Ⓜ Schönhauser Allee (U-bahn, S-bahn), Eberswalderstrasse (U-bahn).*

Muse

$ | International. This casual, colorful spot is tucked into a pleasant, tree-lined, cobblestone street just up the hill from Alexanderplatz. The lunch and dinner menus focus on globally influenced, innovative salads, soups, burgers, and sandwiches, with a few mains like steak frites and chicken tikka masala. **Known for:** global comfort food with American, Mexican, French, Asian, and Indian influences; build-your-own burgers with unique toppings like walnut-spinach pesto; a perfectly juicy southern fried chicken sandwich. *Average main: €8 ⌧ Immanuelkirchstr. 31, Prenzlauer Berg ☏ 030/4005–6289 ⊕ www.muse-berlin.com ◔ Closed Sun. evening Ⓜ Knaackstrasse (tram).*

Pasternak

$$$ | Russian. Russian treats such as dumplings, borscht, blini (Russian pancakes), and much more are the mainstays at this casually refined restaurant with a lovely outdoor terrace for when the weather is nice. There are several set menus available for lunch and dinner, but if you come for the weekend brunch you can try just about all of the delicious dishes, as well as dessert, in an extensive buffet. **Known for:** gourmet takes on old-fashioned Russian dishes; charming setting inside and out; very popular Sunday brunch buffet. *Average main: €21 ⊠ Knaackstr. 22/24, Prenzlauer Berg ☎ 030/441–3399 ⊕ www.restaurant-pasternak.de Ⓜ Senefelder Platz (U-bahn).*

Sasaya

$ | Japanese. In a city that still sometimes struggles to get sushi right, Sasaya's concept can seem groundbreaking: simple, authentic Japanese food in an equally comfortable, no-fuss atmosphere. Don't expect sushi to be the center of the menu, though—the focus is on reasonably priced small plates made for sharing, including pickled vegetables, seaweed salad, and crispy pork belly. **Known for:** soups made with traditional Japanese dashi (fish and seaweed) broth; refined small plates made for sharing; reservations are essential. *Average main: €12 ⊠ Lychenerstr. 50, Prenzlauer Berg ☎ 030/4471–7721 ⊕ www.sasaya-berlin-en.tumblr.com 🗎 No credit cards ⊘ Closed Tues. and Wed. Ⓜ Eberswalder Strasse (U-bahn).*

Wok Show

$ | Chinese. Although there's a full menu of Chinese dishes at this nondescript local favorite, it's the *jiaozi* you want: juicy, perfectly wrapped dumplings with vegetable, pork, or lamb fillings, to be dipped in a sour black vinegar and spicy

WORTH A TRIP

This Uferhallen complex in nearby Wedding, constructed in 1873, was originally part of the Grosse Berliner Pferdeeisenbahn (Great Berlin Horse Railway), before being used for electric trolleys at the beginning of the 20th century, and finally as a bus terminal and repair shop after World War II. In 2010, the Uferhallen were transformed into a series of artists' studios and workshops along the tiny Panke canal. Nowadays, Wedding residents and intrepid visitors can catch a contemporary dance performance at the Uferstudios, an intimate piano concert at the Piano Salon Christophori, or a meal at Café Pförtner. If you're feeling adventurous, just wander around and knock on a few doors.

chili paste. Start with addictive appetizers like tofu with crispy shrimp, cucumber with garlic, or Kaofu—silky tofu skins with bean sprouts and soybean—then dive into the dumplings, which can be ordered in batches of 20 or 40. **Known for:** jiaozi (dumplings filled with vegetable, pork, or lamb); local favorite; affordable menu. *Average main: €8 ⊠ Greifenhagenerstr. 31, Prenzlauer Berg ☎ 030/4391–1857 🗎 No credit cards ⊘ No lunch Mon.–Wed. Ⓜ Schönhauser Allee (U-bahn and S-bahn).*

🍸 Bars and Nightlife

Becketts Kopf

The only indication anything exists behind this bar's curtained facade is a glowing photograph of the head of Samuel Beckett in the window. Press the buzzer and if there's space, you'll be ushered into the dimly lit, gentlemen's club-like surroundings. Settle into a leather armchair and choose from sophisticated cocktails like the Lusitanian or the Widow's Kiss, all crafted with artisanal spirits. Or, try a classic martini—one of the best in town. Reservations are recommended. ✉ *Pappellallee 64, Prenzlauer Berg* ☎ *030/4403–5880 for reservations* ⊕ *www.becketts-kopf.de* Ⓜ *Schönhauser Allee (S-bahn and U-bahn).*

Crossroads

With its jumble of vintage furniture and groovy background music by the likes of Tom Waits and Johnny Cash, this neighborhood bar is undoubtedly cool, but it's also a warm, welcoming, entirely unpretentious spot for a drink. Beer and wine are on offer, but take advantage of the skilled bartenders who mix excellent classic martinis and gimlets. The bar's impressive whiskey selection also makes for top-notch Manhattans and whiskey sours. Be advised that it does get quite smoky as the night goes on. ✉ *Gneiststr. 10, Prenzlauer Berg* ☎ *No phone* ⊕ *crossroadsbarberlin.wordpress. com* Ⓜ *Ebreswalder Strasse (U-bahn).*

★ Prater Garten

This sprawling, 600-seat *biergarten* is where Berliners go when the urge for a hefeweizen and pretzel strikes. Grab a beer and a snack (a bratwurst is the classic choice), squeeze in at one of the long community tables, and get ready for some marathon drinking—at least as a bystander, if not a participant. If the outdoor boisterousness is too much, opt for an indoor table at the slightly more upscale restaurant, which serves an expanded menu of German classics like Wiener schnitzel. The beer garden is open from April to September, while the restaurant operates year-round. ✉ *Kastanienallee 7–9, Prenzlauer Berg* ☎ *030/448–5688 restaurant* ⊕ *www.pratergarten.de* Ⓜ *Eberswalder Strasse (U-bahn).*

Visite Ma Tente

A sweet little French-owned bar with a slightly naughty name, this spot has been a local favorite for several years now—simple and comfortable yet *tres* chic. Come here when you're tired of Berlin's beer-dominated bar culture, and order a kir royal or a glass of excellent French wine, paired with a meat-and-cheese platter. In good weather, nab a rickety sidewalk table; the bar's corner location is great for people-watching. ✉ *Christinenstr. 24, Prenzlauer Berg* ☎ *030/4432–3166* Ⓜ *Senefelderplatz (U-bahn).*

Weinerei Forum

It sounds like a recipe for disaster: pay 2 euro for an empty glass, fill it with your choice of wine from a number of bottles, and when you're ready to leave, pay whatever you think you owe. But this pay-as-you-wish bar has survived for more than 15 years; in fact, Weinerei is one of three such "Communist wine bars," all on the border between Mitte and Prenzlauer Berg. Although the wines aren't extraordinary, the charming concept has attracted cash-strapped Berliners steadily over the years. Note that the pay-what-you-want option is only available after 8 p.m. ✉ *Fehrbellinerstr. 57, Prenzlauer Berg* ☎ *030/440–6983* 🌐 *www.weinerei.com* Ⓜ *Rosenthaler Platz (U-bahn).*

Friedrichshain

GO FOR

Wild nightlife

International
cuisine

East German
history

Sightseeing ★★★★★ | Shopping ★★★★☆ | Dining ★★★★☆ | Nightlife ★★★★★

T he cobblestone streets of Friedrichshain, bustling with bars, cafés, and shops, have an alternative feel. There's plenty to see here, including Karl-Marx-Allee, a long, monumental boulevard lined by grand Stalinist apartment buildings (conceived of as "palaces for the people" that would show the superiority of the Communist system over the capitalist one); the area's funky parks; the East Side Gallery; and lively Simon-Dach-Strasse. It's cool, it's hip, it's historical. If you're into street art, this is a good place to wander. —by Adam Groffman

◉ Sights

Boxhagener Platz
In the heart of Friedrichshain, Boxhagener Platz is the focal point for residents. The square—just a short walk from the trendy Simon-Dach-Strasse—has a small playground and park, but the real attraction is on weekends when it transforms into a bustling market. On Saturday, Boxhagener Platz is home to a farmers' market with fresh vegetables, meats, cheeses, and *imbiss* (snack) stands selling local foods. But on Sunday, Boxhagener Platz is converted into one of Berlin's best flea markets where you can stumble upon old East German artifacts alongside vintage furniture and new, trendy T-shirt shops. If you're looking for an equally hip Berlin flea market experience—but less chaotic than the more touristic one at Mauer Park—Boxhagener Platz on Sunday is the place to be. ⊠ *Boxhagener Pl., Friedrichshain.*

Computerspielemuseum
The world's first permanent exhibition for digital computer games, Berlin's Computerspielemuseum (Computer Games Museum) has hundreds of thousands of historical arcade games, home computer and game console systems, video collections, and other artifacts. The interactive museum is great for children, but also for adults looking to relive and experience their favorite childhood games. ⊠ *Karl-Marx-Allee 93A, Friedrichshain* ☎ *030/6098–8577* ⊕ *www.computerspielemuseum.de/.*

★ East Side Gallery
This 1-km (½-mile) stretch of concrete went from guarded border to open-air gallery within three months. East Berliners breached the wall on November 9, 1989, and between February and June of 1990, 118 artists from around the globe created unique works of art on its longest remaining section. One of the best-known works, by Russian artist Dmitri Vrubel, depicts Brezhnev and Honecker (the former East German leader) kissing, with the caption "My God. Help me

survive this deadly love." The stretch along the Spree Canal runs between the Warschauer Strasse S- and U-bahn station and Ostbahnhof. The redbrick Oberbaumbrücke (an 1896 bridge) at Warschauer Strasse makes that end more scenic. ⊠ *Mühlenstr., Friedrichshain* Ⓜ *Warschauer Strasse (U-bahn and S-bahn), Ostbahnhof (S-bahn).*

Karl-Marx-Allee
The monumental boulevard starts in Alexanderplatz and runs through Friedrichshain into neighboring Lichtenberg. Built by the GDR in the 1950s, it was always symbolic of the state's power; it was even initially called Stalinallee since its reconstruction. Buildings along the boulevard are built in a socialist classic style ("wedding-cake style") with large towers located at Frankfurter Tor and Strausberger Platz. The street was once the sight of the famous 1953 worker uprising which threatened the existence of East Germany at the time. Today, you can easily walk along the boulevard to enjoy the architectural sights and occasional plaques describing historical events along the way. ⊠ *Karl-Marx-Allee, Friedrichshain.*

Michelberger Hotel & Bar
Designed by Werner Aisslinger, the lobby of this three-star hotel is simultaneously ultrahip but ultracozy. Metal bookshelves carve out a casual and comfy place to meet friends or sit alone, with attentive service. Order a cocktail or even one of the craft beers brewed especially for the hotel. Or the health-conscious can get a

> **GETTING HERE**
>
> On the edge of what was once East Germany, Friedrichshain is best accessed by the U5 line from Alexanderplatz which is currently being extended to connect all the way to Hauptbahnhof. However, while the line is being renovated, trams, buses, and the S-bahn serve as the main links to the rest of the city. The M10 tram (locally known as the "party tram") runs regularly and helps to ferry locals and travelers all the way from Oberbaumbrücke at the Kreuzberg-Friedrichshain border to Prenzlauer Berg and Mitte districts.

Fountain of Youth Coconut Water—created by the Michelberger Hotel brand. ⊠ *Warschauer Str. 39-40, Friedrichshain* ☎ *030/2977–8590* ⊕ *michelbergerhotel.com.*

nHow Berlin
This spot bills itself as the music hotel—it hosts regular open-mic nights, has two sound studios overlooking the Spree River, and will send a guitar or keyboard to your room anytime creativity strikes. The space-agey, mod decor is courtesy of celebrated designer Karim Rashid. Other notable features are the hotel's small gallery, which shows work by local and international artists, and numerous elevators, each of which entertains you with a different genre of music. ⊠ *Stralauer Allee 3, Friedrichshain* ☎ *030/290–2990* ⊕ *www.nhow-hotels. com/berlin/en/* Ⓜ *Warschauer Strasse (S-bahn and U-bahn).*

Oberbaumbrücke

The double-decker bridge connecting Friedrichshain to Kreuzberg over the Spree River is probably one of Berlin's most iconic structures besides Brandenburg Gate—and definitely Berlin's most iconic bridge. The bridge connects the two once-divided districts by road and U-bahn and its walkway across offers one of the city's most Instagrammable spots. The bridge has also appeared in *Run Lola Run* and other films. ✉ *Oberbaumbrücke, Friedrichshain.*

RAW-Gelände

The onetime train repair station was shut down in the 1990s and over the past 20 years has become a haven for Berlin's underground culture. Graffiti and street art murals cover the buildings, and various clubs and bars hide between the buildings. There's a swimming-pool club open during the summer, a reggae bar, several cafés, food trucks, and a Sunday flea market for furniture all available in the complex today. Watch your pockets—especially at night—as there have been frequent muggings in the area, though it's still generally safe and comfortable to visit. ✉ *Revaler Str. 99, Friedrichshain.*

Urban Spree

A sprawling arts and event space, Urban Spree includes an exhibition gallery, workshop, art store, and beer garden. Largely focused on urban graffiti, photography, and street art, the space also hosts a number of Berlin's alternative events including ComicInvasion, MidSommar Festival, Berlin Graphic Days, and several food festivals. ✉ *Revaler Str. 99, Friedrichshain* ☎ *030/7407–8597* ⊕ *www.urbanspree.com.*

★ Volkspark Friedrichshain

Berlin's oldest public park, Volkspark Friedrichshain sits on the border between the Friedrichshain and Prenzlauer Berg neighborhoods. As one of the city's largest, it's home to a number of unique attractions. There are several sculptures and monuments, including the iconic Märchenbrunnen (fountain of fairy tales) built in 1913, which depicts German fairy-tale subjects alongside a cascading fountain. There's also a Peace Bell memorializing victims of atomic warfare. The urban park has two small artificial mountains made from bunker ruins which offer panoramic views over the city skyline—and serve as a popular sledding spot for local children on snow days. A pond, grilling area, beach volleyball courts, outdoor amphitheater, running track, and two beer gardens round out the attractions in the park. ✉ *Am Friedrichshain 1, Friedrichshain.*

🛍 Shopping

Grosser Antikmarkt am Ostbahnhof (Antique Market at East Station)

The Sunday Grosser Antikmarkt am Ostbahnhof market is made up almost entirely of antiques and vintage treasures, so it takes little effort but a bit of money to find something truly special to take home. Pre-edited selections of antiquarian books, gramophones, jewelry, and kitschy East German items can be found here. ✉ *Erich-Steinfurth-Str. 1, Friedrichshain* ☎ *030/2900–2010* ⊕ *oldthing.de/Berliner-Flohmarkt/* Ⓜ *Ostbahnhof (S-bahn).*

HHV Store

HHV stands for Hip Hop Vinyl—which is a taste of what you'll find here. Inspired by the '90s hip-hop scene, today you'll find not just music but all aspects of urban culture available for sale—from sneakers and street wear to music records (used and new) and studio gear. ✉ *Grünberger Str. 54, Friedrichshain* ☎ *030/2936–7377* ⊕ *www.hhv.de.*

HUMANA

Germany's popular secondhand shop, HUMANA sells a bit of anything and everything, but their location at Frankfurter Tor is Europe's largest secondhand shop with over 2,000 square meters of shopping space over five floors. ✉ *Frankfurter Tor 3, Friedrichshain* ☎ *030/422–2018* ⊕ *www.humana-second-hand.de* Ⓜ *Frankfurter Tor.*

WORTH A TRIP

In the summer, Berliners love to be outside—and especially so at one of the many lakes in and around Berlin. Berlin's largest lake is just a short ride southeast from Friedrichshain at Müggelsee. Two official bathing areas and beaches are accessible via public transportation (take the S-Bahn S3 and then the tram), including the FKK (nude) beach. At the lake, it's possible to rent canoes, kayaks, or even boats for use on the lake and nearby rivers.

Luccico

This minimal shop keeps an assortment of their own line of Italian leather boots and sandals, along with a good selection of European brands like Swedish Hasbeens clogs and Zalando slip-ons. Popular in Berlin, they also have two shops and an outlet in Mitte, and another outpost in Kreuzberg. ✉ *Bergmannstr. 8, Friedrichshain* ☎ *030/691–3257* ⊕ *www.luccico.de* ⊙ *Closed Sun.* Ⓜ *Samariterstrasse (U-bahn), Warschauer Strasse (S-bahn and U-bahn).*

Shakespeare & Sons

With large glass windows looking out onto Warschauer Strasse and a minimalist interior, Shakespeare & Sons is the perfect place to get lost in another world. The shop sells a variety of English and French books from every genre, though there's a specific slant toward new books covering political topics. Inside, you'll also find coffee and bagels (served by Fine Bagels), though take note that they notoriously limit their Wi-Fi usage for patrons. ⊠ *Warschauerstr. 74, Friedrichshain* ☎ *030/4000–3685* ⊕ *www.shakes-books.de.*

Stereoki
This hip menswear store mixes pieces from Germany, the United States, France, and Switzerland, including major brands like New Balance and Herschel Supply and lower-key designs including Oregon-based Shwood, organic cotton Nudie Jeans, and Norse Projects. ⊠ *Gabriel-Max-Str. 18, Friedrichshain* ☎ *030/5379–4667* ⊕ *www.stereoki.com* ⊘ *Closed Sun.* Ⓜ *Warschauer Strasse (U-bahn and S-bahn).*

Van Liebling
For a piece of Berlin's street-style cool, head to this Friedrichshain shop, where you'll find essentials like caps from The Decades, Herschel bags, and sunglasses from R.T.C.O. The store also stocks a small collection of women's accessories and clothes. ⊠ *Kopernikusstr. 8, Friedrichshain* ☎ *0178/375–0045* ⊕ *www.vanliebling.com/* ⊘ *Closed Sun.* Ⓜ *Frankfurter Tor (U-bahn), Warschauer Strasse (U-bahn and S-bahn).*

Victoria met Albert
A curated concept store with two locations in Berlin, Victoria met Albert offers products for men, women, and children. A mix of home goods and fashion, the shop sells a variety in that unique Berlin aesthetic—at once practical, but überhip. ⊠ *Krossenerstr. 9-10,*

ART IN THE WILD

Everyone visits the East Side Gallery for its public art murals available free for everyone to see, but if you're at the corner of Warschauer Strasse and Mühlenstrasse, where the ESG begins, face the opposite direction and you'll spot a large mural by street artist AliCé (also known as Alice Pasquini) on the side of the building. She's a street artist from Rome and a number of her highly illustrative works are scattered throughout Friedrichshain and Kreuzberg.

Friedrichshain ☎ *030/4467–4772* ⊕ *www.victoriametalbert.com.*

🍵 Coffee and Quick Bites

Cupcake Berlin
$ | **Bakery.** Open since 2007, Cupcake Berlin has survived the trend and continues to serve some of Berlin's best cupcakes in their flagship Friedrichshain café. Alongside their cupcakes, they also serve a number of vegan baked goods. **Known for:** traditional cupcake flavors; cozy interior good for eat-in or take-out; vegan options. *Average main: €4* ⊠ *Krossener Str. 12, Friedrichshain* ☎ *030/2576–8687* ⊕ *www.cupcake-berlin.de.*

Fine Bagels
$ | **Bakery.** Located inside the bookshop Shakespeare & Sons, Fine Bagels is their in-house coffee shop and bakery. They serve hand-rolled and boiled New York–style bagels

(don't miss the Zaatar-spiced bagel) and other traditional Jewish pastries, breads, and cakes. **Known for:** New York style bagels; Jewish food specialties (especially around the Jewish holidays); great casual atmosphere. *Average main: €6* ✉ *Warschauer Str. 74, Friedrichshain* ☎ *030/4679–6332* ⊕ *www.finebagels. com.*

Milja & Schäfa
$ | Mediterranean. Near Friedrichshain's Ostkreuz station, this corner café and restaurant serves Mediterranean dishes in a cozy and casual setting. The menu includes healthy options such as homemade cauliflower spaghetti and plenty of veggie and cheese options. **Known for:** lively café atmosphere; healthy food options; convenient location. *Average main: €9* ✉ *Sonntagstr. 1, Friedrichshain* ☎ *030/5266–2094* ⊕ *www.miljaund-schaefa.com.*

Silo Coffee
$ | Café. Delicious roasted coffees complement a menu of breakfast and brunch dishes. Australian-owned, Silo Coffee has been at the top of the trend for Berlin's third-wave coffee culture. **Known for:** hip Berlin atmosphere of trendy snobs; great brunches; always crowded. *Average main: €9* ✉ *Gabriel-Max-Str. 4, Friedrichshain* ⊕ *www.silo-coffee. com.*

★ Szimpla
$ | Hungarian. While Szimpla isn't best known for its coffee, the Hungarian café, bar, and restaurant is popular at all times of day from breakfast to late. Its pretty interior with fresh flowers on the tables and mismatched furniture make it a quaint hangout anytime of day, though at night it becomes a casual hangout for those looking for craft beers and a place to sit on a Saturday night. **Known for:** Hungarian food and drinks; cool interior with romantic seating; separate room for smokers. *Average main: €8* ✉ *Gärtnerstr. 15, Friedrichshain* ☎ *030/6630–8523* ⊕ *www.szimpla.de.*

Veganz
$ | Vegetarian. Part of the local Berlin vegan grocery chain, the Veganz shop at the edge of the Warschauer Brücke also operates a small café. Fresh smoothies, salads, and sandwiches are available to dine in or at one of the large picnic tables which sit in the sun overlooking the bridge. **Known for:** healthy green smoothies; vegan groceries and light bites; outdoor seating. *Average main: €10* ✉ *Warschauer Str. 33, Friedrichshain* ☎ *030/2900–9435* ⊕ *www.veganz.de.*

🍽 Dining

Briefmarken Weine
$ | Italian. In the grand Berlin tradition of reinventing historical spaces, this lovely wine bar and Italian restaurant has taken over a former stamp shop on beautiful Karl-Marx-Allee. You can pick a regional Italian wine off the shelves (also preserved from the stamp-selling days) or leaf through the extensive list, which separates the wines

into four categories—earth, fire, air, and water—according to their terroirs. **Known for:** Italian wine list; authentic antipasti; homey vibe. *Average main: €14* ⊠ *Karl-Marx-Allee 99, Friedrichshain* ☎ *030/4202–5293* ⊕ *www.briefmarkenweine.de* ⊗ *Closed Sun.* ▤ *No credit cards* Ⓜ *Weberwiese (U-bahn).*

Il Ritrovo

$ | Pizza. Walls here are covered in graffiti, the tablecloths are dirty, and there's always a crowd, but don't be turned off by the hectic atmosphere inside. This is one of Berlin's best pizzerias serving authentic Italian food—and at a great cost. **Known for:** authentic Italian pizza; frenzied atmosphere; Berlin-style interior with colorful walls. *Average main: €11* ⊠ *Gabriel-Max-Str. 2, Friedrichshain* ☎ *0303/2936–4130* ▤ *No credit cards.*

Matreshka

$$ | Russian. A casual restaurant, Matreshka offers small candlelit tables among *matryoshka* dolls on the shelves. The menu comprises homemade Russian and Ukrainian specialties such as *pelmeni,* stroganoff, and Russian soups. **Known for:** homemade Russian and Ukrainian foods; free vodka shots with most meals; candlelit tables and friendly service. *Average main: €14* ⊠ *Boxhagener Str. 60, Friedrichshain* ☎ *163/987–0767* ⊕ *russischessen.de* ▤ *No credit cards.*

Rembrandt Burger

$$ | Burger. Dutch-style burgers are the theme at this local favorite. On a quiet side street, Rembrandt Burger often has a line out the door, though if you arrive early, you can grab a seat at one of the small tables. **Known for:** quality fast food burgers; Dutch food specialties; vegetarian options. *Average main: €11* ⊠ *Richard-Sorge-Str. 21, Friedrichshain* ☎ *030/8999–7296* ⊕ *www.rembrandt-burger.de/* ▤ *No credit cards.*

Santa Cantina

$$ | Mexican Fusion. The lively and sociable extension of the local chain of Mexican eateries under the Santa Maria umbrella, Santa Cantina offers a romantic and sit-down experience for modern Mexican cuisine. Whether it's the cactus ceviche or the beef Rendang tacos, the menu is truly innovative—and delicious! **Known for:** unusual Mexican fusion dishes; great selection of drinks; funky and fun decor. *Average main: €8* ⊠ *Simon-Dach-Str. 22, Friedrichshain* ☎ *030/2336–2333* ⊕ *www.santaberlin. com/santa-cantina/.*

Schneeweiss

$$ | Austrian. Friedrichshain locals have been enjoying this corner spot for years, drawn in by the alpine-inspired new German cuisine and lively atmosphere. Classics like Wiener schnitzel and cheese spätzle share the menu with more inventive dishes like pork belly with scallops or homemade pumpkin and walnut ravioli. **Known for:** modern alpine cuisine; gorgeous all-white decor; Kaiserschmarrn (pancakes torn into pieces, with powdered sugar and blueberry compote). *Average main: €15*

✉ *Simplonstr. 16, Friedrichshain* ☎ *030/2904-9704* ⊕ *www.schnee-weiss-berlin.de* Ⓜ *Warschauer Strasse (S-bahn and U-bahn).*

🍸 Bars and Nightlife

★ Berghain

In an imposing power station in a barren stretch of land between Kreuzberg and Friedrichshain (the name borrows from both neighborhoods), Berghain has achieved international fame as the hedonistic heart of techno music—it was originally a 1990s techno club called Ostgut. It's only open as a club on weekends (for 48-plus hours straight, from midnight on Friday to early Monday), though many international music acts pass through for concert performances during the week. It's become something of a local tradition to arrive on Sunday morning or afternoon and dance until closing. Upstairs, the slightly smaller (but by no means intimate) Panorama Bar opens on Friday at midnight and offers different beats. ✉ *Am Wriezener Bahnhof, Friedrichshain* ✚ *Exit north from Ostbahnhof and follow Str. der Pariser Kommune, then make right on badly marked Am Wriezener Bahnhof and look for line of clubbers* ☎ *030/2936-0210* ⊕ *www.berghain.de* Ⓜ *Ostbahnhof (S-bahn).*

Crush XV

Quality cocktails and bottled craft beers are on offer at this fun and friendly local bar. This is the kind of bar where you might find glitter and neon available on a weeknight, or an all-day mimosa special on weekends. Come for the funky themed movie nights; stay for the chance to chat up friendly locals. ✉ *Gärtnerstr. 15, Friedrichshain* ☎ *1573/428-8961.*

Gin Chilla Bar

Ignore the cheesy name and logo—this gin bar is nothing if not classy. The cocktail bar and gin lounge serves hundreds of gin varieties in both creative and classic cocktails, including an option for a gin tasting. Makeshift tables and chairs make up the seating options, but if you can grab a spot, plan to stay awhile for the opportunity to really learn about gin from the masters behind the bar. ✉ *Warschauer Str. 33, Friedrichshain* ☎ *030/7674-8476* ⊕ *www.gin-chilla-bar.de.*

Holzmarkt Strandbar Pampa

Constructed of recycled materials on the banks of the Spree, Holzmarkt attracts a range of ages (even families) who come to hang out and chill during Berlin's sunny (and not-so-sunny) afternoons and evenings. ✉ *Holzmarktstr. 25, Friedrichshain* ☎ *030/4736-1686* ⊕ *www.holzmarkt.com* Ⓜ *Ostbahnhof (S-bahn), Jannowitzbrücke (U-bahn and S-bahn).*

Hops & Barley

Serving local and regional craft beer, this small brewpub offers a curated taste of seasonal varieties. The building was once a butcher's shop and is the kind of place you can walk in without knowing anyone, and make some friends before you leave. There's a separate smoking room in the back. ✉ *Wuehlischstr.*

22/23, Friedrichshain ☏ 030/2936–7534 ⊕ www.hopsandbarley.eu/.

★ Monster Ronson's Ichiban Karaoke

An underground karaoke bar and club, Monster Ronson's has something going on every night of the week. Besides the private cabins available to rent for karaoke (reserve in advance, if you can), there's also a large dance floor and event space for special programs. Drag queens host special events and shows regularly on Monday and Tuesday throughout the year, and weekends at the bar fill up fast. A funky interior and Korean-style karaoke make this one of Berlin's best nighttime hangouts. ⊠ Warschauer Str. 34, Friedrichshain ☏ 030/8975–1327 ⊕ www.karaoke-monster.de.

Primitiv Bar

This smoky little bar is located directly on Friedrichshain's most popular street for nightlife, Simon-Dach-Strasse. Cheap drinks and a small back room for special events such as burlesque and live music shows make this an especially social place—easy to make new friends and chat with locals. ⊠ Simon-Dach-Str. 28, Friedrichshain.

Salon zur wilden-Renate

In typical Berlin fashion, the Wild Renate club was made out of an unrenovated apartment complex with a large summertime terrace between them and three main dance floors. Music and DJs at the club predominately lay techno music—from trippy disco to house

music. Because of the lackadaisical architecture style, the club feels a lot like a house party—down to the laid-back club goers lounging in the garden in between DJ sets. ⊠ Alt-Stralau 70, Friedrichshain ☏ 030/2504–1426 ⊕ www.renate.cc.

Sisyphos

This sprawling adults' playground, located Spree-side in an old dog-biscuit factory in a former no-go neighborhood, has a cobbled-together feel: you'll find a sandy beach, a man-made pond with a raft in the middle, a camper van, and a number of wooden huts. The club is truly a late-night spot; don't expect much to be happening here before 3 am. ⊠ Hauptstr. 15, Friedrichshain ☏ 030/9836–6839 ⊕ www.sisyphos-berlin.net/.

🎞 Performing Arts

Kino Tilsiter Lichtspiele

A small local cinema (or *kino*), the Tilsiter Lichtspiele has been operating since 1908. While they predominantly show films in German, many also include English subtitles; more mainstream movies are shown in their original language with German subtitles. The cinema also regularly shows alternative, art-house, and political indepen-dent films. Even if you don't come for a film screening, stop by to have a drink in the bar; they serve their own craft beer brewed on the premises. ⊠ Richard-Sorge-Str. 25A, Friedrichshain ☏ 030/426–8129 ⊕ tilsiter-lichtspiele.de.

6 | Neukölln and Alt-Treptow

GO FOR

Underground nightlife

Rich immigrant history

Bars and cafés

Sightseeing ★★☆☆☆ | Shopping ★★★★☆ | Dining ★★★★☆ | Nightlife ★★★★★

f you missed Prenzlauer Berg's heyday, you can still get a good feel for its raw charm and creative flair if you head to ultrahip Neukölln. Just southeast of Kreuzberg below the Landwehr Canal, Neukölln was an impoverished, gritty West Berlin neighborhood until the hip crowd discovered it. It's since been almost completely transformed. Makeshift bar-galleries brighten up semi-abandoned storefronts, and vintage café or breakfast spots put a new twist on old concepts. Everything has a salvaged feel, and the crowds are young and savvy. If you're looking for nightlife, there are bars galore.—by Adam Groffman

◉ Sights

Arena Badeschiff

In summer, a trip to the Arena Badeschiff is a must. The outdoor pool is set on a boat anchored on the river Spree, offering great views of the Kreuzberg skyline. It's open May 1 to late August/September, daily 8–midnight. In winter (September–March) the pool is transformed into an indoor sauna. ✉ Eichenstr. 4 ☎ 0152/0594–5752 ⊕ www.arena.berlin ✆ €5.50 Ⓜ Schlesisches Tor (U-bahn).

Britzer Garten

Named after the surrounding neighborhood of Britz in southern Neukölln, this garden is really more of a large park—albeit one where flowers take center stage year-round in stunning seasonal exhibitions, like the Tulipan tulip festival in April and May or the dahlia festival in late August. Small brooks, streams, and other waterways surround the lake in the center of the park, while hills and meadows provide ample space to amble and play. The rose garden and so-called witches' garden (actually a traditional herb garden) are year-round pleasures. ✉ Buckower Damm 146, Neukölln ☎ 030/700–9060 ⊕ www.gruen-berlin.de ✆ €2; €3 during flower shows Ⓜ Sangerhauser Weg (bus).

Hufeisensiedlung

A working-class housing estate in the south of Neukölln built in the 1920s, the Hufeisensiedlung was listed as a UNESCO World Heritage site for its modernist architecture. The building complex designed by architect Bruno Taut features an idealistic socialist style of terraced garden homes and a large apartment building in the shape of a horseshoe (for which the complex gets its name). The buildings are still private homes today, though it's possible to wander the Horseshoe Estate on your own or through some guided tour companies. ✉ Lowise-Reuter-Ring 1, Neukölln ⊕ www.hufeisensiedlung.info Ⓜ U7 Parchimer Allee.

Insel der Jugend

The name of this tiny island is translated as "Island of Youth." Nestled into a bend in the Spree River between Treptow and the Alt-Stralau peninsula, it was the scene of a youth club during GDR times. Although its heyday is past, there is something dreamy, if not a bit creepy, about the island. It can only be accessed via a narrow, arched footbridge from Treptower Park, so it's devoid of cars, noise, and even much foot traffic. Visitors can enjoy a picnic on the docks, or rent paddleboats and canoes. In the evening, the club Insel Berlin hosts concerts, film screenings, and parties (the club also runs the beer garden and café). ⊠ *Alt-Treptow 6, Treptow* ☎ *030/8096–1850* ⊕ *www.inselberlin.de* Ⓜ *Treptower Park (S-bahn) and Plänterwald (S-bahn).*

Körnerpark

Two blocks west of gritty, noisy Karl-Marx-Strasse, this small, beautifully landscaped park, built in the 1910s, resembles a French chateau garden. Today it remains something of a hidden treasure, cherished by locals but barely known to outsiders. At one end of the park, water cascades down several steps of a multitiered fountain into a round pool; at the other end you'll find the stately former orangerie, which now houses a gallery and café, and presents a concert every Sunday in summer. ⊠ *Schierkerstr. 8, Neukölln* ☎ *030/5682–3939* ⊕ *www.körnerpark.de* Ⓜ *Neukölln (S-bahn and U-bahn).*

GETTING HERE

Located in the southeast of Berlin, the Neukölln neighborhood is relatively well connected via public transportation. Both the U8 and U7 U-bahn lines run north-south through the district, and several useful bus lines intersect the area including the M29 and M41 which provide useful connections. The central transportation hub at Hermannplatz is a popular gateway in Neukölln but beware of pickpockets. Treptow is a little less connected on the U-bahn but the S-bahn and ringbahn run through both Neukölln and Treptow.

Landwehrkanal

Flowing through Tiergarten, Kreuzberg, Neukölln, and Alt-Treptow, the Landwehr Canal connects to the River Spree near the Molecule Man sculpture. Built between 1845 and 1850, the small parks that run alongside the canal and the many frequent bridges offer casual hangout spots and scenic viewpoints through the neighborhoods, especially at its intersection with the Neuköllner Schifffahrtskanal (Neukölln Ship Canal). The Landwehr Canal also serves as the boundary between much of Neukölln and Kreuzberg in the area referred to as Kreuzkölln by locals (along Maybachufer). It's a beautiful walk along this stretch of the canal with a tree-lined dirt path, frequent benches for sitting, and regular runners and cyclists making their way around the canal system. ⊠ *Maybachufer, Neukölln.*

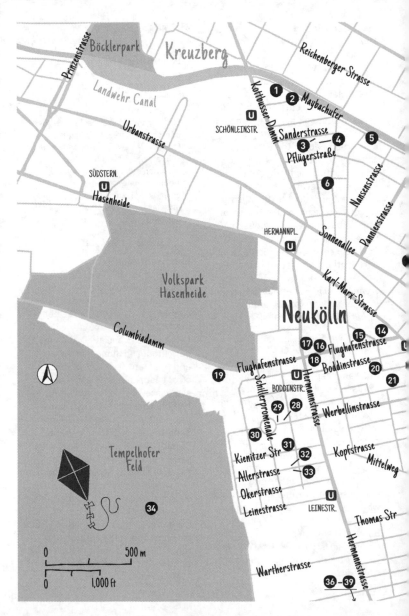

Luisa Catucci Gallery

A small art gallery in the trendy and quickly changing Schillerkiez, the Luisa Catucci Gallery features exhibitions focused on ecological, social, and existential matters through a variety of media such as photography, video, painting, sculpture, and printmaking. The gallery was founded by Italian artist Luisa Catucci but provides space for other European creative professionals and artists—especially from Italy. ✉ *Allerstr. 38, Neukölln* ☎ *0176/2040-4636* ⊕ *www.luisacatucci.com.*

Molecule Man

One of Berlin's most iconic public art sculptures, the Molecule Man was designed by American artist Jonathon Borofsky. The 100-foot-tall aluminum sculpture features three intersecting men with holes throughout their bodies and sits in the middle of the River Spree where East and West Berlin once met. Today, it's at the intersection of the Friedrichshain, Kreuzberg, and Treptow borders. ✉ *An den Treptowers 1, Neukölln.*

Museum Neukölln

Every Berlin neighborhood has a *Heimatmuseum*, which literally translates as "homeland museum" and which acts as a repository for local lore and history. Most are dusty, ill-frequented places, but not the Museum Neukölln, which not only has gone above and beyond in terms of design and organization, but also might be Berlin's most technologically advanced museum. Its permanent exhibition, "99 x Neukölln" is a wonderful grab bag of objects, both old and new, that represent the neighborhood, displayed in cases equipped with computer touch screens that tell each object's history, context, and connection to other objects in the room. The museum is on the grounds of Schloss Britz. ✉ *Schloss Britz, Alt-Britz 81, Neukölln* ☎ *030/6272-77727* ⊕ *www.museumneukoelln.de* 🎫 *Free* Ⓜ *Parchimer Allee (U-bahn).*

Neuköllner Wochenmärkte am Maybachufer

Colloquially referred to as the "Turkish Market," the weekly market on Maybachufer takes place every Tuesday and Friday when the canal-adjacent street turns into a pedestrian street market. Vendors sell everything from Middle Eastern and African food specialties to colorful fabrics and fresh fruit and vegetables. Show up near the end of the day for special, last-minute bargains. ✉ *Maybachufer, Neukölln* ☞ *Open Tues. and Fri. 11–6:30.*

Our/Berlin Vodka

The microdistillery creates a vodka here on-site with local flavors, steps away from the River Spree. Tours and tastings are available during opening hours as well as regularly each Friday afternoon. ⊠ *Am Flutgraben 2, Neukölln* ☎ *030/5360–2227* ⊕ *www.ourberlin.de.*

Richardplatz

Back when this part of Neukölln was a Bohemian village, Richardplatz was its center, and today the square appears virtually untouched by time. Half-timber houses line one side, and some of the grandest turn-of-the-century apartment buildings face them on the other. It's worth exploring the lanes and alleyways running off the square and its extension, Richardstrasse; you'll turn up some secret gardens and hidden buildings along the way. This square is the location of one of the city's most charming Christmas markets, which takes place annually on the second weekend of Advent (usually either the first or second weekend in December): craftsmen and churches sell knitwear, candles, and all sorts of edible goodies under the light of old-fashioned gas lamps. ⊠ *Neukölln* Ⓜ *Neukölln (S-bahn and U-bahn).*

Schillermarkt

The weekly market in Schillerkiez takes place every Saturday from 10–4 and features predominantly organic-food sellers as well as local artists and activists. ⊠ *Herrfurthpl., Neukölln* ☎ *030/2977–2486* Ⓜ *U8 Boddingstrasse.*

Schlesischer Busch

A small park off the trendy Schlesischer Strasse, the spot is popular with young families thanks to its many grilling spots and large open spaces alongside the Landwehr Canal. Most notable in the park is the remaining watch-tower structure from the GDR era. Over 300 watchtowers were constructed in the GDR, mostly along the Berlin Wall, and very few still exist today. At this one in Schlesischer Park, the searchlight and rifle hatches still sit on the roof. ⊠ *Lohmühlenstr. 1, Neukölln.*

Schloss Britz

This sprawling country estate consists of a beautiful early-18th-century Schloss, a manor house, and grounds complete with a working farm—all of which are quite a contrast to the stark, modernist 1960s and 1970s housing that fills the Britz neighborhood. Don't miss the small research library in the manor's attic or the restaurant located in the so-called Schweizer Haus, the old dairyman's living quarters, and manned by Matthias Buchholz, a Michelin-starred chef who left a career in Berlin's top restaurants to make something of this local outpost. The **Museum Neukölln** is on the grounds, too, in the former cow stalls of the Schloss Britz. ⊠ *Alt-Britz 73, Neukölln* ☎ *030/6097–9230* ⊕ *www.schlossbritz.de* 🎟 *€3* Ⓜ *Parchimer Allee (U-bahn).*

Sowjetisches Ehrenmal Treptower Park *(Soviet War Memorial)*

The Sowjetisches Ehrenmal in Treptower Park just might take the hard-earned title of most impressively bombastic monument in Berlin. The size of several city blocks, the memorial celebrates the Soviet WWII victory with inscriptions in both Russian and German, accompanying a series of Socialist realist reliefs lining both sides of an elaborate plaza. At one end stands an enormous bronze of a Russian soldier cradling a child in one arm and wielding a sword with the other, while stomping on a crumpled swastika. Well-placed text and photos educate on the history and importance of the monument, as well as explaining why it was preserved after the fall of the wall. ⊠ *Treptower Park, Treptow* Ⓜ *Treptower Park (S-bahn).*

Spreepark Planterwald

An abandoned amusement park, the Spreepark has a unique history. It opened in 1969 as the GDR's first amusement park, part of the Treptow park along the River Spree. The park closed in 2001 because of a drop in visitor attendance after reunification, and was largely left unattended since then so that the forest overcame many of the attractions. A popular spot for urban explorers (and closely watched by the police), it's now possible to visit on organized tours that avoid potential dangerous spots within the park. Book early to guarantee a spot on the weekend tours (English tours occur every second Saturday). ⊠ *Kiehnwerderallee 1-3, Treptow* ☎ *030/7009-6700* ⊕ *www.gruen-berlin.de/en/spreepark* 💶 *€5.*

Stadtbad Neukölln

In a city dotted with lakes, pools, and thermal baths, this is one of the most attractive public bathing spots, a neoclassical beauty built in 1914 and renovated in 2009. Even if you don't plan on taking a dip, it's worth a peek: the unremarkable, gray concrete exterior, which seems designed to ward off tourists, conceals two stunning swimming halls, their pristine pools lined with columns and decorated with elaborate mosaics and gargoyles spouting water. To make the most of it, get a day pass for the pools and multiple saunas. **Monday is women-only day in the sauna and Sunday evenings are nude-only (FKK).** ⊠ *Ganghoferstr. 3, Neukölln* ☎ *030/682-4980* ⊕ *www. berlinerbaeder.de* 💶 *€3.5* Ⓜ *Rathaus Neukölln (U-bahn), Karl-Marx-Strasse (U-bahn).*

★ Tempelhofer Feld *(Tempelhofer Park)*

Of all Berlin's many transformations, this one—from airport to park—might be the quickest. The iconic airport (it was the site of the 1948–49 Berlin airlift) had its last flight in 2008. Only two years later, it opened as a park, complete

WHAT IS FKK?

FKK is a German naturist (nudist) movement that was once very popular in East German culture. Its full name is Freikörperkultur, which means "Free Body Culture" and, while the tradition isn't as common as it once was, it's still prevalent throughout German society. Many public beaches and parks still have designated FKK zones, and throughout Berlin you'll find a number of very public places where nudism is expected. FKK is also famously part of German spa culture, where men and women are often both naked in the same spa. Nudity in Germany isn't sexualized, and FKK culture is a reminder that our bodies are just that: bodies free of clothing.

Where to try FKK culture in Berlin
Spas, saunas, and public swimming pools—German spas and saunas are almost always nude-only. Often, men and women intermix in these places, but some public swimming pools have designated dates for men and women to allow for more privacy. Visiting a German spa for the first time might seem disconcerting at first, but once you realize everyone else is naked, it's quite easy to get used to the feeling so long as you're a bit open-minded.

Lakes—Many of the lakes on the outskirts of Berlin are in wooded areas with mixed and FKK bathing areas. One of the most common is at Müggelsee—the city's largest lake. You'll sometimes see families of all ages enjoying FKK beaches.

Public parks—FKK doesn't have to be just about bathing in water. It's also common for sunbathers in several of the city parks. In Neukölln, Hasenheide park has a section for FKK near the park's very center, slightly secluded by bushes. Tiergarten also has a few spots for FKK nude sunbathing in several of the open fields, though the largest spot for FKK in Tiergarten is mostly for gay men.

with untouched runways. It's now one of the city's most beloved and impressive outdoor spots, where bikers, skaters, kite flyers, urban gardeners, picnickers, and grillers all gather. Although the Nazi-era airport buildings are not open for wandering, you can explore them on a two-hour tour (book online). ⊠ *Bordered by Columbiadamm and Tempelhoferdamm, Neukölln* ☎ *030/2000–37441* ⊕ *www.thf-berlin.de* ⊠ *Park free; airport*

building guided tour €15 ⊙ *No tours Mon. and Tues.* Ⓜ *Tempelhof (S-bahn and U-bahn).*

Treptower Park
Perhaps best known for the Soviet War Memorial located in it, this Spree-side park is a lovely place for a stroll. True to their outdoorsy reputations, hardy German families don snow boots even during winter's darkest days and traipse around the park's fields and paths, perhaps with a dog in tow, just to get some fresh air. Stick to the waterside promenade for the best people-watching: the elaborate, eccentric

houseboats moored there are a glimpse into yet one more alternative Berlin lifestyle. ⊠ *Treptow* Ⓜ *Treptower Park (S-bahn).*

🛍 Shopping

Arena Indoor Flea Market
Most of Berlin's flea markets operate year-round, regardless of the freezing winter temperatures, but this indoor hall offers some shelter inside an old warehouse near the Arena/Badeschiff complex on the Spree River. The weekend market features tables of kitchenware and rows of old bikes and mechanical parts, which can obscure the real treasures, so be prepared to spend some time digging. ⊠ *Treptow Art Center, Eichenstr. 4, Neukölln* ☎ *0172/303–5775* ⏱ *Open weekends only, 10–4* Ⓜ *Treptower Park (S-bahn).*

Curious Fox
Neukölln's largest English-language bookstore, Curious Fox is a cozy shop selling books and stationery alongside a cute café. They sell a collection of new and used books and even host a regular quiz night every third Tuesday of the month. ⊠ *Flughafenstr. 22,*

Neukölln ☎ *030/5266–4791* ⊕ *www.curiousfoxbooks.com.*

Let Them Eat Cake
A favorite of the vintage shoppers in Neukölln, this delightful shop offers a mixture of handmade pieces and high-quality secondhand clothing for him and her. ⊠ *Weserstr. 164, Neukölln* ☎ *030/6096–5095* Ⓜ *Rathaus Neukölln (U-bahn).*

Nowkoelln Flowmarkt
Pulling on the cutting-edge spirit of Berlin's young, hip inhabitants, this vibrant flea market's offerings place an emphasis on the "now," with a trendy selection of vintage clothing, home goods, music, and original handmade pieces. The canal-side location, tempting food stalls, and live performances are great reasons to visit the bimonthly Sunday event (10–6). Every alternate Sunday you'll find the market at the always lovely Prinzessinengärten (Moritzplatz U-bahn) from 10 to 6. ⊠ *Maybachufer 39–50, Neukölln* ⊕ *www.nowkoelln. de/* ⏱ *Closed Dec.–Apr.* Ⓜ *Schönlein-strasse (U-bahn).*

Shio
This design studio–shop includes items from four designers: the namesake Shio, which stocks new-label sustainable lines, as well as a variety of redesigned secondhand and vintage wear; Treches, which features fun, sustainable clothing in bold colors; Pastperfekt, which refashions recycled materials into jewelry, lamps, furniture, and more; and Pulp Papier, which sells pretty Japanese decorative papers.

✉ *Weichselstr. 59, Neukölln* ⊕ *www.shiostore.com* Ⓜ *Rathaus Neukölln (U-bahn).*

Sing Blackbird

This Kreuzkölln shop, located on the border between Kreuzberg and Neukölln, has become popular for its carefully edited collection of vintage finds, dating back to the 1960s and '70s. The shop also holds a monthly flea market, as well as occasional movie nights, and is home to a popular café, where a menu of homemade cakes and a weekend vegan brunch are served on mismatched vintage china. ✉ *Sanderstr. 11, Neukölln* ☎ *030/5484–5051* Ⓜ *Schönleinstrasse (U-bahn).*

Staalplaat

Amsterdam-based record label Staalplaat opened this eccentric sister record store in Neukölln to help satiate the city's massive music demand, with a specific focus on experimental music and obscure albums. The store also houses a gallery and bookstore where specialty books, handmade fanzines, and limited-edition books and posters are sold. ✉ *Kienitzer Str. 108, Neukölln* ☎ *030/4176–7355* ⊕ *staalplaat.com/* ⊘ *Closed Sun.–Mon.* Ⓜ *Boddinstrasse (U-bahn), Leinestrasse (U-bahn).*

Vintage Galore

Imagine bringing the midcentury European look home with a walk through this shop, which features a collection of Scandinavian furniture and lamps. The shop also has a limited selection of clothing, bags, and accessories, as well as small housewares like teapots and ceramics, which should all fit more comfortably inside a suitcase. ✉ *Sanderstr. 12, Neukölln* ☎ *030/6396–3338* ⊕ *www.vintagegalore.de* Ⓜ *Schönleinstrasse (U-bahn).*

☕ Coffee and Quick Bites

Brammibal's Donuts

$ | Café. Most famous for their vegan doughnuts, Brammibal's on Maybachufer also serves tasty vegan sandwiches. While the decor is a bit bland, their flavors are not—with new doughnut creations regularly. **Known for:** 100% vegan café; great location on Maybachufer; original doughnut flavors. *Average main: €7* ✉ *Maybachufer 8, Neukölln* ☎ *030/2394–8455* ⊕ *www.brammibalsdonuts.com* ▭ *No credit cards.*

Cafe Rix

$$ | German. Located in a small courtyard off the busy Karl-Marx-Strasse in Neukölln, Cafe Rix is a quiet oasis with a golden ceiling—a remnant from the building's heyday as a dance hall. The café is most popular for its all-you-can-eat German breakfast buffet, though there's an extensive menu all day long. **Known for:** historic building; all-you-can-eat breakfast buffet of traditional German foods; relaxed atmosphere. *Average main: €14* ✉ *Karl-Marx-Str. 141, Neukölln* ☎ *030/686–9020* ⊕ *www.caferix.de.*

GORDON

$$ | **Israeli.** Not just a café or restaurant, GORDON serves as a cultural and music hub for artists and performers. With its fresh, local ingredients, the menu consists of many Israeli classics such as shakshuka and hummus (with fresh pita) lovingly made by the self-taught chefs Doron and Nir. **Known for:** closed weekday afternoons between 3–6; modern Middle Eastern cuisine; records for sale and regular music gigs. *Average main: €18* ✉ *Allerstr. 11, Neukölln* ☎ *030/6794–6719* ⊕ *www.gordon-berlin.com/.*

K-Fetisch

$ | **Café.** Located on the perennial favorite Neukölln street of Weserstrasse, this corner café has that authentic Berlin flavor every tourist is looking for. Mismatched furniture and a cozy interior make this the type of place you can spend hours in—not to mention the variety of cakes and quality coffee available. **Known for:** outdoor seating along Weserstrasse; books available to read and borrow; tasty vegan cakes and other snacks. *Average main: €9* ✉ *Wildenbruchstr. 86, Neukölln* ☎ *030/6808–0362* ⊕ *k-fetisch.net.*

Passenger Coffee

$ | **Café.** While this small local chain operates two other cafés (one is just a stand) in Berlin, the roastery in Alt-Treptow is the most worth visiting. A large and spacious café with a retro design, it's a casual spot with a friendly staff willing to share everything they know about coffee roasting. **Known for:** coffee roasted on-site; hipster vibe; limited seating. *Average main: €9* ✉ *Elsenstr. 38, Neukölln* ☎ *030/2357–5667* ⊕ *www.passenger-coffee.de/en* ➡ *No credit cards.*

Two Planets

$ | **Vegetarian.** A small café, but one with a lot of character, Two Planets serves smoothies, coffee, and delicious vegan foods. With a cozy and romantic interior, it's a casual café that's always buzzing. **Known for:** great coffee and fresh fruit smoothies; friendly service; vegan brunches and toasts. *Average main: €9* ✉ *Hermannstr. 230, Neukölln* ⊕ *www.twoplanetsberlin.com* ➡ *No credit cards* Ⓜ *Boddingstrasse.*

White Crow

$ | **Café.** Formerly called the Black Sheep, this all-vegan café serves specialty coffee from nearby Passenger, as well as perennial Berlin favorite roastery The Barn. Snacks and quick bites include homemade vegan cakes, bagels, and sandwiches. **Known for:** kombucha; healthy menu;

BACK IN THE DAY

Don't miss a visit to Tempelhofer Feld. The former airport has been converted into one of the city's best public parks. You'll find community gardens, pop-up cafés, kitesurfers, and even a makeshift mini-golf course made of found objects, all nested between and around the runways. The park is especially beautiful during sunsets.

specialty drinks. *Average main: €9* ✉ *Bouchéstr. 15, Neukölln.*

🍴 Dining

The California Breakfast Slam

$$ | American. What initially started as a pop-up brunch in a bar in 2010 has evolved into a full-scale dining operation. During weekends and mornings, the restaurant serves American brunch classics such as blueberry pancakes, eggs Benedict, and huevos rancheros. **Known for:** Berlin's best pancakes; American brunch classics; humorous menu descriptions. *Average main: €9* ✉ *Innstr. 47, Neukölln* ☎ *030/686–9624* ⊕ *www.cabslam.com* ▭ *No credit cards.*

CODA

$$$$ | Eclectic. Your childhood dream of having dessert for dinner can come true at this intimate "dessert bar" on a pretty street in trendy Neukölln—except at CODA, many of the desserts are more savory than sweet, and all can be paired with alcoholic beverages, from cocktails to beer to wine. Six-course menus use no white flour and very little added sugar or fat in the dishes, but feature plenty of different textures and beautiful presentations to keep things interesting, even for those without a sweet tooth. **Known for:** small-plate "desserts" using natural flavors; intimate, open-kitchen atmosphere; superlative, unusual cocktails. *Average main: €98* ✉ *Friedelstr. 47, Neukölln* ☎ *030/9149–6396* ⊕ *coda-berlin.com* 🕑 *Closed Sun., Mon., and Wed. No lunch* Ⓜ *Schönleinstrasse (U-bahn), Hermannplatz (U-bahn).*

Gastón

$$ | Tapas. In the heart of hip Weserstrasse, tapas bar Gastón is a casual eatery with decent tapas and great wines. On Sundays, they serve a seafood paella in typical Spanish fashion. **Known for:** moderately priced tapas; selection of wines and sangria; Sunday paella. *Average main: €15* ✉ *Weichselstr. 18, Neukölln* ▭ *No credit cards.*

Lavanderia Vecchia

$$$$ | Italian. Hidden away in a courtyard off a busy Neukölln street, in a space that used to contain an old launderette (hence the Italian name), Lavanderia Vecchia offers a prix-fixe-only Italian menu that includes four appetizers, three pasta or risotto *primi,* a meat or fish *secondo,* and dessert, followed by coffee and a digestif; à la carte options, as well as a three-course menu, are available at lunchtime only. The white-painted industrial space is decorated with vintage kerchiefs strung along old wash lines. **Known for:** nine-course set dinner menus changing biweekly; more affordable daily rotating lunch menus; cool setting in former laundromat. *Average main: €65* ✉ *Flughafenstr. 46, Neukölln* ☎ *030/6272–2152* ⊕ *www.lavanderiavecchia.de* 🕑 *Closed Sun.* Ⓜ *Boddinstrasse (U-bahn), Rathaus Neukölln (U-bahn).*

MAMA KALO

$$ | German. Located in the lovely Schillerkiez district of Neukölln, MAMA KALO serves hearty French and German dishes such as quiche, spätzle, and tarte flambé (*flammkuchen* in German) with creative recipes of high-quality ingredients. A well-lit rustic interior with fresh flowers and candles on every table makes it the perfect date spot in the evenings, or a friendly and social casual-dining experience for lunch—if you can get a table in the tiny restaurant. **Known for:** creative flammkuchen (tarte flambé) dishes; large outdoor patio eating; small and cozy atmosphere. *Average main: €15* ⊠ *Herrfurthstr. 23, Neukölln* ☎ *0176/5510–4327* ⊕ *mamakalo.de* ▤ *No credit cards* Ⓜ *Boddingstrasse.*

Mmaah

$ | Korean Barbecue. What started as a small kiosk with no indoor seating on the edge of Tempelhofer Feld in 2013 has expanded to three additional locations in Neukölln and Berlin. The casual dining restaurant serves Korean barbecue from a simple menu of *bulgogi* and other barbecue and vegetarian dishes. **Known for:** big portions served in takeout containers; great location for picnics in Tempelhofer Feld; long queues on sunny days. *Average main: €7* ⊠ *Columbiadamm 160, Neukölln* ☎ *0159/0173–5315* ⊕ *www.mmaah.de.*

SchillerBurger

$$ | Burger. Generally regarded as one of Berlin's best burger joints, SchillerBurger now has stores open around the city, but the one

here in Schillerkiez is its original location. Fresh-baked rolls, home-made sauces, and locally sourced beef make their burgers extra special, but it's their wide variety of quality vegetarian options which make locals come back for new tastes. **Known for:** fresh, quality burgers; large vegetarian selection; quick, casual dining. *Average main: €13* ⊠ *Herrfurthstr. 7, Neukölln* ☎ *030/5587–1716* ⊕ *www.schiller-burger.com.*

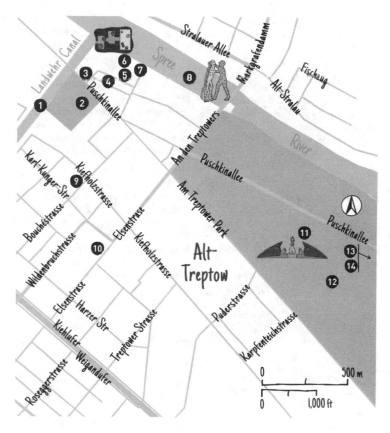

▼ Bars and Nightlife

Bierbaum 2

On the busy Sonnenallee, Bierbaum 2 is the second location of a popular Neukölln bar. It's a typical *Kneipe* (German-style dive bar) that's open 24 hours a day with a convivial atmosphere. Be warned, though: it's smoky inside. But if cheap drinks (or billiards) are your game, it's a great casual hangout. ⊠ *Sonnenallee 86, Neukölln* ☎ *030/686–0488*.

Club der Visionaere

It may not be much more than a series of wooden rafts and a few shoddily constructed shacks, but this club is one of the most beloved outdoor venues in town. The place is packed at all hours, either with clubbers on their last stop of the evening, or with locals and tourists soaking up the sunshine on a Sunday morning. ⊠ *Am Flutgraben 1, Treptow* ✛ *Follow Schlesische Str. east from U-bahn station until you cross two small canals. After second bridge, look left* ☎ *030/6951–8942* ⊕ *clubdervisionaere.com* Ⓜ *Schlesisches Tor (U-bahn)*.

Klunkerkranich

Neukölln's most hipster bar and club, Klunkerkranich used to be a secret rooftop bar, but today it's always drawing a crowd. It's still hard to find, though! Located on the roof of a parking garage for the Neukölln Arkaden shopping mall, there's a small entrance fee after dark so show up early to avoid it. Klunkerkranich offers one of the best panoramic sunset views, and the makeshift wooden-crate seating and picnic tables amidst live plants make the spot as Instagrammable as you can imagine. ⊠ *Karl-Marx-Str. 66, Neukölln* ✛ *Take the elevator in Neukölln Arkaden's parking garage (at the library/post entrance) to the 5th fl. and then walk up the ramp an additional level to get to the rooftop. If you get lost, just follow the crowds* ⊕ *www.klunkerkranich.org* ☞ *Closed Jan. and Feb.* Ⓜ *Rathaus Neukölln*.

MS

Hoppetosse Open regularly in the winter, the docked boat MS *Hoppetosse* rocks steady to reggae and dance hall, house, techno, or hip-hop. A few steps into Treptow from Kreuzberg (if you pass Freischwimmer you're on the right track), there are fantastic views of the Spree River from both the lower-level dance floor or the top deck. The boat is the winter location for Club der Visionaere and hosts occasional parties in summer. ⊠ *Eichenstr. 4, Treptow* ⊕ *www. hoppetosse.berlin*.

Muted Horn

An independent craft beer pub, Muted Horn was opened by Canadian expats in Berlin and has become one of the city's best brewpubs. With 22 rotating taps, a rustic interior of wooden tables, and a bookshelf full of board games, it's easy to stay here for hours. An outdoor patio is open all year as well. Make sure to try a beer flight! ⊠ *Flughafenstr. 49, Neukölln* ☎ *030/9156–9256* ⊕ *www.themuted-horn.com* Ⓜ *Boddingstrasse*.

Prachtwerk

Part café, part craft beer pub, part live music venue, Prachtwerk combines art and music with amazing coffee, daily soups, sandwiches and other pub snacks. During the day, you might bump into young people hard at work on their computers, but in the evenings, there'll be performers on the small stage and usually a DJ in the corner pumping out loud tunes to a lively crowd. ⊠ *Ganghoferstr. 2, Neukölln* ☎ *030/4098-5635* ⊕ *www.prachtwerkberlin.com.*

Sameheads

This bar, club, and performance venue has anchored the district's nightlife scene ever since it was founded by three visionary British brothers in 2006. The upstairs is a straightforward bar, cozy and local, while the cavelike cellar hosts live bands and a range of shows including experimental fashion, open-mic, and underground vinyl parties. ⊠ *Richardstr. 10, Neukölln* ☎ *030/7012-1060* ⊕ *www.sameheads.com.*

SchwuZ

SchwuZ moved to the newly hip Neukölln neighborhood from its original location on Mehringdamm, in Kreuzberg, and the new digs in the old Kindl brewery serve it well: in addition to 1980s music and house dance nights, expect more varied offerings like drag shows, concert performances, and art exhibitions. The venue prides itself on being a "shelter" for queer communities and non-heteronormative lifestyles. ⊠ *Rollbergstr. 26, Neukölln* ☎ *030/5770-2270* ⊕ *www.schwuz.de.*

TiER

On a popular corner of Weserstrasse, the TiER cocktail bar's lively crowd often spills out into the street. It's often crowded and large groups aren't admitted to keep a more intimate atmosphere inside, but if you do get past the door, you'll find a cozy inside with top-quality cocktails. Floor-to-ceiling windows look out onto the street outside. ⊠ *Weserstr. 42, Neukölln* ⊕ *www.tier.bar.*

Twinpigs

A new bar and café opened by a Chilean architect and a Swedish filmmaker, this locals' haunt has quickly become a favorite hideout thanks to it top-quality cocktails and a cozy, raw interior that reminds you more of a friend's home than a trendy nightspot. Friendly bartenders will happily recommend drinks. The candlelit bar is open daily from 4 pm, with small sandwiches served during the afternoon. It's closed Monday. ⊠ *Boddingstr. 57a, Neukölln* Ⓜ *Rathaus Neukölln.*

Performing Arts

Moviemento Kino

An independent cinema, the Moviemento regularly shows documentaries, art-house films, and independent productions from around the world. Over the past century, the site has developed from a small screening room in the back of a restaurant to a cluttered but friendly space in the heart of trendy Kreuzberg and Neukölln. Over the decades, the theater has attracted artists and bohemians to its many events and screenings, such as David Bowie and Tom Tykwer. The cinema also hosts many independent film festivals throughout the year, such as the Porn Film Festival every October (for adults only), the Down Under Berlin Film Festival showcasing Australian and New Zealand films, and the long-running XPOSED International Queer Film Festival. ⊠ *Kottbusser Damm 22, Neukölln* ☎ *030/692-4785* ⊕ *www. moviemento.de* ⌕ *€8.50; €7.50 reduced* Ⓜ *U8 Schönleinstrasse.*

Neuköllner Oper
The small and alternative Neuköllner Oper puts on fun, showy performances of long-forgotten operas as well as humorous musical productions. It also is more likely than other Berlin opera houses to stage productions offering modern social commentary and individual takes on the immigrant experience—which is fitting for this international neighborhood. ⊠ *Karl-Marx-Str. 131–133, Neukölln* ☎ *030/6889-0777* ⊕ *www.neukoell-neroper.de.*

WEDDING
GESUNDBRUNNEN
PRENZLAUER BERG
MOABIT
HANSA-VIERTEL
SPREE
MITTE
CHARLOTTENBURG
TIERGARTEN
FRIEDRICHSHAIN
SPREE
KREUZBERG
HALENSEE
WILMERSDORF
ALT-TREPTOW
SCHÖNEBERG
NEUKÖLLN
PLÄNTERWALD
FRIEDENAU
TEMPELHOF
BAUMSCHULENWEG
MARIENDORF
BRITZ

Sightseeing ★★★★★ | Shopping ★★★★☆ | Dining ★★★★☆ | Nightlife ★★★★★

Hip Kreuzberg, stretching from the West Berlin side of the border crossing at Checkpoint Charlie all the way to the banks of the Spree next to Friedrichshain, is home base for much of Berlin's famed nightclub scene and a great place to get a feel for young Berlin. A large Turkish population shares the residential streets with a variegated assortment of political radicals and bohemians of all nationalities. In the minds of most Berliners, it is split into two even smaller sections: Kreuzberg 61 is a little more upscale, and contains a variety of small and elegant shops and restaurants, while Kreuzberg 36 has stayed grittier, as exemplified by the garbage-strewn, drug-infested, but much-beloved Görlitzer Park. Oranienstrasse, the spine of life in the Kreuzberg 36 district, has mellowed from hard-core to funky since reunification.—*by Adam Groffman*

◉ Sights

★ Berlinische Galerie

Talk about site-specific art: all the modern art, photography, and architecture models and plans here, created between 1870 and the present, were made in Berlin (or in the case of architecture competition models, intended for the city). Russians, secessionists, Dadaists, and expressionists all had their day in Berlin, and individual works by Otto Dix, George Grosz, and Georg Baselitz, as well as artists' archives such as the Dadaist Hannah Höch's, are highlights. There's a set price for the permanent collection, but rates vary for special exhibitions, which are usually well attended and quite worthwhile. ⊠ *Alte Jakobstr. 124–128, Kreuzberg* ☎ *030/7890–2600* ⊕ *www.berlinischegalerie.de* 🎫 *€8* ☾ *Closed Tues.* Ⓜ *Kochstrasse (U-bahn).*

Deutsches Technikmuseum

(German Museum of Technology)
A must if you're traveling with children, this museum will enchant anyone who's interested in technology or fascinated with trains, planes, and automobiles. Set in the remains of Anhalter Bahnhof's industrial yard and enhanced with a glass-enclosed wing, the museum has several floors of machinery, including two airplane rooms on the upper floors crowned with a "Rosinenbomber," one of the beloved airplanes that delivered supplies to Tempelhof Airport during the Berlin Airlift of 1948. Don't miss the train sheds, which are like three-dimensional, walkable timelines of trains throughout history, and the historical

brewery, which has a great rooftop view of today's trains, U-bahn lines U1 and U2, converging at the neighboring Gleisdreieck station. ⊠ *Trebbiner Str. 9, Kreuzberg* ☎ *030/902-540* ⊕ *www.sdtb.de* ☎ *€8* ⊗ *Closed Mon.* Ⓜ *Gleisdreieck (U-bahn), Anhalter Bahnhof (S bahn).*

Jüdisches Museum Berlin *(Jewish Museum)*

The history of Germany's Jews from the Middle Ages through today is chronicled here, from prominent historical figures to the evolution of laws regarding Jews' participation in civil society. A few of the exhibits document the Holocaust itself, but this museum celebrates Jewish life and history far more than it focuses on the atrocities committed during WWII. An attraction in itself is the highly conceptual building, designed by Daniel Libeskind, where various physical "voids" in the oddly constructed and intensely personal modern wing of the building represent the idea that some things can and should never be exhibited when it comes to the Holocaust. The museum's permanent collection is closed until 2019, though a variety of temporary exhibitions can still be viewed. ⊠ *Lindenstr. 9–14, Kreuzberg* ☎ *030/2599–3300* ⊕ *www.jmberlin.de* ☎ *€8* Ⓜ *Hallesches Tor (U-bahn).*

Liquidrom

Germans love their thermal baths and saunas, and this is one of the classiest around. The dramatic main thermal pool lies under a vaulted ceiling, where glowing lights and soothing music that can be heard underwater enhance a feeling of

GETTING HERE

Kreuzberg is centrally located in Berlin and is easily accessible from all major U-bahn lines. The U1 line runs through Kreuzberg crossing most north-south lines at major interchanges and plazas such as Gleisdreick, Hallesches Tor, and Kottbusser Tor, where you'll find plenty of attractions and things to do.

calm. In addition to several saunas and a steam room, take advantage of the outdoor hot tub in the enclosed courtyard, best at night under stars. There's a bar and a healthy snack menu, just in case all that relaxation leaves you hungry. Full nudity is to be expected here, even in coed areas. ⊠ *Möckernstr. 10, Kreuzberg* ☎ *030/2580–07820* ⊕ *www.liquidrom-berlin.de* ☎ *€19.50 for 2 hrs, €24.50 for 4 hrs, €29.50 whole day* Ⓜ *Anhalter Bahnhof (S-bahn).*

Martin-Gropius-Bau

This magnificent palazzo-like exhibition hall first opened in 1881, and once housed Berlin's Arts and Crafts Museum. Its architect, Martin Gropius, was the great-uncle of Walter Gropius, the Bauhaus architect who also worked in Berlin. The international, changing exhibits on art and culture have included archaeology in Germany, Lucien Freud etchings, an expansive Piet Mondrian exhibit, and works from Anish Kapoor and Meret Oppenheim. ⊠ *Niederkirchnerstr. 7, Kreuzberg* ☎ *030/254–860* ⊕ *www. gropiusbau.de* ☎ *Varies with exhibit*

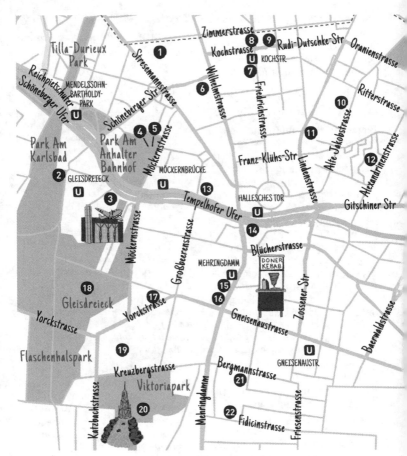

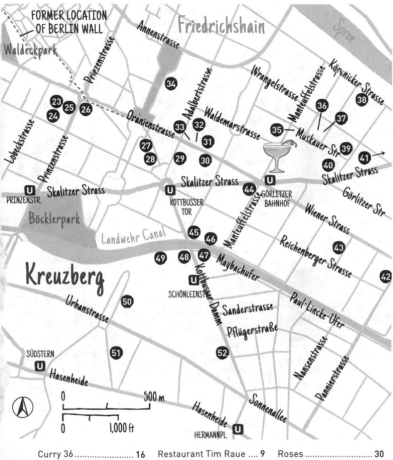

🕙 *Closed Tues.* Ⓜ *Kochstrasse (U-bahn), Potsdamer Platz (U-bahn and S-bahn).*

Mauermuseum-Museum Haus am Checkpoint Charlie

Just steps from the famous crossing point between the two Berlins, the somewhat homespun and slightly disorganized Wall Museum–House at Checkpoint Charlie presents visitors with the story of the wall and, even more riveting, the stories of those who escaped through, under, and over it. This border crossing for non-Germans was manned by the Soviet military in East Berlin's Mitte district and, several yards south, by the U.S. military in West Berlin's Kreuzberg district. Today the touristy intersection consists of a replica of an American guardhouse and signposting, plus cobblestones that mark the old border. The museum reviews the events leading up to the wall's construction and, with original tools and devices, plus recordings and photographs, shows how East Germans escaped to the West (one of the most ingenious contraptions was a miniature submarine). Exhibits about human rights and paintings interpreting the wall round out the experience. Monday, when the state museums are closed, can be particularly crowded. ⊠ *Friedrichstr. 43–45, Kreuzberg* ☎ *030/253–7250* ⊕ *www. mauermuseum.com* 💳 *€15* Ⓜ *Koch-strasse (U-bahn).*

Museum der Dinge

The Museum der Dinge or "Museum of Things" is exactly that—a collection of stuff that represents the best, the worst, and the quirkiest in 20th-century and contemporary design. Although there are a lot of things here, a museum for hoarders this is not. The objects come from the archive of the Deutsches Werkbund (DWB), a hundred-year-old, quasi-utopian consortium that sought perfection in everyday construction and design. The thousands of things are housed in a former factory building on Kreuzberg's busy Oranienstrasse and arranged beautifully by color, material, or use. Browsing the exhibition, one is hit not only by the sheer volume of what was created in the last century, but also by the impressive range—Soviet kitsch toys stand near mobile phones, delicate dishware next to industrial tools. Don't miss the so-called Frankfurt Kitchen a space-saving prototype kitchen from the 1920s that was meant to be replicated over 10,000 times in various housing estates. ⊠ *Oranienstr. 25, Kreuzberg* ☎ *030/9210–6311* ⊕ *www.museum-derdinge.de* 💳 *€6* 🕙 *Closed Tues. and Wed.* Ⓜ *Kottbusser Tor (U-bahn).*

nGbK

The nGbK art association (in English: New Society for Visual Arts) was founded in 1969 and operates a small gallery space on the popular Oranienstrasse behind a bookstore. Exhibitions are always free and the association has a strong ethos in promoting progressive political ideas and social topics. Recent exhibitions cover issues such as labor, migration, xenophobia, and gender. ⊠ *Oranienstr. 25, Kreuzberg* ☏ *030/616–5130* ⊕ *www.ngbk.de* Ⓜ *Kottbusser Tor.*

Park am Gleisdreieck

Like the more glamorous Tempelhof Park, Gleisdreieck, one of Berlin's newest green spaces, was until recently neglected space—in this case, abandoned and over-grown WWII railyards. In between the Kreuzberg and Schöneberg neighborhoods, the park includes playgrounds and open meadows, paths for running and biking, pits for skateboarding, and even a commu-nity garden. Most interesting, however, are the remnants of the park's past: train tracks, signs, and switches have been left intact (if a bit rusty), making this park an urban paradise of the sort Berliners love—one with history hiding in the grass. ⊠ *Kreuzberg* ⊕ *www.gruen-berlin.de* Ⓜ *Gleisdreieck (U-bahn), Yorckstrasse (S-bahn and U-bahn).*

Planet Modulor

Billed as a creative center, this complex of shops, offices, and meeting spaces on Moritzplatz is a step toward revitalizing the once-shabby and still fairly empty square. Its unusual, hulking shape seems designed to attract attention; it may also inspire some local disdain. But one visit is all it takes to appreciate how well the complex represents the Berlin aesthetic: small and mid-size companies share space with craft and designer workshops,

an art bookstore, a café, an outpost of the beloved kitchenware company Coledampf's, and even a kinder-garten. ⊠ *Prinzenstr. 85, Kreuzberg* ☏ *030/690–360* ⊕ *www.modulor.de* Ⓜ *Moritzplatz (U-bahn).*

Prinzessinnengarten

This charming urban garden on the bustling Kreuzberg hub of Moritzplatz perfectly encapsulates the Berlin DIY spirit. Starting with little more than 100 wooden packing crates and an idea, the founders of the Prinzessinnengarten have created an entirely movable source of fruit, vegetables, flowers, and herbs. The café on the premises serves a daily menu of small dishes sourced directly from the garden, while a series of lectures and events facilitate interaction between gardening experts and local enthusiasts. Whether you come just to look, to taste, or to grab a bunch of gardening tools and dig in, the gardens offer a chance to stop, breathe, and enjoy a bit of open space in one of the city's most densely packed quarters. ⊠ *Prinzenstr. 35–38/Prinzessinnenstr. 15, Kreuzberg* ⊕ *prinzessinnengarten. net/* Ⓜ *Moritzplatz (U-bahn).*

St. Agnes Kirche und König Galerie

Hidden away in a part of Kreuzberg most visitors don't reach, St. Agnes, a Catholic church turned contemporary art gallery, is hardly a looker—unless you like the bulky, boxy concrete shapes that char-acterize Brutalist architecture. Gallerist Johann König took over the

1960s building in 2012 and opened it as an exhibition center, which was redesigned again in 2015 by Arno Brandlhuber to include additional gallery space for the König Galerie. ✉ *Alexandrinenstr. 118–121, Kreuzberg* ☎ *030/2610–3080* ⊕ *www. st-agnes.net* Ⓜ *Prinzenstrasse (U-bahn).*

★ Topographie des Terrors
(Topography of Terror)
Topographie des Terrors is partially an open-air exhibit, fully exposed to the elements, and partially a stunning indoor exhibition center, where you can view photos and documents explaining the secret state police and intelligence organizations that planned and executed Nazi crimes against humanity. The fates of both victims and perpetrators are given equal attention here. The cellar remains of the Nazis' Reich Security Main Office (composed of the SS, SD, and Gestapo) contains other exhibitions, which typically run from April to October as this section is outdoors. ✉ *Niederkirchnerstr. 8, Kreuzberg* ☎ *030/2545–0950* ⊕ *www. topographie.de* ☜ *Free* Ⓜ *Kochstrasse (U-bahn), Potsdamer Platz (U-bahn and S-bahn).*

Viktoriapark
A neighborhood favorite, the small Viktoriapark offers one of the highest lookout points in the city center—and definitely the best place to get a free panoramic view. Beginning at the edge of the park, all trails gradually slope upward; at the top stands an elaborate cast-iron monument designed by Karl Friedrich Schinkel in 1821 to commemorate the so-called liberation wars against Napoléon of 1813–15. On the way back down, take the path heading to Kreuzbergstrasse, next to which a lovely little waterfall trips and burbles over rocks and boulders—a favorite splashing spot for local children. ✉ *Kreuzberg* Ⓜ *Yorckstrasse (S-bahn and U-bahn).*

🛍 Shopping

★ Hallesches Haus
Part playfully curated general store and part café, Hallesches Haus is the brainchild of three ex-Fab and Monoqi staffers. Expect to find terrariums, artfully designed gardening tools, Pendleton blankets, housewares, and gifts with a sense of humor. ✉ *Tempelhofer Ufer 1, Kreuzberg* ⊕ *www.hallescheshaus. com* Ⓜ *Hallesches Tor (U-bahn).*

Hardwax
This iconic record store is run by music veteran Mark Ernestus, who handpicks all the vinyl and CDs with a heavy focus on techno, electronic, and dubstep. On the third floor of a heavily graffitied building, it's the true essence of Berlin grunge and totally worth a visit for music lovers. ✉ *Paul-Lincke-Ufer 44a, Kreuzberg* ☎ *030/6113–0111* ⊕ *www.hardwax. com* Ⓜ *Kottbusser Tor (U-bahn).*

Michael Sontag

You'll see a lot of versatile silk shirts and draping dresses to be worn year-round in Berlin-based Michael Sontag's architecturally striking boutique. Often celebrated by the German fashion press, Sontag thinks in terms of timelessness over seasonality. ✉ *Muskauerstr. 41, Kreuzberg* ☎ *0179/971–5932* ⊕ *www. michaelsontag.com* Ⓜ *Görlitzer Bahnhof (U-bahn).*

★ Süper Store

Located in the charming neighborhood of Kreuzberg known as the Graefekiez, this cute little shop supplies a variety of lovely odds and ends, sourced from all over the world, including Turkey, Italy, and Switzerland, as well as locally produced items. Inside you'll find linens, housewares, pantry items, and jewelry. ✉ *Dieffenbachstr. 12, Kreuzberg* ☎ *030/9832–7944* ⊕ *www. sueper-store.de* Ⓜ *Schönleinstrasse (U-bahn).*

Türkischer Markt

On the edge of the Kreuzberg-Neukölln border, this weekly market is a gathering spot for the local Turkish community, and offers many traditional products, including delicious delicacies (olives, cheese, dried fruits, hummus, and fresh breads) and a bazaar of house goods, including an extensive selection of fabrics ✉ *Maybachufer, Kreuzberg* ☎ *030/9170–0700* ⊕ *www. tuerkenmarkt.de* Ⓜ *Schönleinstrasse (U-bahn).*

★ Voo

This "super boutique" in a former locksmith's workshop is a Berlin favorite for women's and men's separates, shoes, accessories, and outerwear, often from rare collections around the world. It's also home to Companion Coffee, for when you need a shopping pick-me-up. ✉ *Oranienstr. 24, Kreuzberg* ☎ *030/6110–1750* ⊕ *www.vooberlin. com* Ⓜ *Kottbusser Tor (U-bahn).*

🍵 Coffee and Quick Bites

Café Morgenland

$ | Middle Eastern. Within view (and earshot) of the elevated U1 line, Café Morgenland is a relatively unremarkable neighborhood haunt on weekdays but on Sundays it devotes an entire room to the extremely popular brunch buffet, which means table space can be scarce. The Turkish-inspired dishes (an ode to the home country of many a Kreuzberg native) are a delicious alternative to the more traditional brunches served elsewhere in Berlin. **Known for:** brunch buffet; sidewalk seating; casual atmosphere. *Average main: €10* ✉ *Skalitzerstr. 35, Kreuzberg* ☎ *030/611–3291* ⊕ *www.morgenland-berlin.de* 🚫 *No credit cards* Ⓜ *Görlitzer Bahnhof (U-bahn).*

The Visit Coffee Roastery

$ | Café. Set inside a quiet courtyard off the busy Adalbertstrasse, The Visit Coffee Roastery is a small oasis with excellent coffee and breakfast dishes in a sleek, whitewashed café. A neon sign at the courtyard entrance introduces you to the café, and stadium-style seating in the entrance is typical of the Berlin café and bar style—a cozy environment for that perfect cup of coffee. **Known for:** sleek modernist design; large breakfast and brunch dishes; great coffee. *Average main: €7* ✉ *Adalbertstr. 9, Kreuzberg* ⊕ *kontakt@visit-coffee.com* Ⓜ *Kottbusser Tor.*

Westberlin
$ | Café. A coffee bar and shop, this modern café has a stylish Scandinavian-inspired design. Besides the light meals and lunches available, Westberlin also sells a wide variety of fashion, art, and design magazines. **Known for:** modern architectural design; hipster magazine selection; Five Elephant coffee. *Average main: €7* ✉ *Friedrichstr. 215, Kreuzberg* ☎ *030/2592-2745* ⊕ *www.westberlin-bar-shop.de/* Ⓜ *Kochstrasse.*

🍴 Dining

★ BRLO Brwhouse
$$ | Eclectic. A cross between a craft brewery, a hip outdoor beer garden (spring through fall only), and a casual indoor restaurant inside reused shipping containers, BRLO is a quintessential Berlin spot to spend an afternoon drinking and eating. If the weather's nice, grab a striped lounge chair outside and choose from a range of modern bar snacks at the beer garden, open every day except in winter; other-wise, head indoors for a choice of vegetable-focused mains along with meats cooked in their own smoker. **Known for:** cool, fun outdoor and indoor setting; tasty barbecue and vegetables; beers brewed on-site. *Average main: €18* ✉ *Schöneberger Str. 16, Kreuzberg* ☎ *151/7437-4235* ⊕ *www.brlo-brwhouse.de* 🕐 *Closed Mon. No lunch Tues.–Fri.* Ⓜ *Gleis-dreieck (U-bahn).*

★ Curry 36
$ | Fast Food. This currywurst stand in Kreuzberg has a cult following and just about any time of day or night you'll find yourself amid a crowd of cab drivers, students, and lawyers munching on currywurst *mit Darm* (with skin) or *ohne Darm* (without skin). Go local and order your sausage with a big pile of crispy fries served *rot-weiss* (red and white)—with curry ketchup and mayonnaise. **Known for:** Berlin's most famous currywurst; vegan currywurst for non-meat eaters; late-night eats (open till 5 am). *Average main: €2* ✉ *Mehringdamm 36, Kreuzberg* ☎ *030/251-7368* ⊕ *www.curry36.de* ▭ *No credit cards* Ⓜ *Mehringdamm (U-bahn).*

Defne
$$ | Turkish. In a city full of Turkish restaurants, Defne stands out for its exquisitely prepared food, friendly service, and pleasant setting. Beyond simple kebabs, the fresh and healthy menu here includes a selection of hard-to-find fish dishes from the Bosphorus, such as *acili ahtapot* (spicy octopus served with mushrooms and olives in a white-wine-and-tomato sauce), as

well as delicious meze and typical Turkish dishes like "the Imam Fainted," one of many eggplant preparations. **Known for:** large selection of traditional Turkish meat and seafood plates; delicious vegetarian dishes; lovely location on the bank of the Landwehrkanal, with outdoor terrace. *Average main: €15* ✉ *Planufer 92c, Kreuzberg* ☎ *030/8179–7111* ⊕ *www.defne-restaurant.de* ⊘ *No lunch* Ⓜ *Kottbusser Tor (U-bahn).*

★ Die Henne

$ | **German.** The 100-plus-year-old Kreuzberg stalwart has managed to stick around thanks in part to its most famous dish, which is still just about all it serves: a crispy, fried half chicken. The rest of the menu is short: coleslaw, potato salad, a few *boulette* (meat patty) options, and several beers on tap; for "dessert," look to the impressive selection of locally sourced brandies and fruit schnapps. **Known for:** scrumptious fried chicken; front-yard beer garden; charming historic setting. *Average main: €9* ✉ *Leuschnerdamm 25, Kreuzberg* ☎ *030/614–7730* ⊕ *www.henne-berlin.de* ⊘ *Closed Mon.* Ⓜ *Moritzplatz (U-bahn), Kottbusser Tor (U-bahn).*

Jolesch

$$ | **Austrian.** The front bar area and a cozy dining room are usually filled with chattering locals and the occasional dog peeking out from under the table (pets are allowed in unexpected places in Berlin, including many restaurants). The house specialties include Viennese

classics like Wiener schnitzel and apple strudel, along with a few "modern" Austrian dishes, but look for surprises, too, on the seasonal weekly menu, which is full of interesting ingredients and unusual combinations. **Known for:** a mixture of traditional and contemporary

Austrian cooking; some of the best Wiener schnitzel in Berlin; classic Viennese desserts like Sacher torte and apple strudel. *Average main: €18 ⊠ Muskauerstr. 1, Kreuzberg* ☎ *030/612–3581* ⊕ *www.jolesch.de* ⊘ *No lunch Sat.* Ⓜ *Görlitzer Bahnhof (U-bahn).*

La Lucha

$$ | Mexican. This modern Mexican restaurant opened in 2017 with a lot of fanfare and has continuously lived up to its hype. Friendly service and original recipes make the restaurant stand out among other international dining in Berlin—especially with the funky, colorful design inside. **Known for:** contemporary and creative Mexican dishes; strong cocktails; colorful interior, lively atmosphere, and friendly service. *Average main: €13* ⊠ *Paul-Lincke-Ufer 39/41, Kreuzberg* ☎ *030/5520–0914* ⊕ *laluchaberlin. com* Ⓜ *Kottbusser Tor.*

Mariona

$ | Spanish. This bright, welcoming space just off Kreuzberg's Lausitzer Platz serves tasty Catalonian tapas created from locally sourced ingredients that put a bit of sunshine on the plate during the dreary months. The colorful dishes on the daily changing menu are often unique pairings of sweet and savory ingredients, which combine well with the list of Spanish wines. **Known for:** fresh seafood tapas from Catalonia; dinner only; friendly service. *Average main: €12* ⊠ *Skalitzerstr. 94b, Kreuzberg* ☎ *030/6167–1214* ⊕ *www.mariona-berlin.de* ▭ *No credit cards* Ⓜ *Görlitzer Bahnhof (U-bahn).*

★ Markthalle Neun

$ | International. Thanks to the efforts of local activists, this century-old market hall was saved from becoming a chain supermarket and instead turned into a center for local food vendors, chefs, wine dealers, and brewers. From Tuesday to Saturday, a large and rotating variety of food and drink is on offer for lunch and all afternoon; Thursday evening is the hugely popular Street Food Thursday; Friday and Saturday find the weekly market with tempting food products for sale, from fruits and vegetables to bread and fish; and the space also hosts a dazzling array of rotating events, so it's best to check what's on before heading there. **Known for:** tasty and varied food choices from local entrepreneurs, from barbecue to crepes to tapas; a fun, hipster scene; a good selection of beer, wine, and coffee. *Average main: €8* ⊠ *Eisenbahnstr. 42/43, Kreuzberg* ☎ *030/6107–3473* ⊕ *www. markthalleneun.de* ⊘ *Closed Sun.* Ⓜ *Görlitzer Bahnhof (U-bahn).*

Marqués Rene Maschkiwitz

$$ | Spanish. In a city where it seems as if 10 new restaurants open every day, this Spanish and Portuguese tapas spot has been spared much of the hype, but that's a good thing: Marqués serves high-end, inventive food and Mediterranean wines, without pretension. The menu is extensive, so talk it over with friendly staff, who will advise and serve you delights like sizzling plates of chorizo, and salted, fried *pimientos* *de padron,* the small, green, Spanish peppers. **Known for:** speciality cocktails; outdoor seating; classic Spanish tapas. *Average main: €15* ⊠ *Graefestr. 92, Kreuzberg* ☎ *030/6162–5906* 🖃 *No credit cards* Ⓜ *Schönleinstrasse (U-bahn).*

Mustafa's Gemüse Kebab
$ | Turkish. For the traditional *döner kebab,* head to Mustafa's for mouthwateringly delicious vegetable kebabs (also available with chicken for those who can't resist a bit of protein, but the vegetarian is what people rave about). The line can sometimes stretch down the block, but it's well worth the wait, and this is a traditional street stand, so no seating. **Known for:** toasted pita bread stuffed full of roasted veggies with sauce and feta cheese; döner kebab (seasoned meat in a wrap with salad); long lines at all hours. *Average main: €3* ⊠ *Mehringdamm 32, Kreuzberg* ☎ *283/2153* ⊕ *www.mustafas.de* 🖃 *No credit cards* 🕒 *Closed Sun.* Ⓜ *Mehringdamm (U-bahn).*

Restaurant Tim Raue
$$$$ | Asian Fusion. The conservative decor belies the artistry on offer at this Michelin-starred restaurant from Germany's most famous celebrity chef. Asian ingredients such as wasabi, miso, and dashi find their way into traditional German dishes including veal and pork knuckle, as well as more explicitly fusion dishes; four-, six-, or eight-course tasting menus can be paired with splendid wines from one of the most comprehensive lists in Berlin. **Known for:** Peking duck "TR" (duck three ways); langoustine with wasabi Cantonese-style; yuzu cheesecake with caramel beurre salé. *Average main: €66* ⊠ *Rudi-Dutschke-Str. 26, Kreuzberg* ☎ *030/2593–7930* ⊕ *tim-raue.com* 🕒 *Closed Sun. and Mon. No lunch Tues.* Ⓜ *Kochstrasse (U-bahn).*

Richard
$$$ | French. On an industrial Kreuzberg street, Richard isn't relying on foot traffic to bring in customers; but everyone who knows about it raves. The unassuming facade hides an elegant white interior with stained-glass windows, an intricate, carved wood ceiling, and modern paintings. **Known for:** elegant decor; classic French cuisine; roast suckling pig. *Average main: €22* ⊠ *Köpenickerstr. 174, Kreuzberg* ☎ *030/4920–7242* ⊕ *www.restaurant-richard.de* 🖃 *No credit cards* 🕒 *Closed Sun. and Mon.* Ⓜ *Schlesisches Tor (U-bahn).*

★ Tulus Lotrek

$$$$ | **Eclectic.** Tucked onto a charming, leafy street, this quirky Michelin-starred restaurant decked out in green jungle wallpaper and wood floral details, with a cozy outdoor terrace, focuses on the "experience" of their food, serving up beautiful and interesting dishes using unusual ingredient combinations. Diners can choose from a six- to eight-course tasting menu, and vivacious co-owner Ilona Scholl will happily suggest (and encourage) whimsical international wine pairings to match. **Known for:** relaxed, fun service; only six- or eight-course tasting menus; large selection of nonstandard wines. *Average main: €110* ⊠ *Fichtestr. 24, Kreuzberg* ☎ *030/4195–6687* ⊕ *tuluslotrek.de* ⊘ *Closed Wed. and Thurs. No lunch* Ⓜ *Südstern (U-bahn), Schönleinstrasse (U-bahn).*

🍸 Bars and Nightlife

Bellmann Bar

The candlelit, rough-wood tables, water-stained walls, and frequent appearances by local musicians just dropping by for a few tunes give this cozy cocktail bar an artsy, old-world feel. Lovingly nicknamed "the Gramophone Bar" for the old gramophone that sits in its window, Bellmann is a place to linger and chat over a glass of wine or a whiskey from the outstanding collection. ⊠ *Reichenbergerstr. 103, Kreuzberg* ⊕ *www.bellmanbar. de/*Ⓜ *Schlönleinstrasse (U-bahn), Görlitzer Bahnhof (U-bahn).*

ART IN THE WILD

Some of Berlin's best street art is located in Kreuzberg. Once on the fringe of West Berlin, the alternative neighborhood has always attracted artists to paint on its walls. One of Berlin's most iconic urban art murals is the towering Astronaut/Cosmonaut, painted by Victor Ash in 2007, located near Kottbusser Tor on Skalizter Strasse. But you'll also find iconic works in Kreuzberg by ROA on Oranienstrasse, by Brazilian Os Gemos near the Schleissches Tor U-bahn, and the remnants of Blu's iconic murals on Schlesische Strasse (he removed the paintings in 2014 but left an outline out of protest).

Facciola

Facciola looks like a lovely little wine bar from the outside—large windows with some greenery, a red awning, a handful of Berliners sitting on the stoop. Inside, the bartenders make the environment more than cozy, though. Fresh Italian foods and snacks are available on candelit tables, but it's the impressive selection of Italian wines that make the place stand out—and the over-the-top-friendly bartenders. Don't miss Aperitivo Thursdays, when light Italian snacks are served with every drink. ⊠ *Forster Str. 5, Kreuzberg* ⊕ *www.facciola-berlin.de* Ⓜ *Görlitzer Bahnhof.*

Heidenpeters

Named after owner and head brewer Johannes Heidenpeter, this brewery has transformed its little corner of the bustling Markthalle Neun market hall into a pleasant taproom (the brewing happens just below, in the basement). Enjoy the six beers on tap here, or take them with you in hand-labeled bottles; choices typically include an IPA and a couple of seasonal ales. Open Tuesday and Thursday–Saturday only. ⊠ *Eisenbahnstr. 42–43, in Markthalle Neun, Kreuzberg* ⊕ *www. heidenpeters.de/.*

Prince Charles

This club, located under the multipurpose art space Planet Modulor Aufbau Haus, has become a neighborhood hangout. DJs, live bands, flea markets, and even food events have all found a home in here. The club is a bit hard to find—look for the ramp leading down to what seems like a parking garage off Prinzenstrasse. It's next to Parker Bowles restaurant, which the club also operates. ⊠ *Prinzenstr. 85F, Kreuzberg* ⊕ *www.princecharles-berlin.com/.*

Ritter Butzke

This club may not enjoy the breathless hype of some of its brethren, but it has consistency, and perhaps staying power (it's been open since 2007—a lifetime in Berlin). Only the determined will find the place: it's in an old factory that you reach via a courtyard off a quiet street. Three dance floors with different kinds of music allow you to pick and choose, and the club's decor includes some Alice-in-Wonderland-like objects like a giant teapot, strangely illuminated stacked cubes, and a ceiling

made of umbrellas. ⊠ *Ritterstr. 24, Kreuzberg* ⊕ *www.ritterbutzke.de.*

Roses

If you don't find any eye candy at tiny Roses there are always the furry red walls and kitschy paraphernalia to admire. It opens at 10 pm and keeps going until very late (and is usually very smoky). ⊠ *Oranienstr. 187, Kreuzberg* ☏ *030/615–6570* Ⓜ *Kottbusser Tor (U-bahn), Görlitzer Bahnhof (U-bahn).*

Watergate

The elegant Watergate is a club for people who usually don't like clubbing. It sits languidly at the base of the Oberbaumbrücke, on the Kreuzberg side, and has two dance floors with bars. The terrace extending over the River Spree is one of the city's best chill-out spaces. In addition to hosting internationally renowned DJs, the club is the beautiful and intimate setting for infrequent but popular classical music nights. ⊠ *Falckensteinstr. 49, Kreuzberg* ☏ *030/6128–0396* ⊕ *water-gate.de* Ⓜ *Schlesisches Tor (U-bahn), Warschauer Strasse (U-bahn and S-bahn).*

Würgeengel

Named after a 1962 surrealist film by Luis Buñuel (known as *The Exterminating Angel* in English), this classy joint offers an elaborate cocktail menu in a well-designed space off Kottbusser Tor. The bar's loyal fans spill out onto the streets on busy nights, and an evening tapas menu comes from the neighboring restaurant, Gorgonzola Club. ⊠ *Dresdenerstr. 122,*

Kreuzberg 🕾 *030/615–5560* ⊕ *www. wuergeengel.de* Ⓜ *Kottbusser Tor (U-bahn).*

Yorckschlösschen
A bit rougher around the edges than most Berlin jazz clubs, Yorckschlösschen ("little York castle") has become the unofficial living room of the area's musicians and jazz aficionados. The club is plastered with posters and decorated with old instruments, and the stage isn't much more than a slightly raised platform—but some of the area's best play here. The Thursday-night jam session is free; other nights, a music charge will be added to your bill. ⊠ *Yorckstr. 15, Kreuzberg* 🕾 *030/215–8070* ⊕ *www. yorckschloesschen.de.*

 **Performing Arts**

Babylon
Partially hidden behind Kottbusser Tor, Babylon shows original-language films with English/German subtitles. Ticket prices vary according to the day of the week, with Monday being the cheapest at €7. ⊠ *Dresdener Str. 126, Kreuzberg* 🕾 *030/6160–9693* ⊕ *www.yorck.de.*

English Theatre Berlin
The English Theatre presents dramas and comedies in English as well as hosting independent productions, concerts, events, and comedies for Berlin's international community. ⊠ *Fidicinstr. 40, Kreuzberg* 🕾 *030/691–1211* ⊕ *www. etberlin.de.*

Hebbel am Ufer Theater *(HAU)*
This theater consists of three houses (HAU 1, 2, 3) within a five-minute walk of one another. Fringe theater, international modern dance, and solo performers share the stages. ⊠ *HAU1, Stresemannstr. 29, Kreuzberg* 🕾 *030/2590–0427* ⊕ *www.hebbel-am-ufer.de.*

Tanzfabrik
The Tanzfabrik is Berlin's best venue to see young dance talent and the latest from Europe's avant-garde. Additionally, contemporary artists come to learn and practice here in dance classes and workshops. The company holds dance festivals at Uferstrasse 8/23 in Wedding on occasion. ⊠ *Studio, Möckernstr. 68, Kreuzberg* 🕾 *030/786–5861* ⊕ *www. tanzfabrik-berlin.de.*

Tempodrom
The white, tentlike Tempodrom, beyond the ruined facade of Anhalter Bahnhof, showcases international music and rock stars. ⊠ *Möckernstr. 10, behind Askanischer Pl., Kreuzberg* 🕾 *030/747–370* ⊕ *www. tempodrom.de.*

Sightseeing ★★☆☆☆ | Shopping ★★★★☆ | Dining ★★★★☆ | Nightlife ★★★★☆

Long known as Berlin's gay neighborhood, these days Schöneberg also attracts young families. You'll find many stylish shops and cafés in and around Nollendorfplatz, steps away from Winterfeldtplatz, where a weekly food and flea market takes place Wednesday and Saturday.—*by Liz Humphreys*

◉ Sights

Blain|Southern
The Berlin branch of a swish London gallery, Blain|Southern occupies a breathtaking loft space that once housed the printing presses of *Tagesspiegel,* the daily Berlin newspaper. Since opening in 2010, the gallery has highlighted star artists like Douglas Gordon, Lawrence Weiner, and Jannis Kounellis. ⊠ *Potsdamerstr. 77–87, Schöneberg* ☎ *030/6449-31510* ⊕ *www.blainsouthern.com* Ⓜ *Kurfürstenstrasse (U-bahn).*

Galeria Plan B
In March 2012, Romanian gallery Plan B moved into an industrial space deep within the *Tagesspiegel* building complex. This is the place to see offbeat Eastern European art. ⊠ *Potsdamerstr. 77–87, Bldg. G, 2nd courtyard, Schöneberg* ☎ *030/3980-5236* ⊕ *www.plan-b.ro* Ⓜ *Kurfürstenstrasse (U-bahn).*

Galerie Isabella Bortolozzi
Bortolozzi consistently spots and cultivates the hottest young talent in the city (like Danh Vo), showing their work in a quirky, wood-paneled space. ⊠ *Schöneberger Ufer 61, Schöneberg* ☎ *030/2639-7620* ⊕ *www.bortolozzi.com* Ⓜ *Potsdamer Platz (U-bahn and S-bahn) or Mendelssohn-Bartholdy Park (U-bahn).*

Galerie Verein Berliner Künstler
Founded in 1841, this is the oldest artist association in Germany. Its lavish townhouse gallery spaces often highlight the work of its 120-odd artist members. ⊠ *Schöneberger Ufer 57, Schöneberg* ☎ *030/261-2399* ⊕ *vbk-art. de* Ⓜ *Potsdamer Platz (U-bahn and S-bahn) or Mendelssohn-Bartholdy Park (U-bahn).*

Schwules Museum *(Gay Museum)*
This compact museum examines LGBTQ life both in Germany and internationally—most exhibits are in English as well as German—and also features temporary exhibitions ranging from feminist porn and erotic video art to a queer history of video games. There's also a library and archive, which includes more than 16,000 volumes of material, a café, and a bookshop. ⊠ *Lützowstr. 73, Schöneberg* ☎ *030/6959-9050* ⊕ *www. schwulesmuseum.de* ⊘ *Museum: Closed Tues., and before 2 pm Wed.–Sun. Library and archive: Closed Tues., Sat., and Sun.* Ⓜ *Potsdamer Platz (U-bahn, S-bahn), Mendelssohn-Bartholdy-Park (U-bahn).*

GETTING HERE

Schöneberg's transit hub is the U-bahn station at Nollendorfplatz, from which it's an easy walk to the Winterfeldtplatz market, the Urban Nation Museum for Urban Contemporary Art, the LGBTQ bars clustered on Motzstrasse, and many other cocktail bars and restaurants nearby. The U-bahn stops at Eisenacher Strasse and Bülowstrasse can also be convenient depending on where in the neighborhood you're staying or visiting.

Sommer & Kohl
In what was once a mattress factory, Patricia Kohl and Salome Sommer show mostly young, international artists. ⊠ *Kurfurstenstr. 13/14, Schöneberg* ☎ *030/2300–5581* ⊕ *www.sommerkohl.com* Ⓜ *Kurfürsten-strasse and Bülowstrasse (U-bahn).*

Supportico Lopez
Recently joining Sommer + Kohl's courtyard (in the empire owned by Scottish artist Douglas Gordon, whose studio is upstairs), Supportico Lopez is a curator's and art-lover's dream. No wonder: it started as a curatorial project in Naples, and reflects curators Gigiotto Del Vecchio and Stefania Palumbo's vision. ⊠ *Kurfürstenstr. 14/b, Schöneberg* ☎ *030/3198–9387* ⊕ *www.supporti-colopez.com* Ⓜ *Kurfürstenstrasse and Bülowstrasse (U-bahn).*

Urban Nation Museum for Urban Contemporary Art
The largest organized display of street art in the world, this museum features original creations from more than 100 street artists,

including well-known names like Shepard Fairey. Outdoors you'll find transportable panels displaying 8,000-square-foot murals that can be rotated regularly. ⊠ *Bülowstr. 7, Schöneberg* ☎ *030/3229–5989* ⊕ *urban-nation.com* ⊠ *Free* ⊗ *Closed Mon.* Ⓜ *Nollendorfplatz (U-bahn).*

🛍 Shopping

★ Markt am Winterfeldtplatz
Berlin's largest farmers' market features stalls brimming with fruit, vegetables, and cheese, along with an international selection of prepared foods, including Korean, Turkish, Thai, and Indian, plus home goods, clothes, and jewelry. It's held every Wednesday from 8 am to 1 pm and Saturday from 8 am to 4 pm. ⊠ *Winterfeldtpl., Schöneberg* Ⓜ *Nol-lendorfplatz (U-bahn).*

★ Winterfeldt Schokoladen
A historic wood-paneled pharmacy dating from 1892 has been turned into an adorable chocolate shop with a fabulous selection of chocolate bars from around the world. There's also a lovely café in the back where you can enjoy hot chocolate, coffee, or tea along with tasty cakes and pastries. ⊠ *Goltzstr. 23, Schöneberg* ☎ *030/2362–3256* ⊕ *www.winterfeldt-schokoladen.de* Ⓜ *Nollendorfplatz (U-bahn).*

☕ Coffee and Quick Bites

★ Café Einstein Stammhaus
$$$ | Austrian. In the historic grand villa of silent movie star Henny Porten, the Einstein is one of the

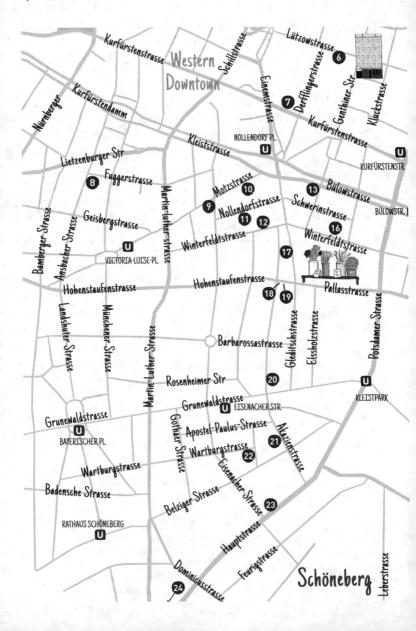

Schöneberg

leading coffeehouses in town, and it charmingly recalls the elegant days of the Austro-Hungarian Empire, complete with an artsy, high-brow clientele and slightly snobbish waiters gliding across the parquet floors. Order Austrian delicacies such as *Tafelspitz* or schnitzel (the small order is plenty large), coffee, and, of course, some cake, best enjoyed in summer in the shady garden behind the villa. **Known for:** schnitzel and Tafelspitz (boiled beef); apple strudel with vanilla sauce; outdoor seating in a beautiful courtyard. *Average main: €24* ⊠ *Kurfürstenstr. 58, Schöneberg* ☎ *030/263–9190* ⊕ *www.cafeeinstein. com* Ⓜ *Kurfürstenstrasse (U-bahn), Nollendorfplatz (U-bahn).*

Double Eye

$ | Café. Try this tiny, always buzzing neighborhood coffee joint for delicious brews (with dark or light roast options) and delectable pastries, including Portuguese *pasteis de nata* (egg custard tarts). **Known for:** friendly service; expertly brewed coffee; outdoor people-watching. *Average main: €5* ⊠ *Akazienstr. 22, Schöneberg* ☎ *0179/456–6960* ⊕ *doubleeye.de* Ⓜ *Eisenacher Strasse (U-bahn), Julius-Leber-Brücke (S-bahn).*

Hisar Fresh Food

$ | Turkish. The lines here are often long, but they move fast and the combination of seasoned, salty meat with crunchy salad and warm bread is unbeatable. Most people come here for a quick döner kebab, line up outside on the sidewalk, and order from the window; there's

ART IN THE WILD

While the Urban Nation Museum for Urban Contemporary Art shows works from international street artists in an indoor space, the museum also maintains an Art Map that directs people to fascinating street art around the city—including several large-scale pieces on the sides of buildings not far from the museum in Schöneberg. Don't miss seeing them on your own self-guided art walk.

also a good choice of other Turkish specialties. **Known for:** döner kebabs, made with beef, chicken, or vegetables; beef, chicken, or veggie dürüm (wrapped in Turkish flatbread); quick, easy, and cheap meals. *Average main: €3* ⊠ *Yorckstr. 49, Schöneberg* ☎ *030/216–5125* ⊕ *www.hisarfreshfood.de* ▭ *No credit cards* Ⓜ *Yorckstrasse (U-bahn and S-bahn).*

Jones Ice Cream

$ | Café. In her airy, brick-walled shop, ice cream maker extraordinaire Gabrielle Jones whips up small batch ice cream, sorbet, and frozen yogurt in tempting flavors like lemon and blueberry jam, whiskey and pecan, and salted butter caramel. **Known for:** arguably the best ice cream in town; handmade waffle cones; ice cream served between two cookies (in flavors like matcha and white chocolate, and peanut butter and glazed bacon). *Average main: €3* ⊠ *Goltzstr. 3, Schöneberg* ☎ *0171/833–5780* ⊕ *www.jonesicecream.com* Ⓜ *Eisenacher Strasse (U-bahn).*

🍴 Dining

Café Aroma

$$ | Italian. On a small winding street in an area between Kreuzberg and Schöneberg known as *Rote Insel* (Red Island) because of its location between two S-bahn tracks and its socialist, working-class history, this neighborhood institution was an early advocate of the slow-food movement. The food is Italian and focuses on high quality, locally sourced ingredients and every-thing—whether it's an innovative preparation of artichokes or beef fillet with green peppercorns—is tasty. **Known for:** popular brunch with Italian delicacies; slow-food principles using seasonal ingredi-ents; tagliatelle pirata (with seafood) and spaghetti saporiti (with rabbit). *Average main: €18 ⊠ Hochkirchstr. 8, Schöneberg ☎ 030/782–5821 ⊕ www. cafe-aroma.de ⊘ No lunch weekdays* Ⓜ *Yorckstrasse (S-bahn and U-bahn).*

Ixthys

$ | Korean. This tiny Korean hole-in-the-wall serves what many claim is the best bibimbap (rice topped with veggies, optional meat, and egg) in town, plus a short list of other rice bowl and soup options. There's limited seating, no public bathroom, and sparse, strange decor (with Bible quotes in German papering the walls), but if you're looking for a deli-cious, filling meal that won't break the bank, Ixthys is a solid choice for a casual lunch or dinner. **Known for:** home-style Korean cooking; cash only; cheerful, if sometimes slow, service. *Average main: €9 ⊠ Pallasstr.*

21, Schöneberg ☎ 030/8147–4769 ⊘ Closed Sun. ▭ No credit cards Ⓜ *Nollendorfplatz (U-bahn).*

Malafemmena

$ | Neapolitan. Venture to Schöenberg's far southern reaches to find one of the most talked-about pizza-focused Italian joints in Berlin, which serves up Neapolitan-style pizza along with tempting appe-tizers such as eggplant in tomato sauce with Parmesan and aran-cini (stuffed rice balls). There's a lovely outdoor terrace that attracts a young, lively crowd when the weather's nice. **Known for:** top-notch pizza with seasonal toppings; Neapolitan dishes including pasta, fish, and meat; wines to wash it all down. *Average main: €10 ⊠ Hauptstr. 85, Schöneberg ☎ 030/8418–3182 ⊕ malafemmena.restaurant* Ⓜ *Inns-brucker Platz (S-bahn).*

Renger-Patzsch

$$ | German. Black-and-white photographs by the German landscape photographer Albert Renger-Patzsch, the restaurant's namesake, decorate the dark-wood-paneled dining room at this beloved local gathering place that focuses on top-notch ingredients, respecting the classics while also reinventing them. The menu changes daily but might feature blood sausage with lentils or perhaps venison with choucroute, along with lighter bites like a selection of *Flammkuchen* (Alsatian flatbread tarts) that are perfect for sharing. **Known for:** daily changing seasonal specials; Alsatian Flammkuchen in savory and sweet options; lovely outdoor terrace seating. *Average main: €20* ✉ *Wartburgstr. 54, Schöneberg* ☎ *030/784–2059* ⊕ *www.renger-patzsch.com* ⊘ *Closed Sun. No lunch* Ⓜ *Eisenacher Strasse (U-bahn).*

 Bars and Nightlife

Connection Club
Just south of Wittenbergplatz, the dance club Connection is known for heavy house music and lots of dark corners. ✉ *Fuggerstr. 33, Schöneberg* ☎ *030/218–1432* ⊕ *www.connection-club.de* Ⓜ *Bahnhof Wittenbergplatz (U-bahn), Nollendorfplatz (U-bahn), Viktoria-Luise-Platz (U-bahn).*

Green Door
A grown-up crowd focused on conversation and appreciating outstanding cocktails heads to Green Door, a Schöneberg classic (note that smoking is allowed). The decor is retro 1960s style, with gingham walls and stand-alone lamps. ✉ *Winterfeldstr. 50, Schöneberg* ☎ *030/215–2515* ⊕ *www.greendoor.de* Ⓜ *Nollendorfplatz (U-bahn), Viktoria-Luise-Platz (U-bahn).*

Hafen
The stylish decor and the energetic crowd at Hafen make it a popular singles hangout. ✉ *Motzstr. 19, Schöneberg* ☎ *030/211–4118* ⊕ *www.hafen-berlin.de* Ⓜ *Nollendorfplatz (U-bahn), Viktoria-Luise-Platz (U-bahn).*

Havanna Club
Berlin's multiculti crowd frequents the Havanna Club, where you can dance to soul, R&B, or hip-hop on four different dance floors. The week's highlights are the wild salsa and merengue nights (Wednesday at 9 pm, Friday and Saturday at 10 pm). If your Latin steps are weak, come an hour early for a lesson. Friday and Saturday are "ladies free" nights until 11. ✉ *Hauptstr. 30, Schöneberg* ☎ *030/784–8565* ⊕ *www.havanna-berlin.de.*

Heile Welt
This relaxed gay bar-café, an institution in Schöneberg, makes a great stop for a predinner drink. ✉ *Motzstr. 5, Schöneberg* ☎ *030/2191–7507* Ⓜ *Nollendorfplatz (U-bahn).*

★ Stagger Lee
In the atmosphere of an old Western saloon, with red patterned wallpaper and brown leather couches, you can choose from a large selection of expertly mixed cocktails heavy on the tequila, rum, and whiskey. ✉ *Nollendorfstr. 27, Schöneberg* ☎ *030/2903–6158* ⊕ *www.staggerlee.de* Ⓜ *Nollendorfplatz (U-bahn).*

Voima
Run by charming Berlin bar legend Barbara Piri Ettel, this Finnish-influenced cocktail bar is named after the ship where Ettel spent her honeymoon. The sleek, nautical-themed decor includes model ships, while the drinks feature classic cocktails as well as those using Finnish ingredients. ✉ *Winterfeldtstr. 22, Schöneberg* ☎ *030/2098–5435* ⊕ *www.voima.de* Ⓜ *Bülowstrasse (U-bahn), Nollendorfplatz (U-bahn).*

Tiergarten and Potsdamer Strasse

WEDDING

GESUNDBRUNNEN

PRENZLAUER BERG

MOABIT

HANSA-VIERTEL

SPREE

MITTE

CHARLOTTENBURG

TIERGARTEN

FRIEDRICHSHAIN

SPREE

HALENSEE

KREUZBERG

WILMERSDORF

SCHÖNEBERG

ALT-TREPTOW

FRIEDENAU

NEUKÖLLN

PLÄNTERWALD

TEMPELHOF

BAUMSCHULENWEG

MARIENDORF

BRITZ

Sightseeing ★ ★ ★ ☆ ☆ | Shopping ★ ★ ★ ☆ ☆ | Dining ★ ★ ★ ★ ☆ | Nightlife ★ ★ ★ ★ ☆

T he Tiergarten, a bucolic 630-acre park with lakes, meadows, and wide paths, is the "green heart" of Berlin. In the 17th century it served as the hunting grounds of the Great Elector (its name translates into "animal garden"). Now it's Berlin's backyard for sunbathing and summer strolls. The government district, Potsdamer Platz, and the embassy district ring the park from its eastern to southern edges. Potsdamer Strasse, which runs from Potsdamer Platz down to Schöneberg, is home to the state museums and cultural institutes of the Kulturforum; farther south, the once-sleazy street turns into a fashionable boulevard of galleries, shops, and restaurants. —by Liz Humphreys

👁 Sights

Berlin Zoological Garden and Aquarium Berlin

There are more than 19,000 animals to see here, and more varied species than any other zoo in Europe, including many that are rare and endangered, which the zoo has been successful at breeding. The animals' enclosures are designed to resemble natural habitats, though some structures are ornate, such as the 1910 Arabian-style Zebra House. Pythons, frogs, turtles, invertebrates, Komodo dragons, and an amazing array of strange and colorful fish are part of the three-floor aquarium. Check the feeding times posted to watch creatures such as seals, apes, hippos, penguins, and pelicans during their favorite time of day. ✉ *Hardenbergpl. 8 and Budapester Str. 32, Tiergarten* ☎ *030/254-010* ⊕ *www.zoo-berlin. de* 🎟 *Zoo or aquarium from €16* Ⓜ *Zoologischer Garten (U-bahn and S-bahn).*

Das Stue

History meets contemporary style in the heart of Berlin, in a building that once housed the Royal Danish Embassy and still retains governmental grandeur—from the classical facade to the dramatic entry staircase—now mixed with warming touches like cozy nooks designed by Patricia Uriquola. Public spaces of the hotel showcase the leafy neighborhood through walls of windows and the photography of noted shutterbugs like Helmut Newton, Henri Cartier-Bresson, and Diane Arbus. Michelin-starred Catalonian chef Paco Perez oversees two on-site eateries—one casual, one fine dining—that draw upon the Mediterranean flavors of his homeland, while the zoo-view bar-and-tapas lounge serves everything from cocktails of the 1920s and '30s to a list of 400 German and Spanish wines. ✉ *Drakestr. 1, Tiergarten* ☎ *030/311-7220* ⊕ *www.das-stue. com/en/.*

Deutsche Kinemathek Museum für Film und Fernsehen

Within the Sony Center is the small but fun Museum für Film und Fernsehen, which presents the groundbreaking history of German moviemaking with eye-catching displays. Descriptions are in English, and there's an audio guide as well. Memorabilia include personal belongings of Marlene Dietrich and other German stars, while special exhibitions go into depth about outstanding directors, movements, and studios. A good selection of films, from the best classics to virtually unknown art-house finds, are shown in the theater on the lower level. A shop on the ground floor sells books and other media for cinephiles. ⊠ *Sony Bldg., Potsdamer Str. 2, Potsdamer Platz* ☎ *030/300–9030* ⊕ *www.deutsche-kinemathek.de* ☒ *€7* Ⓜ *Potsdamer Platz (U-bahn and S-bahn).*

★ Gedenkstätte Deutscher Widerstand *(German Resistance Memorial Center)*

This fascinating museum tells the story of the German resistance movement against the Nazis during World War II. It includes the courtyard where the German officers who attempted to assassinate Hitler in July 1944—including Claus von Stauffenberg, depicted in the movie Valkyrie—were themselves executed when the coup failed. There are also rotating temporary exhibitions such as stories of rescue during the Holocaust. ⊠ *Stauffenbergstr. 13-14, Tiergarten* ☎ *030/2699–5000* ⊕ *www.*

GETTING HERE

Potsdamer Platz is one of Berlin's major transit centers; take a U-bahn or S-bahn there to visit any of the Kulturforum museums or the Berlin Philharmonie. From Potsdamer Platz, it's only a short bus ride or moderate walk down to the cultural and culinary sights of Potsdamer Strasse. Zoologischer Garten, on the west side of Tiergarten, is another major U-bahn stop, or if you're not short on time, a leisurely walk from the Reichstag through the Tiergarten to Zoo Station takes about 90 minutes.

gdw-berlin.de ☒ *Free* Ⓜ *Potsdamer Platz (U-bahn, S-bahn), Mendelssohn-Bartholdy-Park (U-bahn).*

Gemäldegalerie *(Picture Gallery)*
The Kulturforum's Gemäldegalerie reunites formerly separated collections from East and West Berlin. It's one of Germany's finest art galleries, and has an extensive selection of European paintings from the 13th to 18th centuries. Seven rooms are reserved for paintings by German masters, among them Dürer, Cranach the Elder, and Holbein. A special collection has works of the Italian masters—Botticelli, Titian, Giotto, Lippi, and

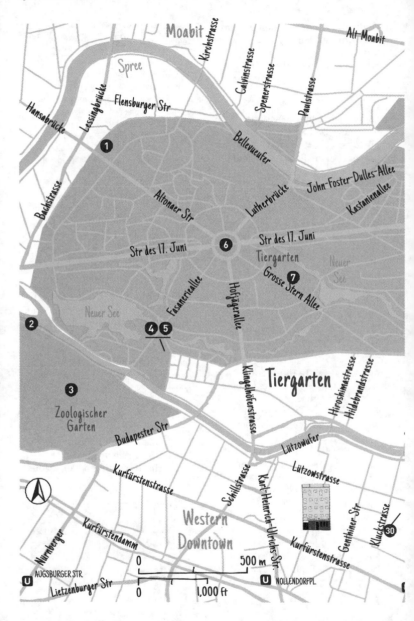

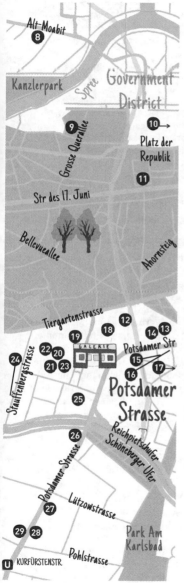

SIGHTS

DINING

BARS & NIGHTLIFE

PERFORMING ARTS

SHOPPING

COFFEE & QUICK BITES

Raphael—as well as paintings by Dutch and Flemish masters of the 15th and 16th centuries: Van Eyck, Bosch, Bruegel the Elder, and Van der Weyden. The museum also holds the world's second-largest Rembrandt collection. ⊠ *Kulturforum, Matthäikirchpl., Potsdamer Platz* ☎ *030/2664–24242* ⊕ *www.smb.museum* ✉ *€10* ⊙ *Closed Mon.* Ⓜ *Potsdamer Platz (U-bahn and S-bahn).*

German Spy Museum *(Deutsches Spionage Museum)*
This museum dedicated to the world of espionage features interactive exhibits from the time of the Bible to the present day, covering topics that include military interrogation techniques and the world of secret services. The museum even touches on celebrated fictional spies, James Bond among them. An exhibit on the Enigma machine and the history of code breaking, as well as a laser maze that visitors can navigate, are two of the museum's biggest draws. ⊠ *Leipziger Pl. 9, Potsdamer Platz* ☎ *030/3982–00451* ⊕ *www.deutsches-spionagemuseum.de* ✉ *€12* Ⓜ *Potsdamer Platz (U-bahn and S-bahn).*

★ **Kulturforum** *(Cultural Forum)*
This unique ensemble of museums, galleries, and the Philharmonic Hall was long in the making. The first designs were submitted in the 1960s and the last building completed in 1998. Now it forms a welcome modern counterpoint to the thoroughly restored Prussian splendor of Museum Island, although Berliners and tourists alike hold drastically differing

opinions on the area's architectural aesthetics. Whatever your opinion, Kulturforum's artistic holdings are unparalleled and worth at least a day of your time, if not more. The Kulturforum includes the **Gemäldegalerie** (Picture Gallery), the **Kunstbibliothek** (Art Library), the **Kupferstichkabinett** (Print Cabinet), the **Kunstgewerbemuseum** (Museum of Decorative Arts), the **Philharmonie**, the **Musikinstrumenten-Museum** (Musical Instruments Museum), the **Staatsbibliothek** (National Library), and the **Neue Nationalgalerie** (New National Gallery), which is closed for renovations until sometime in 2019. ⊠ *Potsdamer Platz* ⊕ *www. smb.museum/en/museums-institutions/kulturforum/home.html* ✉ *€16 for all Kulturforum exhibitions* ⊙ *Closed Mon.* Ⓜ *Potsdamer Platz (U-bahn and S-bahn).*

Kunstbibliothek *(Art Library)*
With more than 400,000 volumes on the history of European art, the Kunstbibliothek in the Kulturforum is one of Germany's most impor-

tant institutions on the subject. It contains art posters and advertisements, examples of graphic design and book design, ornamental engravings, prints and drawings, and a costume library. Visitors can view items in the reading rooms, but many samples from the collections are also shown in rotating special exhibitions. ⊠ *Kulturforum, Matthäikirchpl., Potsdamer Platz* ☎ *030/2664–24242* ⊕ *www.smb. museum* ⊠ *Varies according to exhibition* ☉ *Closed Mon.* Ⓜ *Potsdamer Platz (U-bahn and S-bahn).*

Kunstgewerbemuseum *(Museum of Decorative Arts)*
Inside the Kulturforum's Kunstgewerbemuseum are European arts and crafts from the Middle Ages to the present. Among the notable exhibits are the Welfenschatz (Welfen Treasure), a collection of 16th-century gold and silver plates from Nuremberg; a floor dedicated to design and furniture; and extensive holdings of ceramics and porcelain. Though there is a free English-language audio guide, the mazelike museum is difficult to navigate and most signposting is in German. ⊠ *Kulturforum, Herbert-von-Karajan-Str. 10, Potsdamer Platz* ☎ *030/266–2902* ⊕ *www.smb.museum* ⊠ *€8* ☉ *Closed Mon.* Ⓜ *Potsdamer Platz (U-bahn and S-bahn).*

Kupferstichkabinett *(Drawings and Prints Collection)*
One of the Kulturforum's smaller museums, Kupferstichkabinett has occasional exhibits, which include European woodcuts, engravings,

and illustrated books from the 15th century to the present (highlights of its holdings are pen-and-ink drawings by Dürer and drawings by Rembrandt). You can request to see one or two drawings in the study room. Another building displays paintings dating from the late Middle Ages to 1800. ⊠ *Kulturforum, Matthäikirchpl. 4, Potsdamer Platz* ☎ *030/2664–24242* ⊕ *www.smb. museum* ⊠ *Varies depending on exhibition* ☉ *Closed Mon.* Ⓜ *Potsdamer Platz (U-bahn and S-bahn).*

Musikinstrumenten-Museum
(Musical Instruments Museum)
Across the parking lot from the Philharmonie, the Kulturforum's Musikinstrumenten-Museum has a fascinating collection of keyboard, string, wind, and percussion instruments. These are demonstrated during an 11 am tour on Saturday, which closes with a 35-minute Wurlitzer organ concert for an extra fee. ⊠ *Kulturforum, Ben-Gurion-Str. 1, Potsdamer Platz* ☎ *030/254–810* ⊕ *www.sim.spk-berlin.de* ⊠ €6; *organ concert €3* ⊙ *Closed Mon.* Ⓜ *Potsdamer Platz (U-bahn and S-bahn).*

Neue Nationalgalerie *(New National Gallery)*
Bauhaus member Ludwig Mies van der Rohe originally designed this glass-box structure for Bacardi Rum in Cuba, but Berlin became the site of its realization in 1968. Highlights of the collection of 20th-century paintings, sculptures, and drawings include works by expressionists Otto Dix, Ernst Ludwig Kirchner, and Georg Grosz; special exhibits often take precedence over the permanent collection. The museum is scheduled to reopen in 2019 after four years of renovations. ⊠ *Potsdamer Str. 50, Potsdamer Platz* ☎ *030/2664–24242* ⊕ *www. smb.museum* ⊠ *Varies according to exhibition* Ⓜ *Potsdamer Platz (U-bahn and S-bahn).*

Panoramapunkt
Located 300 feet above Potsdamer Platz at the top of one of its tallest towers, the Panoramapunkt (Panoramic Viewing Point) not only features the world's highest-standing original piece of the Berlin Wall, but also a fascinating, multi-media exhibit about the dramatic history of Berlin's former urban center. A café and a sun terrace facing west make this open-air viewing platform one of the city's most romantic. Purchase a VIP ticket to bypass the elevator queues. ⊠ *Potsdamer Pl. 1, Potsdamer Platz* ☎ *030/2593–7080* ⊕ *www.panorama-punkt.de* ⊠ *From €7.50* Ⓜ *Potsdamer Platz (U-bahn and S-bahn).*

★ **Reichstag** *(Parliament Building)*
The Bundestag, Germany's federal parliament, returned to its traditional seat in the spring of 1999 for the first time since 1933. British architect Sir Norman Foster lightened up the gray monolith with a glass dome: you can circle up a gently rising ramp while taking in the rooftops of Berlin and the parliamentary chamber below. At the base of the dome is an exhibit on the Reichstag's history. Completed in 1894, the Reichstag housed the imperial German parliament and later served a similar function during the ill-fated Weimar Republic. On the night of February 27, 1933, the Reichstag was burned down in an act of arson, a pivotal event in Third Reich history. It was rebuilt but again badly damaged in 1945. All visitors must register their names and birth dates in advance and reserve a place on a guided tour, which you can do online. A riverwalk with great views of the government buildings begins behind

the Reichstag. ⊠ *Pl. der Republik 1, Tiergarten* ☎ *030/2273–2152* ⊕ *www.bundestag.de* 🎫 *Free with prior registration online* Ⓜ *Unter den Linden (S-bahn), Bundestag (U-bahn).*

Siegessäule *(Victory Column)* The 227-foot granite, sandstone, and bronze column is topped by a winged, golden goddess and has a splendid view of Berlin. It was erected in front of the Reichstag in 1873 to commemorate Prussia's military successes and then moved to the Tiergarten in 1938–39. You have to climb 270 steps up through the column to reach the observation platform, but the view is rewarding. The gold-tipped cannons surrounding the column are those the Prussians captured from the French in the Franco-Prussian War. ⊠ *Str. des 17. Juni/Am Grossen Stern, Tiergarten* ☎ *030/391–2961* 🎫 *€3* Ⓜ *Tiergarten (S-bahn), Bellevue (S-bahn).*

Sowjetisches Ehrenmal Tiergarten *(Soviet Memorial)* Built immediately after World War II, this monument stands as a reminder of the Soviet victory over the shattered German army in Berlin in May 1945. The Battle of Berlin was one of the deadliest on the European front. A hulking bronze statue of a soldier stands atop a marble plinth taken from Hitler's former *Reichkanzlei* (headquarters). The memorial is flanked by what are said to be the first two T-34 tanks to have fought their way into the city. ⊠ *Str. des 17.*

Juni, Tiergarten Ⓜ *Unter den Linden (S-bahn).*

Staatsbibliothek *(National Library)* The Kulturforum's Staatsbibliothek is one of the largest libraries in Europe, and was one of the Berlin settings in Wim Wenders's 1987 film *Wings of Desire.* ⊠ *Kulturforum, Potsdamer Str. 33, Potsdamer Platz* ☎ *030/2664–33888* ⊕ *staatsbibliothek-berlin.de* Ⓜ *Potsdamer Platz (U-bahn and S-bahn).*

Tiergarten The quiet greenery of the 520-acre Tiergarten, originally planned as the royal family's private hunting grounds, is a beloved oasis today, with some 23 km (14 miles) of footpaths, meadows, and two beer gardens, making it the third-largest urban green space in Germany. The inner park's 6½ acres of lakes and ponds were landscaped by garden architect Peter Joseph Lenné in the mid-1800s. The park's most popular attraction is the 85-acre Berlin Zoo (Tiergarten literally translates to "animal garden"). ⊠ *Tiergarten* Ⓜ *Zoologischer Garten (S-bahn and U-bahn), Bellevue (S-bahn), Hansaplatz (U-bahn), Potsdamer Platz (U-bahn).*

🛍 Shopping

★ **Andreas Murkudis** Inside the former *Taggespiegel* newspaper office space, you'll find this cool concept store featuring handpicked men's, women's, and children's clothing, including designs by brother Kostas

Murkudis, Dries van Noten, and Christian Haas, as well as accessories and contemporary housewares. ⊠ *Potsdamer Str. 81e, Tiergarten* ☎ *030/6807–98306* ⊕ *andreas-murkudis.com* Ⓜ *Kurfürstenstrasse (U-bahn).*

★ Fiona Bennett

For a unique hat no matter what the season or occasion, for both men and women, stop by this sleek shop run by master milliner (and British expat) Fiona Bennett. You can see hatmakers at work in the attached atelier, and even have a hat made to order, if you choose. ⊠ *Potsdamer Str. 81-83, Tiergarten* ☎ *030/2809–6330* ⊕ *fionabennett.de* Ⓜ *Kurfürstenstrasse (U-bahn).*

🍵 Coffee and Quick Bites

Schleusenkrug

$ | **German.** Forget the fast-food options at Zoo Station. Instead, follow the train tracks to the back of the taxi and bus queues, where you'll enter Tiergarten and within 100 yards come upon the best hideaway in the area: Schleusenkrug. **Known for:** outdoor drinking and dining; good choice of beer and wine; flammkuchen and schnitzel. *Average main: €12* ⊠ *Tiergarten, Müller-Breslau-Str., Tiergarten* ☎ *030/313–9909* ⊕ *www.schleusenkrug.de* 🚫 *No credit cards* Ⓜ *Zoologischer Garten (S-bahn and U-bahn).*

🍴 Dining

★ Facil

$$$$ | **Eclectic.** One of Germany's top restaurants, Facil is also one of the more relaxed of its class: the elegant, minimalist setting—it's in the fifth-floor courtyard of the Mandala Hotel, with exquisite wall panels and a glass roof that opens in summer—and impeccable service make this feel like something of an oasis in the busy city. Diners can count on a careful combination of German classics and inspiration from across the globe; you can choose from the four- to eight-course set meals, or order à la carte. **Known for:** seasonal tasting menus with mainly regional ingredients; beautiful rooftop setting; extensive wine list. *Average main: €66* ⊠ *The Mandala Hotel, Potsdamer Str. 3, Tiergarten* ☎ *030/5900–51234* ⊕ *www.facil.de* 🕐 *Closed weekends* Ⓜ *Potsdamer Platz (U-bahn and S-bahn).*

5 - Cinco by Paco Pérez

$$$$ | **Spanish.** Catalan chef Paco Pérez, a disciple of Ferran Adrià of Spain's legendary elBulli, offers two tasting menus of colorful and playful food, highlighting the maximum flavor of each ingredient and containing some fun surprises; you can also order à la carte. If you are curious and want something less dear, try a less expensive sampling of the chef's food next door at The Casual. **Known for:** high-end Spanish-style molecular gastronomy; good selection of Spanish wines; cheaper, simpler options at The Casual next door.

Average main: €43 ⊠ Das Stue Hotel, Drakestr. 1, Tiergarten ☎ 030/311–7220 ⊕ www.5-cinco.com ⊘ Closed Sun. and Mon. No lunch Ⓜ *Zoologischer Garten (S-bahn and U-bahn).*

Golvet

$$$$ | International. It's all about the Berlin skyline views at this Michelin-starred restaurant high atop a nondescript building on up-and-coming Potsdamer Strasse; enjoy them from your table or on the expansive outdoor deck while dining on classic dishes with global flavors, all made with ingredients sourced from Germany and throughout Europe. Though à la carte dishes are available, it's best to choose from the four- to seven-course menus to sample the seasonal cuisine, especially when paired with wines chosen by the knowledgeable sommelier. **Known for:** homemade bread served with caramel butter; intriguing cocktails inspired by Northern and Central Europe; splashes of urban art created by local artists. *Average main: €45 ⊠ Potsdamer Str. 58, Tiergarten ☎ 030/8906–4222 ⊕ golvet.de ⊘ Closed Sun. and Mon. No lunch* Ⓜ *Mendelssohn-Bartholdy-Park (U-bahn).*

Kin Dee

$$$$ | Thai. High-quality Thai food is hard to find in Berlin, so chef Dalad Kambhu, after spending years in NYC, opened this compact, modern eatery that balances Thai flavors with German ingredients, such as white asparagus in spring. Dishes are only available in a set menu of 8 to 10 courses and are made to share (though they run a bit on the small side), so come with a dining partner or two for the full experience. **Known for:** contemporary Thai cuisine; small plates to share; frequently changing set menus. *Average main: €49 ⊠ Lützowstr. 81, Tiergarten ☎ 030/215–5294 ⊕ kindee-berlin.com ⊘ Closed Sun. and Mon. No lunch* Ⓜ *Mendelssohn-Bartholdy-Park (U-bahn), Gleisdreieck (U-bahn).*

★ Panama

$ | Eclectic. Tucked into a courtyard in the emerging Tiergarten district near galleries and cool boutiques, Panama has a contemporary, artsy decor that perfectly matches its eclectic international cuisine—think small, shareable plates of "leaves and flowers," "grains and vegetables," or "meat and fish." Hip Berliners and in-the-know tourists enjoy seasonal cocktails or a glass of wine with their meal, or you can pop into the sister Tiger Bar next door for a postdinner tipple. **Known for:** well-presented, family-style small plates; inventive, unique flavor combinations; fun vibe with charming waitstaff. *Average main: €14 ⊠ Potsdamer Str. 91, Tiergarten ☎ 030/9832–08435 ⊕ oh-panama.com ⊘ Closed Sun. and Mon. No lunch* Ⓜ *Kurfürstenstrasse (U-bahn), Gleisdreieck (U-bahn), Mendelssohn-Bartholdy-Park (U-bahn).*

Paris-Moskau

$$$$ | Eclectic. If you're looking for a one-of-a-kind dining experience, head to this half-timber house—built more than 100 years ago as a pub and guesthouse along the Paris–Moscow railway—that stands dwarfed by a government complex and the hotels and office buildings around Hauptbahnhof. Today, it serves dishes so intricately prepared they look like works of art, with unique flavor combinations; in addition to the à la carte menu, there is a three-course set menu and a four-course set vegetarian menu in the evening. **Known for:** quaint historic setting; artfully presented international dishes; well-chosen wine list. *Average main: €30* ⊠ *Alt-Moabit 141, Tiergarten* ☎ *030/394-2081* ⊕ *www.paris-moskau.de* ☾ *Closed Sun. No lunch Sat.* Ⓜ *Berlin Hauptbahnhof (S-bahn).*

Ⴘ Bars and Nightlife

★ Victoria Bar
The elegant Victoria Bar is a stylish homage to 1960s and '70s jet-setters, and the cocktails are mixed with care. It typically attracts a middle-age, affluent, and artsy crowd. ⊠ *Potsdamer Str. 102, Tiergarten* ☎ *030/2575-9977* ⊕ *www.victoriabar.de* Ⓜ *Kurfürstenstrasse (U-bahn).*

Performing Arts

★ Berliner Philharmonie
The Berlin Philharmonic Orchestra is one of the world's best and their resident venue is the Philharmonie, comprising the Grosser Saal, or large main hall, and the smaller Kammermusiksaal, dedicated to chamber music. Tickets sell out in advance for the nights when star maestros conduct, but other orchestras and artists appear here as well. Tuesday's free Lunchtime Concerts fill the foyer with eager listeners of all ages at 1 pm. Show up early as these concerts can get very crowded. Daily guided tours (€5) also take place at 1:30 pm. ⊠ *Herbert-von-Karajan-Str. 1, Tiergarten* ☎ *030/2548-8999 ticket office* ⊕ *www.berliner-philharmoniker.de.*

CineStar im Sony Center
Mainstream U.S. and British movies are screened in their original versions at the CineStar im Sony Center. Tuesday is a discount evening. ⊠ *Potsdamer Str. 4, Tiergarten* ☎ *0451/7030-200* ⊕ *www.cinestar.de.*

Grips Theater
For children's theater, head to the world-famous Grips Theater, whose musical hit *Linie 1,* about life in Berlin viewed through the subway, is just as appealing for adults. ⊠ *Altonaer Str. 22, Tiergarten* ☎ *030/397-4740* ⊕ *www.grips-theater.de.*

Tipi am Kanzleramt *(Tipi am Kanzleramt)*
Tipi is a tent venue between the Kanzleramt (Chancellor's Office) and Haus der Kulturen der Welt. Artists featured are well suited for an international audience, and you can opt to dine here before the show. Even the back-row seats are good. ⊠ *Grosse Queralle, Tiergarten* ☎ *030/3906-6550* ⊕ *www.tipi-am-kanzleramt.de.*

WEDDING

GESUNDBRUNNEN

PRENZLAUER BERG

MOABIT

HANSA-VIERTEL

SPREE

CHARLOTTENBURG

MITTE

FRIEDRICHSHAIN

TIERGARTEN

SPREE

HALENSEE

KREUZBERG

ALT-TREPTOW

WILMERSDORF

SCHÖNEBERG

PLÄNTERWALD

NEUKÖLLN

FRIEDENAU

TEMPELHOF

BAUMSCHULENWEG

MARIENDORF

BRITZ

Sightseeing ★ ★ ★ ★ ★ | Shopping ★ ★ ★ ★ ★ | Dining ★ ★ ★ ☆ ☆ | Nightlife ★ ★ ☆ ☆ ☆

An important part of former West Berlin but now a western district of the united city, Charlottenburg has retained its old-world charm. Elegance is the keyword here. Whether you're strolling around leafy Savignyplatz or pausing for a refreshment at the LiteraturHaus, you'll be impressed with the dignity of both the neighborhood's architecture and its inhabitants. Kurfürstendamm (or Ku'damm, as the locals call it) is the central shopping mile, where you'll find an international clientele browsing brand-name designers, or drinking coffee at sidewalk cafés.—*by Jennifer Ceaser*

◉ Sights

Bröhan-Museum
This enjoyable, lesser-known museum of art deco, art nouveau, and functionalist furniture, dishware, jewelry, and paintings is hidden away in plain sight, just across the street from Schloss Charlottenburg. It provides a lovely glimpse into a time when every object was made with great care and artistic creativity—and when artists in booming creative cities like Berlin and Vienna were at the top of their game. ⊠ *Schlossstr. 1a, Charlottenburg* ☎ *030/3269-0600* ⊕ *www.broehan-museum.de* 🖃 *€8* 🕓 *Closed Mon.* Ⓜ *Richard-Wagner-Platz (U-bahn).*

C/O Berlin
Set in the renovated 1950s-era Amerika Haus building, C/O Berlin focuses on contemporary photography by established and emerging international artists. The gallery's rotating exhibitions have profiled legendary photographers such as Annie Leibovitz and Irving Penn, while its themed group shows have featured the likes of Nan Goldin, Gerhard Richter, and Weegee. ⊠ *Hardenbergstr. 22–24, Charlottenburg* ☎ *030/2844–41662* ⊕ *www.co-berlin.org* 🖃 *€10* Ⓜ *Zoologischer Garten (S-bahn and U-bahn).*

Ellington Hotel Berlin
Tucked away behind the beautiful, historic facade of a grand Bauhaus-style office building—and just around the corner from prime shopping at KaDeWe and Kurfürstendamm—this sleek, modern hotel is accentuated with modern art and is home to a stylish jazz bar. ⊠ *Nürnbergerstr. 50–55, Charlottenburg* ☎ *030/683–150* ⊕ *www.ellington-hotel.com* Ⓜ *Wittenbergplatz (U-bahn).*

Kaiser-Wilhelm-Gedächtnis-Kirche *(Kaiser Wilhelm Memorial Church)*
A dramatic reminder of World War II's destruction, the ruined bell tower is all that remains of this once massive church, which was completed in

1895 and dedicated to the emperor, Kaiser Wilhelm I. The Hohenzollern dynasty is depicted inside a gilded mosaic whose damage, like that of the building, will not be repaired. The exhibition revisits World War II's devastation throughout Europe. On the hour, the tower chimes out a melody composed by the last emperor's great-grandson, the late Prince Louis Ferdinand von Hohenzollern. In stark contrast to the old bell tower, dubbed the "Hollow Tooth" (under restoration), are the adjoining Memorial Church and Tower, designed by the noted German architect Egon Eiermann and finished in 1961. Church music and organ concerts are presented in the church regularly. ⊠ *Breitscheidpl., Charlottenburg* ⊕ *www.gedaechtni-skirche-berlin.de* ⊠ *Free* Ⓜ *Zoolo-gischer Garten (U-bahn and S-bahn).*

Kurfürstendamm

This busy thoroughfare began as a riding path in the 16th century. The elector Joachim II of Brandenburg used it to travel between his palace on the Spree River and his hunting lodge in the Grunewald. The Kurfürstendamm (Elector's Causeway) was transformed into a major route in the late 19th century, thanks to the initiative of Bismarck, Prussia's Iron Chancellor. Even in the 1920s, Ku'damm (as it's commonly known) was still relatively new and by no means elegant; its prewar fame was due mainly to its rowdy bars and dance halls, as well as to the cafés where the cultural avant-garde of Europe gathered. Almost half of its 245

GETTING HERE

Bordering Charlottenburg is one of the city's biggest attractions, the Berlin Zoo, around which cluster many of the district's shopping and dining options, as well as museums and hotels—especially along the posh shopping street, Ku'damm. Multiple U-bahn, S-bahn, and national train lines run through the Zoologischer Garten station, which is also a hub for area buses (there are no trams in West Berlin). Charlottenburg Palace, surrounded by a host of fine state art museums, can be reached by U-bahn (Richard-Wagner-Platz station).

late-19th-century buildings were completely destroyed in the 1940s, and the remaining buildings were damaged to varying degrees; what you see today is either restored or newly constructed. Although Ku'damm is still known as the best shopping street in Berlin, many of its establishments have declined in elegance and prestige over the years. Nowadays you'll want to visit just to check it off your list. ⊠ *Kurfürstendamm, Charlottenburg* Ⓜ *Kurfürstendamm (U-bahn).*

Museum Berggruen

This small modern-art museum holds works by Matisse, Klee, Giacometti, and Picasso, who is particularly well represented with more than 120 works. Heinz Berggruen (1914–2007), a businessman who left Berlin in the 1930s, amassed this fine collection of paintings and sculpture. ⊠ *Schlossstr. 1, Charlottenburg*

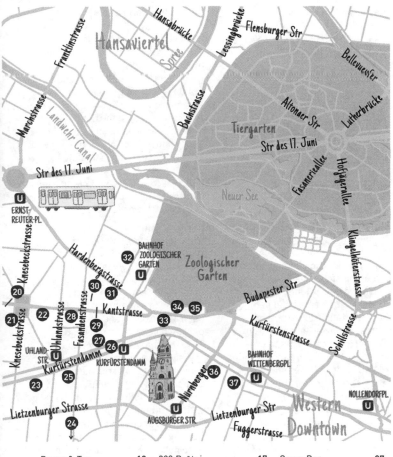

☎ 030/2664–24242 ⊕ www.smb.
museum 🎟 €10 ☉ Closed Mon.
Ⓜ Sophie-Charlotte-Platz (U-bahn),
Richard-Wagner-Platz (U-bahn).

Museum für Fotografie–Helmut Newton Stiftung (Museum of Photography–Helmut Newton Foundation)

Native son Helmut Newton
(1920–2004) pledged this collection of 1,000 photographs to Berlin
months before his unexpected
death. The man who defined fashion
photography in the 1960s through
the 1980s was an apprentice to Yva,
a Jewish fashion photographer in
Berlin in the 1930s. Newton fled
Berlin with his family in 1938, and
his mentor was killed in a concentration camp. The photographs, now
part of the state museum collection,
are shown on a rotating basis in the
huge Wilhelmine building behind
the train station Zoologischer
Garten. You'll see anything from
racy portraits of models to serene
landscapes. There are also rotating
exhibitions from other photographers, such as Mario Testino
and Jean Pigozzi. ✉ Jebensstr. 2,
Charlottenburg ☎ 030/6642–4242
⊕ www.smb.museum 🎟 €10
☉ Closed Mon. Ⓜ Zoologischer Garten
(U-bahn and S-bahn).

Olympiastadion (Olympic Stadium)

Berlin's famous sports attraction
is the 1936 Olympic Stadium, which
received a thorough modernization
in 2004. American sprinter Jesse
Owens won his stunning four gold
medals here in 1936; these days,
the local soccer team Hertha BSC is
the star of the arena. The stadium
hosted the World Cup soccer final
match in July 2006 and served as
a spectacular backdrop to the first
European Athletics Championships
in 2018. Different themed tours are
offered throughout the year; one
option is touring on your own with
an audio guide, but only a guided
tour will show you the nonpublic
areas. Tours in English are offered
less frequently, so check the website
or call ahead for the schedule.
✉ Olympischer Pl. 3, Charlottenburg
☎ 030/3068–8100 ⊕ www.olympiasta-
dion-berlin.de 🎟 €8, tours from €11
Ⓜ Olympiastadion (U-bahn).

Schloss Charlottenburg (Charlottenburg Palace)

A grand reminder of imperial days,
this showplace served as a city
residence for the Prussian rulers.
In the 18th century Frederick the
Great made a number of additions,
such as the dome and several wings
designed in the rococo style. By
1790 the complex had evolved into a
massive royal domain that could take
a whole day to explore. The **Altes
Schloss** is the main building of the
Schloss Charlottenburg complex,
with the ground-floor suites of
Friedrich I and Sophie-Charlotte.
Paintings include royal portraits by
Antoine Pesne, a noted court painter
of the 18th century. The upper floor
has the apartments of Friedrich
Wilhelm IV, a silver treasury, and
Berlin and Meissen porcelain and

can be seen on its own. The **Neuer Flügel** (New Building), where Frederick the Great once lived, was designed by Knobelsdorff, who also built Sanssouci, and houses a ballroom called the Golden Gallery and the Silver Vault with beautiful tableware. The lovely gardens include a mausoleum and the Belvedere tea house, which holds a porcelain collection. ⊠ *Spandauer Damm 20–24, Charlottenburg* ☎ *030/3319–694200* ⊕ *www.spsg.de* 🎫 *€17 Tageskarte (day card) for all buildings; gardens free* ⊙ *Closed Mon.* Ⓜ *Richard-Wagner-Platz (U-bahn).*

The Story of Berlin

You can't miss this multimedia museum—just look for the airplane wing exhibited in front. It was once part of a "Raisin bomber," a U.S. Air Force DC-3 that supplied Berlin during the Berlin Airlift in 1948 and 1949. Eight hundred years of the city's history, from the first settlers casting their fishing lines to Berliners heaving sledgehammers at the wall, are conveyed through hands-on exhibits, film footage, and multimedia devices in this unusual venue. The sound of footsteps over broken glass follows your path through the exhibit on the *Kristallnacht* pogrom, and to pass through the section on the Nazis' book-burning on Bebelplatz, you must walk over book bindings. Many original artifacts are on display, such as the stretch Volvo that served as Erich Honecker's state carriage in East Germany. The eeriest relic is the 1974 nuclear shelter, which you can visit by guided tour

WORTH A TRIP

The lush Grunewald forest, where villas peep out between the trees, is just outside Charlottenburg. You can swim in bucolic Schlachtensee Lake or visit the odd site of Teufelsberg, a man-made hill. When it comes to the strange history of Teufelsberg, it's hard to separate truth from rumor and legend. Constructed from the rubble left by World War II bombings, the hill became the site of an important U.S. listening station during the Cold War, the otherworldly ruins of which still stand today, topped with globular, mosquelike roofs. ⊕ www.berliner-teufelsberg.com

on the hour. Museum placards are also in English. ⊠ *Ku'damm Karree, Kurfürstendamm 207–208, Charlottenburg* ☎ *030/8872–0100* ⊕ *www.story-of-berlin.de* 🎫 *€12* Ⓜ *Uhlandstrasse (U-bahn).*

🛍 Shopping

Ariane

A great place to look for designer secondhand finds, this tiny shop is tucked away near West Berlin's Savignyplatz. You'll find labels like Hermès, Versace, Chanel, and Jil Sander on the racks. ⊠ *Wielandstr. 37, Charlottenburg* ☎ *030/881-7436* ⊕ *www.ariane-secondhand.de* ⊙ *Closed Sun.* Ⓜ *Savignyplatz (S-bahn).*

★ Bücherbogen

Peek under the railway tracks of Charlottenburg's Savignyplatz station and you'll find this much-loved bookstore. The large selection of books, many of them special editions or out of print, include numerous titles on art, design, and architecture, and the international offerings are extensive. ✉ *Stadtbahnbogen 593, Charlottenburg* ☎ *303/3186–9511* ⊕ *www.buecherbogen.com* ☾ *Closed Sun.* Ⓜ *Savignyplatz (S-bahn).*

★ Chelsea Farmers Club

This living-room-like space is the go-to for sophisticated menswear with a British posh edge; you'll find everything from tuxedoes to hunting jackets on their shelves. The owners manufacture their own line of quality British-style smoking jackets, and the inventory also includes top brands and small fashion accessories. There's a small bar in the back, where you can toast your latest purchase in style. ✉ *Schlüterstr. 49, Charlottenburg* ☎ *030/8872–7474* ⊕ *www.chelseafarmersclub.de* ☾ *Closed Sun.* Ⓜ *Uhlandstrasse (U-bahn), Savignyplatz (S-bahn).*

Frank Leder

Part showroom, part cabinet of curiosities, the German menswear designer has turned his Charlottenburg apartment into a bespoke shopping experience. Expect expertly tailored blazers and trousers that nod to military uniforms and traditional work wear, plus an assortment of locally produced oils and perfumes. Appointments are preferred. ✉ *Kantstr. 139, Charlottenburg* ☎ *030/6956–7548* ⊕ *www.frank-leder.com* Ⓜ *Savignyplatz (S-bahn).*

Harry Lehmann

If you want a taste—or rather, a smell—of old Berlin, head to Harry Lehmann. The shopkeeper will greet you in a white lab coat, helpfully explaining the origin and inspiration of the expertly mixed perfumes, which fill large apothecary jars along a mirrored wall. This is definitely old-school—the shop was opened in 1926. ✉ *Kantstr. 106, Charlottenburg* ☎ *030/324–3582* ⊕ *www.parfum-individual.de* ☾ *Closed Sun.* Ⓜ *Wilmersdorfer Strasse (U-bahn), Berlin-Charlottenburg (S-bahn).*

Jil Sander

The sleek, minimalist flagship store of German designer Jil Sander carries the newest collections from this iconic, understated brand, including fashions for men. ✉ *Kurfürstendamm 185, Charlottenburg* ☎ *030/886–7020* ⊕ *www.jilsander.com* ☾ *Closed Sun.* Ⓜ *Adenauerplatz (U-bahn), Savignyplatz (S-bahn).*

Kaufhaus Des Westens (KaDeWe)

Opened in 1907, classy Kaufhaus des Westens (known colloquially as KaDeWe) is one of the largest department stores in Europe, with a grand selection of upscale goods spread over seven floors. It's perhaps best known for its sixth-floor gourmet food hall, with a vast variety of international cuisine as well as wine, champagne, and beer bars. Along with fashion, home goods, and cosmetics, the store offers a wealth of services including luxury gift basket arrangements, a hair salon, currency exchange, and tailoring. ⊠ *Tauentzienstr. 21–24, Charlottenburg* ☎ *030/21210* ⊕ *www. kadewe.de* ⊘ *Closed Sun.* Ⓜ *Wittenbergplatz (U-bahn).*

Mientus

The trendsetting outfitter Mientus stocks Armani, Dolce & Gabbana, and Hugo Boss and has an in-house tailor. The Wilmersdorfer Strasse location is their flagship, carrying both women's and men's fashion, and there's also a men's-only branch at Kurfürstendamm 52. ⊠ *Wilmersdorfer Str. 73, Charlottenburg* ☎ *030/323–9077* ⊕ *www.mientus.com* ⊘ *Closed Sun.* Ⓜ *Berlin-Charlottenburg (S-bahn), Wilmersdorfer Strasse (U-bahn).*

Mykita Shop Berlin West

Handcrafted in Berlin, Mykita has been at the forefront of innovative eyewear since 2003. Luckily, their hefty price tag comes with perks like free eye exams, and your pick of designs—like frame collaborations with Maison Margiela and Bernhard Wilhelm. There is another location on Rosa-Luxemburg-Strasse in Mitte and an outpost at the Andreas Murkudis shop on Potsdamerstrasse. ⊠ *Bikini Berlin, Budapester Str. 38–50, Charlottenburg* ☎ *030/2847–4114* ⊕ *mykita.com* ⊘ *Closed Sun.* Ⓜ *Zoologischer Garten (S-bahn and U-bahn).*

★ Paper & Tea

Enter this serene shop just off Kantstrasse and you'll be stepping into a world of high-quality loose-leaf teas. The stylish store displays its teas in museumlike cases, where you can smell the wares, and there are tasting areas where expert attendants brew and explain the teas. There is also a Mitte shop on Alte Schönhauser Strasse. ⊠ *Bleibtreust. 4, Charlottenburg* ☎ *030/5557–98080* ⊕ *www.paper-andtea.com* ⊘ *Closed Sun.* Ⓜ *Savignyplatz (S-bahn).*

★ Wald Königsberger Marzipan

This third-generation artisan shop offers a taste of the old-world treat marzipan, using a family recipe that dates back to the turn of the 20th century. The vintage-style shop features candy-striped wall paper, vintage tools, and rows of handmade marzipan, all wrapped in delicate packaging. ⊠ *Pestalozzistr. 54a, Charlottenburg* ☎ *030/323–8254* ⊕ *www.wald-koenigsberger-marzipan.de* ⊘ *Closed Sun.* Ⓜ *Sophie-Charlotte-Platz (U-bahn).*

🍴 Coffee and Quick Bites

Café-Restaurant Wintergarten im Literaturhaus

$ | **Café.** Ideal for a leisurely lunch or a coffee and cake break after shopping on nearby Ku'damm, this lovely café is set in a 19th-century villa that is home to literary-related events. In warm weather, the premium tables are outside in the flowering garden; in chilly months, the glassed-in winter garden is popular with well-heeled locals. *Average main: €10* ⊠ *Fasanenstr. 23, Charlottenburg* ☎ *030/882–5414* ⊕ *www.literaturhaus-berlin.de/cafe-buchhandlung* Ⓜ *Uhlandstrasse (U-bahn).*

Schwarzes Cafe

$ | **Café.** In otherwise upscale Savignyplatz, this laid-back café is a throwback to edgier times, when artists, actors, and musicians like David Bowie and Iggy Pop frequented the area. Opened in the 1970s, the dual-level spot still attracts young, artsy types, and is especially bustling late in the evening (it stays open 24 hours most days). *Average main: €10* ⊠ *Kantstr. 148, Charlottenburg* ☎ *030/313–8038* ⊕ *www.schwarzescafe-berlin.de* ▭ *No credit cards* Ⓜ *Savignyplatz (S-bahn), Uhlandstrasse (U-bahn).*

🍴 Dining

The Butcher Berlin

$ | **Burger.** Marked by an enormous cow sculpture in the window, this trendy burger joint near Savignyplatz grills up one of the best burgers in the city. Inventive toppings include baba ganoush or fried egg and hollandaise sauce (the Benedict), but the juicy Aberdeen Angus patties stand on their own with just pickles and onions. **Known for:** excellent burgers; trendy industrial interior; fashionable local crowd. *Average main: €10* ⊠ *Kantstr. 144, Charlottenburg* ☎ *030/3230–15673* ⊕ *the-butcher. com/kantstrasse/menu* Ⓜ *Savignyplatz (S-bahn).*

★ 893 Ryotei

$$ | **Japanese.** Chic foodies frequent this sleek Japanese-Peruvian fusion restaurant from renowned Berlin restaurateur Duc Ngo, which sits behind a graffiti-covered door. The cocktails are top-notch, the sushi and sashimi some of the freshest in town, and the food is wonderfully prepared. **Known for:** tiradito and ceviche (Peruvian marinated raw fish); sashimi taquitos (raw fish rolled into tortillas); enticing cocktail, sake, and wine list. *Average main: €20* ⊠ *Kantstr. 135, Charlottenburg* ☎ *030/9170–3121* ⊕ *893ryotei.de* ⊙ *Closed Sun. and Mon. No lunch* Ⓜ *Savignyplatz (S-bahn).*

Hot Spot

$$ | **Chinese.** In a city that's unfortunately full of mediocre pseudo-Asian restaurants that serve bland versions of curries, noodles, and rice dishes, Hot Spot stands out for its daring and authenticity. The menu features recipes from the provinces of Sichuan, Jiangsu, and Shanghai, and the freshest ingredients are guaranteed; *mala* dishes (numbing and spicy) are a specialty here, and the excellent selection of German wines—particularly Riesling—goes well with the spicy food. **Known for:** amazing wine list, unusual to find in an Asian restaurant; much spicier food than normal for Berlin; quick, friendly service. *Average main: €16* ⊠ *Eisenzahnstr. 66, Charlottenburg* ☎ *030/8900–6878* ⊕ *www.restaurant-hotspot.de* Ⓜ *Adenauerplatz (U-bahn).*

★ Kushinoya

$$$ | **Japanese.** This eatery makes culinary art from the Japanese snack, *kushiage,* breaded and fried skewers of meat, fish, and vegetables, accompanied by an array of colorful dipping sauces. The Kushinoya team uses a special cooking process to

deep-fry the doughy exteriors of the skewered ingredients without letting them get oily, and offers at least 30 different skewers daily, using fresh, local ingredients. **Known for.** kushiage (Japanese breaded, fried skewers of meat, seafood, and veggies); interesting sake selection; upscale setting. *Average main: €25 ⊠ Bleibtreustr. 6, Charlottenburg ☎ 030/3180–9897 ⊕ www.kushinoya. de ⊗ Closed Mon.* Ⓜ *Savignyplatz (S-bahn).*

Lubitsch
$$ | German. Named after the famous Berlin film director Ernst Lubitsch, this sophisticated restaurant attracts an equally refined crowd with its hearty local fare (and lighter international options) that's hard to find these days. Dishes like *Königsberger Klopse* (German meatballs in a creamy caper sauce), fried calf's liver, and Wiener schnitzel are examples of the home-style German cooking, plus there are frequently rotating seasonal specials, and breakfast on weekends. **Known for:** well-prepared classic German dishes; elegant old-fashioned atmosphere; good location off of lively Savignyplatz. *Average main: €20 ⊠ Bleibtreustr. 47, Charlottenburg ☎ 030/882–3756 ⊕ www.restaurant-lubitsch.de* Ⓜ *Savignyplatz (S-bahn).*

Ottenthal
$$$ | Austrian. This intimate restaurant with white tablecloths is owned by Austrians from the small village of Ottenthal and serves as an homage to their country, with interesting and delicious combinations using many organic ingredients. It's a good option for a leisurely meal before catching a show at Theater des Westens around the corner. **Known for:** huge Wiener schnitzel that extends past the plate's rim; homemade pasta and strudel; excellent Austrian wine list. *Average main: €25 ⊠ Kantstr. 153, Charlottenburg ☎ 030/313–3162 ⊕ www.ottenthal.com ⊗ No lunch* Ⓜ *Zoologischer Garten (U-bahn and S-bahn).*

★ Thai Park
$ | Thai. Every weekend from spring to autumn, in decent weather, the main lawn at Preussenpark in Wilmersdorf fills up with Southeast Asian families (mostly Thai, but some Vietnamese, Malaysian, and Indonesian) who set up cooking equipment and prepare authentic delicacies like beef noodle soup, skewered fried meat, and spicy green-papaya salad. Come with a picnic blanket, cash, and a lot of napkins, and stay for the afternoon. *Average main: €5 ⊠ Preussenpark, Brandenburgische Str., Charlottenburg ⊕ www.thaipark. de ⊟ No credit cards ⊗ Runs Apr.– Nov.* Ⓜ *Fehrbelliner Platz (U-bahn).*

⏱ Bars and Nightlife

A-Trane
A-Trane in West Berlin has hosted countless greats throughout the years, including Herbie Hancock and Wynton Marsalis. Numerous free events make it a good place to see jazz on a budget. ⊠ *Bleibtreustr. 1, Charlottenburg ☎ 030/313–2550 ⊕ www.a-trane.de* Ⓜ *Savignyplatz (S-bahn).*

Grace Bar

Fashionable locals flock to this swanky cocktail bar in the Hotel Zoo—both to its ground-floor, speakeasy-style space and in warmer weather, to the rooftop terrace. The drinks list leans toward the light and fruity, with signature cocktails that artfully fuse South American and Asian flavors. Dress to impress, especially on busy Friday and Saturday nights, when DJs spin house music. ⊠ *Kurfürstendamm 25, Charlottenburg* ☎ *030/8843–7750* ⊕ *www.hotelzoo.de* Ⓜ *Kurfürstendamm (U-bahn).*

★ Monkey Bar

On the rooftop of the 25hours Hotel Bikini Berlin, this often-packed watering hole affords scenic views over the Berlin Zoo and Tiergarten Park and an impressive range of well-crafted cocktails. Expect a crowd at the ground-floor entrance (no matter what day of the week)—this place is worth the wait. ⊠ *Budapester Str. 40, Charlottenburg* ☎ *030/1202–21210* ⊕ *www.25hourshotels.com* Ⓜ *Zoologischer Garten (U-bahn and S-bahn).*

Quasimodo

To get to Quasimodo, the most established and popular jazz venue in the city, you'll need to descend a small staircase to the basement of the Theater des Westens. Despite its college-town pub feel, the club has hosted many Berlin and international greats. Seats are few, but there's plenty of standing room in the front. ⊠ *Kantstr. 12a, Charlottenburg* ☎ *030/3180–4560* ⊕ *quasimodo.de* Ⓜ *Zoologischer Garten (S-bahn and U-bahn).*

Rum Trader

This cocktail bar, which bills itself as the oldest in Berlin (it opened in 1975), may have the right to be a bit snooty: there is only room for around 30 people, and if they're full you'll be waiting outside in the cold. But inside, the bar is classic and cozy, with built-in shelves for spirits, and every patron has a front-row seat to the bartenders' show. The drinks, too, are worth the wait—just don't let the bartender catch you showing ignorance about alcohol or, God forbid, treating your cocktail as anything less than a work of art. ⊠ *Fasanenstr. 40, Wilmersdorf* ☎ *030/881–1428.*

🎭 Performing Arts

Deutsche Oper Berlin

Of the many composers represented in the repertoire of Deutsche Oper Berlin, Verdi and Wagner are the most frequently presented. ⊠ *Bismarckstr. 35, Charlottenburg* ☎ *030/343–8401, 030/343–84343 tickets* ⊕ *www.deutscheoperberlin.de* Ⓜ *Deutsche Oper (U-bahn).*

Theater des Westens

The late-19th-century Theater des Westens, one of Germany's oldest musical theaters, features international musicals such as *Ghost* and *Dance of the Vampires.* ⊠ *Kantstr. 12, Charlottenburg* ☎ *030/01805–4444* ⊕ *www.stage-entertainment.de* Ⓜ *Berlin Zoologischer Garten (S-bahn and U-bahn).*

Potsdam ◆ BERLIN

BRANDENBURG

Sightseeing ★★★★★ | Shopping ★☆☆☆☆ | Dining ★★★☆☆ | Nightlife ★★☆☆☆

A trip to Berlin wouldn't be complete without paying a visit to Potsdam, known for its 18th-century baroque architecture, especially Sanssouci Park, the former residence of the Prussian royals. The town center offers historical landmarks, charming boutiques, and café-lined cobblestone streets. The bonus is that it's only a half-hour trip from Berlin.—*by Robin Raven*

Potsdam is the state capital of Brandenburg (the region surrounding Berlin), and although it was severely damaged by bombing during World War II, much of the city has been restored to its former glory and still retains the imperial character it accrued during the many years it served as a royal residence and garrison quarters. The city center has stately Prussian architecture as well as a charming Dutch quarter, while Sanssouci Park, the city's main tourist attraction and sometimes called the Versailles of Potsdam, is a short bus ride away. Just north of Sanssouci Park is Neuer Garten, where the Schloss Cecilienhof was the site of the Potsdam Conference in 1945. Both are home to manicured gardens, stunning architecture, lakes and fountains, and several palaces, galleries, and former royal buildings. An enthusiastic history buff could happily spend several days exploring the palaces and landmarks of Sanssouci Park and Neuer Garten, but considering that most of the palace interiors are quite similar, and that the city is quite compact and well connected with public transport, one day is generally sufficient for a visit.

Potsdam is on the Havel River, and its small harbor area showing off modern and vintage-style boats is a casting-off point for boat tours around the area or back to Berlin.

The main attraction for Potsdam visitors is the sprawling Sanssouci Park, a World Heritage site since 1990. The former summer residence of the Prussian royals, the park is home to numerous palaces, landscaped gardens, and eye-catching architecture. Your best bet is to hop on Bus 695 or X15, which stops right outside the train station and will get you to the park in 10 minutes. Otherwise it's about a half-hour walk. Note that if you want to see many of the palaces inside the park, your best bet is to buy a sanssouci+ ticket, which includes timed entry to Sanssouci Palace and anytime-entry to the others; buy it in advance online or at any of the palaces or visitor centers on-site.

Most visitors to Potsdam come for the castles, but the town itself is picturesque, elegant, and compact enough to be explored in an hour or two. It contains both Alter Markt (Old Market) and Neuer Markt (New Market) squares, which show off stately Prussian architecture, while the Holländisches Viertel (Dutch Quarter) is home to a collection of redbrick, gable-roofed buildings, many of which now house popular restaurants, boutiques, and cafés. Friedrich-Ebert-Strasse, the town's main thoroughfare, is full of coffee shops and restaurants, and Brandenburger Strasse, the pedestrian walking street, often has outdoor café seating and street musicians. Leafy Hegelallee, to the north, with its tree-lined central pedestrian strip, is where you will find Potsdam's historic gates. Potsdam's city center is easily reached by foot or tram from the main train station.

Just north of the city center, the Neuer Garten (New Garden) is along the west shore of the Heiliger See (Holy Lake), with beautiful views. The park is home to the Marmorpalais (Marble Palace) and Schloss Cecilienhof, the last palace built by the Prussian Hohenzollern family. To get here from the Potsdam train station, take Tram 92 and then walk 10–15 minutes; another option is to take a taxi.

◉ Sights

Alter Markt *(Old Market Square)*
The hub of Potsdam's historical center was home to the city's baroque palace for three centuries. The area was heavily damaged by Allied bombing in World War II and then further destroyed by the East German regime in 1960. After reunification, Potsdam decided to rebuild its palace, and the re-created struc-

GETTING HERE

Potsdam is 20 km (12 miles) southwest of Berlin's center and a half-hour journey by car or bus. From Zoo Station to Potsdam's main train station, the regional train RE 1 takes 17 minutes, and the S7 line of the S-bahn takes about 30 minutes; use an ABC zone ticket for either service. City traffic can be heavy, so a train journey is recommended.

ture, with a combination of modern and historic elements, has housed the state parliament since 2013. Thanks to private donors, a magnificent replica of the Fortunaportal, or Fortune's Gate, now stands proudly at the center of the square. A gilded figure of Atlas tops the tower of the **Altes Rathaus** (Old City Hall), built in 1755 in the model of an Italian palazzo, its dome meant to mimic the Pantheon's in Rome. The **Potsdam Museum** contains a large collection of paintings, photographs, and historical objects. Karl Friedrich Schinkel designed the Alter Markt's domed **Nikolaikirche** (St. Nicholas Church), which was also heavily damaged in the war and only reopened in 1981 after extensive renovations. ⊠*Alter Markt, Potsdam.*

Belvedere auf dem Pfingstberg
Commissioned by King Friedrich Wilhelm IV, the Belvedere on Pfingstberg was built in the Italian Renaissance style with grand staircases, colonnades, and perfect symmetry. It served as a pleasure palace and lofty observation platform for the royals, and the

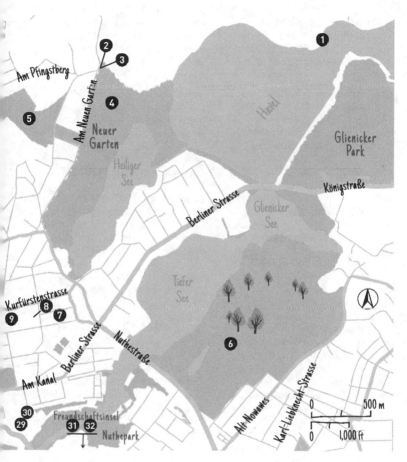

towers still offer one of the best views of Potsdam. ✉ *Am Pfingstberg, Potsdam* ☎ *0331/2005–7930* ⊕ *www. pfingstberg.de* 💶 *€5* 🕑 *Closed weekdays Nov.–Mar.*

Brandenburger Tor, Jägertor, and Nauener Tor

These gates (translated as the Brandenburg Gate, the Hunter's Gate, and the Nauen Gate) are three of the original seven gates that were incorporated into the old city walls. They were mostly ornamental, erected by noblemen to show off their prowess and accomplishments, and were meant to direct the eye along various axes from the center of the city to grand boulevards radiating outwards.
If you follow the promenade that traces the now-demolished city walls, you can see all three of these gates in a 10-minute walk.
The **Brandenburger Tor** sits at one edge of Luisenplatz, between the pedestrian streets of the old town and an entrance to Sanssouci Park. Commissioned by Frederick the Great to celebrate his victory in the Seven Years' War, it was built by Karl von Gontard as a Roman triumphal arch. The small **Jägertor** is really nothing more than a simple archway, crowned by a statue of a deer set upon by hunting dogs. Its diminutive size, however, belies its historical importance: it's the only gate in Potsdam still in its original form instead of a restored version. The sandstone **Nauener Tor**, which sits at the northern edge of the bustling, shop-filled main corridor Friedrich-Ebert-Strasse, is the

oldest example of a neo-Gothic structure in continental Europe. It looks something like a mini-castle with its twin turrets. ✉ *Potsdam* ⊕ *www.potsdam.de*.

Heilandskirche Sacrow

You'd be forgiven for wondering if you'd been transported to Italy when you first glimpse this dreamy lakeside church, complete with a campanile (bell tower) and mosaic-adorned colonnade, from across the Havel Lake or through the Sacrower Schlosspark near Potsdam.
Actually, the church suffered a grim fate for many years, trapped in the no-man's-land of the outer Berlin Wall. From 1961 to 1989, the East German government closed the church, fearing that it would serve as a hiding place for those trying to flee. Now it is restored and again in use, and makes the perfect endpoint to a scenic walk from the lakeside village of Kladow. To reach it, take the S75 train from Central Berlin to S-bahnhof Heerstrasse, then the X34 Bus to Alt-Kladow, then follow Sakrower Landstrasse until it turns into Kladower Strasse and ends at Schloss Sacrow. The path out to the water will take you to the church. ✉ *Fährstr., Potsdam* ☎ *0331/505–2144* ⊕ *www.heilandskirche-sacrow.de*.

Holländisches Viertel

The center of the small Holländisches Viertel—the Dutch Quarter—is an easy walk north along Friedrich-Ebert-Strasse to Mittelstrasse. Friedrich Wilhelm I built the settlement in the 1730s to entice Dutch artisans who would be able to support the city's rapid growth. The 134 gabled, mansard-roof brick houses make up the largest Dutch housing development outside of the Netherlands today. Antiques shops, boutiques, and restaurants fill the buildings now, and the area is one of Potsdam's most visited. ⊠ *Potsdam*.

Neuer Markt *(New Market Square)* Neuer Markt (New Market) square has baroque-style architecture similar to that of the Alter Markt square and a handful of the city's best-preserved buildings, some of which date back to the 18th century. ⊠ *Neuer Markt, Potsdam*.

★ **Neues Palais** *(New Palace)* A larger and grander palace than Sanssouci, the Neues Palace stands at the end of the long avenue that runs through Sanssouci Park. It was built after the Seven Years' War (1756–63). Impressive interiors include the Grotto Hall with walls and columns set with shells, coral, and other aquatic decorations. The royals' upper apartments have paintings by 17th-century Italian masters. You can tour the palace yourself, with an audio guide, from April through October; the rest of the year you must be accompanied by a tour guide. All visits are at scheduled times when you buy a ticket. ⊠ *Sanssouci Park, Potsdam* ☎ *0331/969–4200* ⊕ *www.spsg.de* 🎫 *€8* ⊗ *Closed Tues*.

Park Babelsberg Less well known than the gleaming Sanssouci but still impressive, the Schloss Babelsberg was once the summer residence of Wilhelm I. The expansive park surrounding it has acres and acres of charm, with expansive views, a waterfront promenade, and plenty of historical buildings. Although the castle itself is currently under extensive renovation, there's still plenty to explore, such as the Dampfmaschinenhaus, a 19th-century steam-engine building right on the water, or the Kleines Schloss, which literally translates as "small castle" and today houses an elegant, wood-paneled café. Climb the Flatowturm (Flatow Tower) for a 360-degree view of the surrounding parkland and waterways, and the city of Potsdam in the distance. The tower frequently showcases small historical exhibitions, like a recent one about park landscaping in Germany through the ages, detailing how Park Babelsberg has been restored to its former glory after the fall of the Berlin Wall. ⊠ *Schlosspark Babelsberg 10, Potsdam* ☎ *0331/969–4200* ⊕ *www.spsg.de* Ⓜ *Wannsee (S-bahn) and Schloss Babelsberg (Bus)*.

Potsdam Filmmuseum Inside this beautiful baroque building, originally the Marstall or Prussian royal stables, film buffs can look into the history of film production in the area—many early silent films, including Fritz Lang's *Metropolis*, were made in the town of Babelsberg, right next to Potsdam, and modern-day filmmakers continue to use the studios. A permanent exhibition called "Traumfabrik" ("The

Dream Factory") details 100 years of filmmaking in Babelsberg. The cinema screens contemporary and historic films, and includes an old film organ, which is still used today to provide music and sound effects alongside silent film screenings. ✉ *Breitestr. 1A, Potsdam* ☎ *0331/271–810* ⊕ *www.filmmuseum-potsdam.de* 🎫 *Permanent exhibition €5, temporary exhibitions €3.*

Schloss Cecilienhof (Cecilienhof Palace)

Resembling a rambling Tudor manor house, Schloss Cecilienhof was built for Crown Prince Wilhelm in 1913, on what was then the newly laid-out stretch of park called the Neuer Garten. It was here, in the last palace built by the Hohenzollerns, that the leaders of the allied forces—Stalin, Truman, and Churchill (later Attlee)—hammered out the fate of postwar Germany at the 1945 Potsdam Conference. ✉ *Im Neuen Garten 11, Potsdam* ☎ *0331/969–4200* ⊕ *www.spsg.de* 🎫 *From €8.*

Schloss Charlottenhof

After Frederick the Great died in 1786, the ambitious Sanssouci building program ground to a halt, and the park fell into neglect. It was 50 years before another Prussian king, Friedrich Wilhelm IV, restored Sanssouci's earlier glory, engaging the great Berlin architect Karl Friedrich Schinkel to build the small **Schloss Charlottenhof** for the crown prince. Schinkel's demure interiors are preserved, and the most fanciful room is the bedroom, decorated like a Roman tent, with walls and ceiling draped in striped canvas. Friedrich Wilhelm IV also commissioned the **Römische Bäder** (Roman Baths), about a five-minute walk north of Schloss Charlottenhof. It was also designed by Schinkel, and built between 1829 and 1840. Like many other structures in Potsdam, this one is more romantic than authentic. Half Italian villa, half Greek temple, it is nevertheless a charming addition to the park. ✉ *Geschwister-Scholl-Str. 34a, Potsdam* ☎ *0331/969–4200* ⊕ *www.spsg.de* 🎫 *Schloss Charlottenhof €6 with guided tour; Roman Baths €5; combination ticket €8* ⏲ *Closed Nov.–Apr., and Mon. May–Oct.*

★ Schloss Sanssouci

Prussia's most famous king, Friedrich II—Frederick the Great—spent more time at his summer residence, **Schloss Sanssouci,** than in the capital of Berlin. Executed according to Frederick's impeccable French-influenced taste, the palace, which lies on the northeastern edge of Sanssouci Park, was built between 1745 and 1747. It is extravagantly rococo, with scarcely a patch of wall left unadorned. Visits to the palace are only allowed at fixed times scheduled when tickets are purchased. During peak tourist months, timed tickets can sell out before noon, so book online in advance.

From Schloss Sanssouci, you can wander down the extravagant terraced

gardens, filled with climbing grapevines, trellises, and fountains to reach the Italianate **Friedenskirche,** or "Peace Church," which was completed in 1854, and houses a 13th-century Byzantine mosaic taken from an island near Venice. ⊠ *Park Sanssouci, Potsdam* ☎ *0331/969–4200* ⊕ *www. spsg.de* ⌖ *Schloss Sanssouci €12; Friedenskirche free* ⊙ *Schloss Sanssouci closed Mon. Friedenskirche closed weekdays Nov.–mid-Mar.*

☕ Coffee and Quick Bites

Café Guam

$ | Café. Tucked into a small street of antiques shops and boutiques in the Dutch Quarter, Café Guam is a charming bakeshop that offers visitors a taste of German-style cheesecake. The daily selection includes 6 to 10 different varieties, which rotate among 30 different flavors, including poppy seed, marbled chocolate, and caramelized almond. *Average main: €7* ⊠ *Mittelstr. 38, Potsdam* ⊕ *www.cafe-guam.de* ⊟ *No credit cards.*

Café Heider

$ | European. Just across from the Nauener Tor, Café Heider has been serving coffee in this Viennese-style café since 1878. In warmer weather, the outdoor seating has views of the gate; the indoor dining room has large bay windows and plush seating. *Average main: €13* ⊠ *Friedrich-Ebert-Str. 29, Potsdam* ☎ *0331/270–5596* ⊕ *www.cafeheider. de* ⊟ *No credit cards.*

🍴 Dining

Assaggi

$$$ | Italian. Situated on the Luisenplatz, Assaggi offers authentic Italian dishes with plenty of seafood and vegetarian options. The ambience is fun and upbeat at this spacious, modern eatery with open lighting and a black-and-white checkered floor. **Known for:** carpaccio; vongole pasta; steak. *Average main: €20* ⊠ *Luisenpl. 3, Potsdam* ☎ *0331/2879–5452* ⊕ *www. assaggi-potsdam.de.*

Brasserie zu Gutenberg

$$ | Contemporary. The Brasserie zu Gutenberg is an authentic brasserie in the heart of the city center. The eatery has a clean, open look with plenty of natural light from its many windows, and the focus here is on fresh German-French cuisine that includes pork schnitzel "Wiener Art," tarte flambé, and crêpes. **Known for:** filet mignon; steaks cooked on a lava-stone grill; fine selection of both French and German wines. *Average* *main: €20* ⊠ *Jägerstr. 10, Potsdam* ☏ *0331/7403–6878* ⊕ *www.brasserie-zu-gutenberg.de.*

Der Butt

$$$ | Seafood. Potsdam is surrounded by lakes and rivers so the fish served here is almost always local—try the rainbow trout or the eel, fresh from the Havel River; the house beer is brewed in Potsdam. It's just a block from the busy pedestrian shopping area, and has a casual, friendly atmosphere that makes this an excellent spot for a light meal. **Known for:** fresh fish from the Havel; sustainable seafood; local wines and beers. *Average main: €21* ⊠ *Gutenbergstr. 25, Potsdam* ☏ *0331/200–6066* ⊕ *www.der-butt.de.*

Maison Charlotte

$$ | Bistro. This Dutch Quarter restaurant captures the essence of old-world France with its rustic decor and bistro classics, including Breton-style fish soup and coq au vin. The small outdoor area is the perfect spot to people-watch and enjoy a glass of wine on a sunny afternoon. *Average main: €20* ⊠ *Mittelstr. 20, Potsdam* ☏ *0331/280–5450* ⊕ *www.maison-charlotte.de* ▭ *No credit cards.*

Meierei Brauhaus

$ | Burger. Situated next to the Cecilienhof landing on the banks of the Jungfernsee River, the historical Meierei Brauhaus is an inviting brewpub with a food menu that's as revered as its drink one. Don't miss the beautiful views from the terrace in warm weather.

Known for: veggie burgers; bratwurst; local beer. *Average main: €10* ⊠ *Im Neuen Garten 10, Potsdam* ☏ *0331/704–3211* ⊕ *www.meierei-potsdam.de* ☾ *Closed Mon.*

Meierei im Neuen Garten

$ | German. At the tip of the Neuer Garten, Meierei brewery serves classic German beer and local cuisine, with hearty dishes like schnitzel and roast pork knuckle. The outdoor terrace has great views of the lake and boats during the warm weather; the indoor tavern seating has rustic charm. *Average main: €5* ⊠ *Im Neuen Garten 10, Potsdam* ☏ *0331/704–3211* ⊕ *www.meierei-potsdam.de* ▭ *No credit cards* ☾ *Closed Mon.*

Old Town Hanoi

$ | Vietnamese. Old Town Hanoi is a Vietnamese restaurant with a casual atmosphere that serves up tofu and rice dishes alongside fresh sushi. The upbeat, efficient staff serves up family-style platters and multiple-course dinners all day. **Known for:** soups; sushi; bun bo nam bo (Vietnamese beef noodle salad). *Average main: €8* ⊠ *Friedrich-Ebert-Str. 92, Potsdam* ☏ *0331/8170–9640* ⊕ *www.old-town-hanoi.de.*

Peter Pane

$ | American. The fun, whimsical Peter Pane offers comfort food with a twist with a huge selection of burgers and creative toppings. Indoor picnic-style tables contribute to the casual vibe at Peter Pane, and guests flock to the eatery to enjoy combo meals from its large menu. **Known for:** fried avocados;

sweet-potato fries; vegan burgers. *Average main: €9 ⊠ Humboldtstr. 1, Potsdam ☎ 0331/5817–7980 ⊕ www.peterpane.de.*

Restaurant & Café Drachenhaus
$$ | German. Drachenhaus, which translates to Dragon House, is named after the dragon imagery on its roof and is housed in a Chinese-style palace in Sanssouci Park. Enjoy the opulent dining room with a historic ambience or dine in one of the three sun terraces during the warmer months to enjoy fresh, creative German seasonal cuisine. **Known for:** locally sourced fish; delectable baked goods from the in-house pastry shop; unbelievable setting in Sanssouci Park. *Average main: €18 ⊠ Maulbeerallee 4, Potsdam ⊕ www.drachenhaus-potsdam.de.*

Restaurant Fiore
$$$ | Modern European. For a taste of Potsdam's finer side, enjoy a meal at Hotel am Jägertor's restaurant. Chef Rene Tinz highlights regional products and local recipes in creative dishes like rabbit liver with wasabi foam or a deconstructed Waldorf salad with apple gel and walnut oil. *Average main: €23 ⊠ Hotel am Jägertor, Hegelallee 11, Potsdam ☎ 0331/201–1100 ⊕ www.hotel-am-jaegertor.de ▭ No credit cards.*

Restaurant Juliette
$$$$ | French. Potsdam is proud of its past French influences, and the highly praised French food at this intimate restaurant on the edge of the Dutch Quarter is served in a lovely space, with brick walls and a fireplace. Restaurant Juliette is affiliated with four other more casual French restaurants in Potsdam, including a creperie and a café. **Known for:** three- to six-course tasting menus, plus à la carte choices; starter plate of seasonal foie-gras preparations; more than 120 wines from Germany and France. *Average main: €26 ⊠ Jägerstr. 39, Potsdam ☎ 0331/270–1791 ⊕ www.restaurant-juliette.de ⊘ Closed Mon. and Tues.*

Rosenberg
$$ | Vegetarian. This cozy, comfortable vegan café will appeal to all with hearty soups and pasta dishes. With fresh, seasonal ingredients, it's easy to chow down, but diners should save room for the decadent desserts and high-quality coffee with plant-based milk. **Known for:** tasty cakes; seasonal brunch menu; superior sandwiches. *Average main: €12 ⊠ Dortustr. 15, Potsdam ☎ 0151/1605–0600 ⊕ www.rosenberg-potsdam.de ⊘ Closed Sun.*

Speckers Landhaus
$$$ | German. This restored Tudor-style cottage is a 10-minute walk from the town center, and well worth a visit for its charming historic architecture and relaxing, farmhouse-style dining room. The menu is unfailingly local, emphasizing produce like white asparagus in spring and pumpkin in fall. **Known for:** monthly changing dishes with regional ingredients; homemade pastas, local game, and German specialties; three spacious

guest rooms decorated in a simple, country-home style. *Average main: €25* ⊠ *Jägerallee 13, Potsdam* ☎ *0331/280–4311* ⊕ *www.speckers.de* ☉ *Closed Sun. and Mon. No lunch.*

Wiener Restaurant and Café
$$$ | Austrian. Diners get a taste of Vienna in Potsdam at the Wiener Restaurant and Café. Just a short distance from Sanssouci Park, the café has a nice garden area for warmer weather, and its beloved German and Austrian dishes include *soljanka* soup with meat and cabbage and sauerbraten. **Known for:** Wiener schnitzel; weekend brunches; seasonal German ingredients. *Average main: €20* ⊠ *Luisenpl. 4, Potsdam* ☎ *0331/6014–9904* ⊕ *wiener-potsdam.de.*

🍸 Bars and Nightlife

BAR-O-meter
This small vaulted cellar lounge, whose comprehensive cocktail list offers more than 180 classics and house creations, is much loved by both locals and visitors. ⊠ *Gutenbergerstr. 103, Potsdam* ☎ *0331/270–2880.*

Kneipe Hafthorn
$$ | American. With seasonal drink and food specials made with the freshest ingredients, Kneipe Hafthorn is a pub with comfort food and refreshing beers. The candlelight, metal lamps, and simple tables set a fun scene indoors; picnic-style tables and benches offer outdoor seating in the warmer months. **Known for:** burgers,

including cheeseburgers, veggie burgers, and chicken burgers; vibrant local vibe; outdoor dining. *Average main:* ⊠ *Friedrich-Ebert-Str. 90, Potsdam* ☎ *0331/280–0820.*

🛍 Shopping

P&B Books
P&B Books is a book-lover's dream with an eclectic and large selection of books, blank journals, and magazines. Discover local authors with books in both English and German. ⊠ *Press & Books, Station Potsdam, Babelsberger Str. 16, Potsdam* ☎ *0331/233–7841.*

Waldstadt-Center
You're likely to find all the basics you need at the Waldstadt-Center. Situated in Potsdam's eponymous district, this shopping center has so many small shops to explore that you could easily spend an afternoon here. There's also a large supermarket where you can get fresh, seasonal fruits and vegetables or dessert after dining in one of the center's bistros. ⊠ *Am Moosfenn 1, Potsdam* ☉ *Closed Sun.*

Writers Heaven
Selling more than just paint, Writers Heaven is an art supply shop that sells artwork based on graffiti, design, and textiles. The friendly, attentive staff members can help customers design their own T-shirts for a truly one-of-a-kind souvenir. ⊠ *Brandenburger Str. 4, Potsdam* ☎ *0176/5635-8331* ⊕ *www.writers-heaven.de* ☉ *Closed Sun.*

INDEX

Photo Credits

Chapter 3: Mitte North of the Spree River: canadastock/Shutterstock (67). **Chapter 6:** Neukölln and Alt-Treptow: Dagmar Schwelle/visitBerlin (124). **Chapter 7:** Kreuzberg: Julien Lanoo (139). **Chapter 9:** Tiergarten and Potsdamer Strasse: Mariia Golovianko/Shutterstock (159).

NOTES

NOTES

NOTES

NOTES

NOTES

NOTES

NOTES

NOTES

NOTES

NOTES

NOTES

Fodor's INSIDE BERLIN

Editorial: Douglas Stallings, *Editorial Director;* Margaret Kelly, Jacinta O'Halloran, Amanda Sadlowski, *Senior Editors;* Kayla Becker, Alexis Kelly, Teddy Minford, Rachael Roth, *Editors;* Jeremy Tarr, *Fodors. com Editorial Director;* Rachael Levitt, *Fodors.com Managing Editor*

Design: Tina Malaney, *Design and Production Director;* Jessica Gonzalez, *Graphic Designer;* Mariana Tabares, *Design & Production Intern*

Production: Jennifer DePrima, *Editorial Production Manager;* Carrie Parker, *Senior Production Editor;* Elyse Rozelle, *Production Editor;* Jackson Pranica, *Editorial Production Assistant*

Maps: Rebecca Baer, *Senior Map Editor;* Mark Stroud (Moon Street Cartography) *Cartographer*

Photography: Jill Krueger, *Director of Photo;* Namrata Aggarwal, Ashok Kumar, Carl Yu, *Photo Editors;* Rebecca Rimmer, *Photo Intern*

Business & Operations: Chuck Hoover, *Chief Marketing Officer;* Robert Ames, *General Manager;* Stephen Horowitz, *Director of Business Development and Revenue Operations;* Tara McCrillis, *Director of Publishing Operations*

Public Relations and Marketing: Joe Ewaskiw, *Senior Director Communications & Public Relations;* Esther Su, *Senior Marketing Manager;* Ryan Garcia, Thomas Talarico, Miranda Villalobos, *Marketing Specialists*

Technology: Jon Atkinson, *Director of Technology;* Rudresh Teotia, *Lead Developer;* Jacob Ashpis, *Content Operations Manager*

Illustrator: Kathryn Holeman

Writers: Jennifer Ceaser, Adam Groffman, Liz Humphreys, Giulia Pines, Robin Raven

Editor: Teddy Minford

Production Editor: Jennifer DePrima

Designers: Tina Malaney, Chie Ushio

1st Edition
ISBN 978-1-64097-148-6
ISSN 2379-8076
Library of Congress Control Number 2018914622

SPECIAL SALES

This book is available at special discounts for bulk purchases for sales promotions or premiums. For more information, e-mail SpecialMarkets@fodors.com.

PRINTED IN THE UNITED STATES OF AMERICA

10 9 8 7 6 5 4 3 2 1

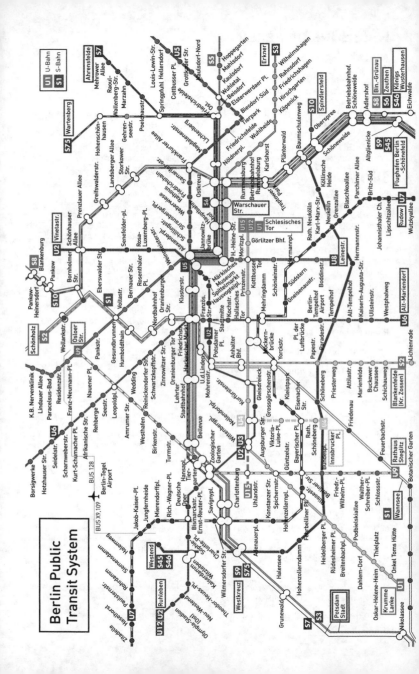

RESOURCES

Berlin has an integrated network of subway (U-bahn), suburban (S-bahn) train lines, buses, ferries, and trams (almost exclusively in eastern Berlin) divided into three zones. Zone A covers central Berlin, B includes the suburbs, and C extends into Brandenburg. Most visitor destinations are in the broad reach of the fare zones A and B, which can be covered with a €2.80 ticket (valid for two hours). The €1.70 Kurzstrecke tickets are used for trips up to three train and subway stops. A day ticket costs €7.00 in zones AB and €7.70 for ABC. The Berlin Welcome Card includes unlimited public travel. Make sure to validate your ticket in the small yellow or red box on the platform—ticket inspectors may ask to see your ticket. Being caught without a ticket will get you a €40 fine. Berlin's transit authority BVG ([web]www.bvg. de) has up-to- date information and a "Journey Planner" function in English. The free "Fahrinfo Mobil" app can also help plan your journey. Note that ticket agents and machines only take cash.

For cyclists, designated bike lanes and relatively flat topography make Berlin a pleasure to explore on two wheels. The same traffic laws apply to bicyclists as motorists, and police have been known to give out tickets.

⊕ www.berlin-welcomecard.de/en
⊕ www.visitberlin.de/en

ABOUT OUR WRITERS & ILLUSTRATOR

Jennifer Ceaser has been a free-lance writer and editor for 20 years. A former New Yorker and editor at the *New York Post*, Jennifer now splits her time between Germany and Spain. She regularly contributes to *Condé Nast Traveler*, *AFAR*, *New York Magazine*, *Evening Standard UK*, *Time Out*, and a number of other U.S. and U.K. publications. She updated the Prenzlauer Berg and Charlottenburg chapters.

Adam Groffman is an award-winning writer, marketer, and travel blogger based between Berlin and NYC. He covers city trips around the world, expat life, LGBT issues, festivals, and nightlife. His writing has been featured in *National Geographic Traveler*, *The Guardian*, *AFAR*, *Condé Nast Traveler*, and countless online publications including his own travel blog, *Travels of Adam*. Follow him on social media @travelsofadam for embarrassing, in-the-moment travel stories. He updated the Kreuzberg, Friedrichshain, and Neukölln chapters.

Liz Humphreys made the move to the creative hub of Berlin in 2017 after spending several years in Amsterdam and London. Before that, she lived in New York City, where she worked in editorial for Condé Nast, Time Inc., and other media companies. She currently writes and edits for publications including *Condé Nast Traveler*, *Time Out International*, and *Forbes*. Liz updated the Mitte, Schöneberg, and Tiergarten chapters for this edition.

Giulia Pines is a freelance journalist who cultivated an in-depth knowledge of Berlin's food, culture, and history over 10 years of living there. She has since moved back to New York City but will always hold a place in her heart for the Hauptstadt. Guilia updated the Experience chapter.

Robin Raven is a travel journalist and author. She studied writing at the School of Visual Arts. Her work can be seen in *Reader's Digest*, USAToday.com, *Grok Nation*, *HelloGiggles*, *Paste Magazine*, and many other publications. She can often be found roaming the world in pursuit of delicious vegan food and she's the author of *Santa's First Vegan Christmas*. Robin updated the Potsdam chapter.

Kathryn Holeman is an illustrator and print designer based in Greater Philadelphia. She loves to create art every day, bringing history to life with her educational coloring books about Tudor England and her literary gift line on Etsy. Kathryn shares her wanderlust for far off places with her husband and two young sons.